SME Funding

Gianluca Oricchio • Andrea Crovetto •
Sergio Lugaresi • Stefano Fontana

SME Funding

The Role of Shadow Banking and Alternative Funding Options

Gianluca Oricchio
Springgrowth SGR
Milan, Italy

Sergio Lugaresi
ABI
Rome, Italy

Andrea Crovetto
EPIC SIM
Milan, Italy

Stefano Fontana
Sapienza Università di Roma
Rome, Italy

ISBN 978-1-137-58607-0   ISBN 978-1-137-58608-7   (eBook)
DOI 10.1057/978-1-137-58608-7

Library of Congress Control Number: 2016957417

This Palgrave Macmillan imprint is published by Springer Nature
The registered company is Macmillan Publishers Ltd.
The registered company address is: The Campus, 4 Crinan Street, London, N1 9XW, United Kingdom

To our families for their love and support

Foreword

In spring 2014, on the way back from a Saturday morning jog along the marvellous paths of Monte San Fruttuoso nearby Camogli, Liguria, a successful entrepreneur and friend of mine told me something which did not entirely surprise me, but, for sure, made me think. He described a blooming economic-environment for his business, which was enjoying a positive net financial position. Despite it had no needs of funding, his company was receiving many offers of credit at very favorabe rates, and was taking advantage of "treasury arbitrages" by making short-term deposits to Italian banks, funded by cheaper liquidity received from other Italian and Eurozone banks.

Since they were firstly introduced in late 2011, most of Italian banks took full advantage of the long term refinancing facilities (LTRO) operated by the ECB. Banks borrowed significant amounts from the ECB and entered in "carry trades" by buying Italian Govies, which had among the highest spreads (and the lowest prices) in the euro area. For a while, these financial strategies helped the P&L of Italian banks and, by reducing the spreads of Govies against Bunds, contributed to save the country from the risk of default. Although unconventionally and indirectly, these strategies were crucial (also) for the real economy. Thereafter, the ECB monetary stimulus have struggled to transmit to the real economy at the pace and for the amounts which were hoped. A combination of high stocks of non-performing loans (NPL), weak capital positions, rating models and risk management choices have reduced the appetite of Banks to lend to the part of the economy which needs it the most. Distortions like the one described in the anecdote have occurred. Yes, expansionary monetary policies are known to be less effective than contractionary ones. Yet, it is disappointing to witness the failure of such important stimulating measures, especially in an economy in desperate search of growth and employment. Paradoxically, liquidity is abundant for large and healthy companies (which do not need funding), and scarce for SMEs (which need it the most, both short term and long term). This is particularly frustrating as SMEs represent the backbone of the European economy (99.8 % of EU companies, 60 % of EU GDP and 70 % of EU employment).

Why is this? Is there anything the different stakeholders (policymakers, banks, financial markets, rating agencies, SMEs, etc.) can innovate, or do better, or do differently?

Should Europe at large develop towards the Anglo-Saxon model, where the role of capital markets instruments and that of non-banks in funding the real economy – overall and in respect of SMEs – is much more pronounced?

Are there any lessons to be learned from the digital economy and the digital platforms that are flourishing in financial services?

What are the key pillars of an effective short- and long-term funding ecosystem for SMEs?

By means of the contributions of a formidable blend of financial services academics and practitioners, this book analyzes and suggests some concrete and promising ways forward in regard to three key pillars underpinning the growth agenda of an SME.

Pillar I: Valuing SMEs' credit risk. How much of the credit crunch for SMEs is genuinely based on a proper assessment of their risks, and how much it is simply due to the lack of the information to be able to do so in an effective and efficient manner? What contribution to the above issues can come from the development of rating systems dedicated to SMEs, taking advantage also of the new frontiers offered by real-time analytics, structured and unstructured big data mining, and information pooling and sharing?

Pillar II: Policies for SMEs lending. What are the measures in place at EU and country levels? What are the successes, failures, contradictions and potential remedies for a higher harmonization of Basel III banking regulation, ECB monetary measures, EU policies and efforts to develop lending to SMEs? How does one limit the unwanted effects of pro-cyclicality amplified by banking capital requirements and prevailing accounting standards, in both the financial sector and the real economy? What is still lacking for the support of a healthier capital position for SMEs and to satisfy their funding requirements?

Pillar III: The potential role of so-called "shadow banking". Why and how are new players entering the lending market? What value propositions do they provide of which banks are not capable? Is it already possible to identify some patterns in this new lending landscape? What is the positioning of these players? Are they banks' competitors or banks' potential partners? And, in the latter case, how can one deal with asymmetric information?

In addressing the above questions, the authors suggest that a sound growth of the SME sector can come from the combination of dedicated and reliable information and tools for the proper assessment of the risk, a clear framework of proven policies and the sound development of new lending players for SMEs.

One final consideration on "shadow banking". The term was first introduced to describe the damages caused by non-regulated or poorly regulated financial intermediaries in the US crises of 2007–2008. Sometimes, and improperly, the definition is also applied to regulated non-banking players; for example, alternative asset managers such as specialized SME credit (closed-end) funds, and SME-lending brokerage platforms. Players in the first category pool long-term resources from institutional investors – mostly pension funds, endowments and insurers – and, without taking any mismatched risk, allocate those resources to the funding needs of the SMEs, according to agreed investment criteria (detailed in the prospectus). Platforms in the second category provide a marketplace where quality of information, streamlined digital processes and the market forces of supply and demand meet the financial needs of SMEs.

The contribution of these, and other similar players, to SMEs can further grow and complement the array of financial providers available to the sector. They deserve to be brought "out of the shadow", and to take a greater role in developing bright and sound financial solutions for SMEs.

Andrea Moneta
Apollo Management International
Senior Advisor Italy and Operating Partner FS

Contents

List of Figures

List of Tables

1

Banking Crisis and SME Credit Risk Assessment

1.1   Introduction

The financial crisis that began in 2008 unveiled the connection between the economic cycle and the frequency of default. The combination of the procyclical nature of credit ratings and the volatility of evaluations based on fair value or mark-to-market has brought about the contraction of bank capital while also requiring an increase in capital absorption (risk-weighted assets: RWAs).

The effects of the new Basel III regulations will become apparent over time. Nonetheless, the contraction of RWAs in order to strengthen bank core tier capital has induced a severe reduction of the credit available to enterprises, and this is particularly true regarding SME funding needs.

SMEs are significant for the real economy: enterprises with fewer than 250 employees are estimated to have accounted for 99.8 % of the total number of enterprises across Europe, 66 % of employment, 57 % of turnover and 58 % of added value.

There is a strong relationship between bank capital buffers and lending growth in the fringe countries of the European Union (EU). The lower the bank capital buffer, the lower the lending growth rate (IMF 2013a).

© The Author(s) 2017
G. Oricchio et al., *SME Funding*,
DOI 10.1057/978-1-137-58608-7_1

The percentage of reduction in loans granted before the crisis in 2007, and again in June 2015, is acute in Ireland, Spain, Portugal, France, The Netherlands and Italy (in the range 50–20 %). Access to credit represents the second biggest problem faced by entrepreneurs, falling just behind the ability to find customers.

It is straightforward to compute the cost of having a loan as an asset on a bank balance sheet. If we assume a Tier 1 ratio of 10 % and a Return on Equity of 10 % (and a tax rate of 50 %), it is easy to affirm that the bank needs at least 200 basis points of income to satisfy both (1) capital requirements; and (2) targeted Return on Equity [10 % × 10 %/(1 − 50 %)]. From a banking perspective, a 200 basis point income floor must be assumed in addition to the expected loss estimation of the loan.

If we compare the bank cost of having a loan as an asset before and after Basel III, we can see a material increase in this cost; over the same period, credit derivative indexes show a strong increase followed by a huge reduction in the cost of credit risk protection. In Fig. 1.1, we can see the dynamics of credit cost in terms of remuneration of capital requirements and the cost of a credit risk protection based on i-Traxx Europe 5 years.

In Fig. 1.1, three time periods are identified:

1. Before 2007: The bank cost of having an investment grade loan as an asset was more expensive than selling the loan (and the credit risk). Before 2007, the banking industry had conceived the Originate-to-Distribute model and active credit portfolio management (ACPM)/ Credit Treasury played a central role in the new banking business model.

2. 2008–2012: The cost of credit risk protection was very high and volatile. The financial crisis became a crisis in the real economy, to which the regulators responded through three different actions: (i) new higher capital requirements and one Banking Union; (ii) an abundance of liquidity to avoid any bank default risk (such as the long-term refinancing operation, LTRO etc.); and (iii) setting the conditions to favor non-bank actors entering the loan origination market.

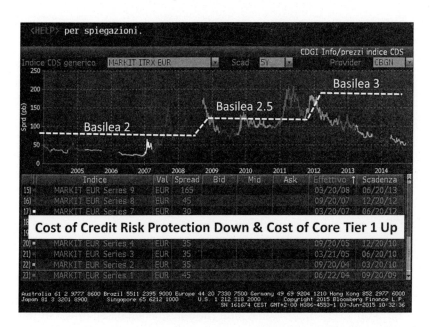

Fig. 1.1 Cost of credit for a bank and cost of buying credit risk protection (Source: Our elaboration on regulatory capital and Bloomberg data)

3. 2013–2016: The bank cost of having an investment grade loan as an asset is now more expensive than selling the loan (and the credit risk). Could this mean a return to the Originate-to-Distribute Model? Perhaps not. However, we do believe that there is plenty of space for non-bank investors to enter the business of granting, repackaging, buying and selling loans.

A new credit market, complementary to bank credit, is necessary for the development of the real economy. Non-bank investors would be able to finance SMEs; such investors would need a better understanding of the SME credit risk and opportunities than that of commercial banks, which is a not an easy task. To this extent, the ability to read the information held in Central Credit Registers (CCRs) takes on an important role for non-bank investors in reducing imbalances in the availability of information, thus making these new credit channels more efficient and capable.

- CCRs play a key role in supporting supervisory activity and improving the banking and financial sectors. These systems gained greater importance during Basel II/Basel III, establishing the first reliable information repositories able to provide data and test assumptions for new regulation. During the current crisis, and given the existence of information gaps, the importance of complete, accurate and timely credit information in the financial system is evident (Gutierrez and Hwang 2010).
- CCRs are a means of: (1) helping to impose discipline on borrowers, (2) facilitating appropriate analysis of their creditworthiness, and (3) fostering greater transparency and more competition between banks (Artigas 2004).
- CCRs operated by central banks exist in 14 EU countries, covering approximately 13 million bank–SME relationships.

It is relevant to note that the lower the turnover of the SME, the lower the accuracy ratio on the Financial Module and the higher the accuracy ratio on CCR-Based Behavioral Modules, when based on CCR data more generally (see Fig. 1.2):

1. SMEs – the lower the turnover, the greater the role of banks in funding and the higher the value added by analysis of CCR data;

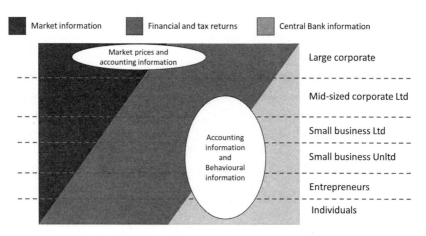

Fig. 1.2 Source of information and typology of valuation

2. Large corporations – the higher the turnover, the lesser the role of banks in funding and the lower the value added by analysis of CCR data.

In other words, the role of the CCR in estimating SME credit risk is, in a certain sense, equivalent to the role of market prices in estimating credit risk in public and large corporations. This is due to: (1) the reliability of CCR data; (2) its strong correlation with a 90-days past due definition of default; and (3) the immediacy of data availability.

The purpose of this volume is to offer an operative guide for non-bank investors.

1.2   The structure of the book

Chapter 2 (Stefano Fontana) presents an overview of the significance of SMEs in Europe and discusses the new funding channels and actors that are rapidly entering the SME funding market in the EU.

Chapter 3 (Stefano Fontana) offers an introduction to the funding of European SMEs through securitization and discusses the key role played by Central Credit Registers in supporting supervisory activity and improving the banking and financial sectors.

Chapter 4 (Gianluca Oricchio) presents corporate and SME credit rating models, discussing the main steps in developing a rating model. The chapter goes on to present SME sub-segment models related to the probability of default (PD) encountered in corporate entities. The chapter also considers the term structure of probability of default, the production of European transition matrices based on the different phases of the cycle itself, validation of internal credit rating models and the validation of the PD model. The chapter closes with a section on the performance assessment of PD and the backtesting related to the model.

Chapter 5 (Gianluca Oricchio) describes the methodology and the estimation and validation processes of a proprietary SME Credit Rating Model (DefaultMetrics™ 2.0), which is able to differentiate the relationships between SMEs and hausbanks (or leading banks) from those between SMEs and multiple banks (non-leading banks). This approach has proven to be very effective in improving the performance and accuracy of the quantitative model developed for Italy, as well as in testing its applicability in other EU countries.

Chapter 6 (Sergio Lugaresi) discusses the large set of tools now in place in order to restart the SME credit engine in Europe. This chapter describes in great detail all the measures proposed and the steps taken to head the economy in a more stable and productive direction.

Chapter 7 (Andrea Crovetto) investigates E-platforms as alternative funding options for SMEs. This model is based on low costs, technological performance and the leverage afforded by intermediation facilities Internet capabilities offer. The chapter provides an in-depth examination of the interaction between alternative and traditional funding channels.

Chapter 8 (Andrea Crovetto) presents a case study undertaken on Epic – an investment company (SIM) authorized and regulated by Consob and Bank of Italy that was established in 2014. Epic is Italy's first FinTech platform where Italian SMEs can present their development projects to a selected audience of institutional investors (investment funds, family offices, banks, insurance companies, investment companies, pension funds) and private investors classified as qualified under the Markets in Financial Instruments Directive (MiFID) (Directive 2004/39/EC), which has been in force since November 2007.

2

SMEs in Europe: An Overview

2.1 Introduction

In his *Principles of Economics*, first published in 1890, Alfred Marshall concluded that, in an industrial society, profit is achievable not only through capitalistic enterprise, but also through alternative economic systems. Profit, in particular, becomes possible through the distribution of a multitude of firms, each of which is specialized in a given phase of the production process. The beneficial effects of a similar process would be measurable not only in economic terms, but also in terms of the enhancement of living standards, triggering a sort of virtuous cycle among workers, thus creating a community based on general scientific and technical knowledge aimed towards productivity. Hence, large and small businesses would be able to prosper by interacting within their local territory. Expanding opportunities for small and medium-sized enterprises (SMEs) has been subject to different interpretations in economic literature over time, such expansion being considered as both essential to the survival of SMEs and an obstacle to the flexibility of the firms themselves.

There have been many studies of SMEs based on the contributions of classics: for example, Rostow (1960), Chandler (1962), McGuire (1963)

© The Author(s) 2017
G. Oricchio et al., *SME Funding*,
DOI 10.1057/978-1-137-58608-7_2

and Greiner (1972). These studies have as a common denominator a vision of the small business not as a finished entity but, rather, as a mandatory phase in a natural and ineluctable process of growth, in which a small business can grow or, alternatively, become extinct.

A different approach appeared in the 1970s. The economic crisis, with the managerial and organizational distress of many large companies that had become too imposing and marked by officialism, led to a revaluation of the small business model. It came to be considered as a more flexible form of organization and, therefore, particularly suitable to function in a more complex and turbulent social-economic environment. In 1973, *Small is Beautiful. A Study of Economics as if People Mattered* by E.F. Shumacher strongly echoed this. The book criticized the Fordistic development of capitalism as materialistic, efficiency-minded and oriented towards an idolatry of excess. The focus of the book was on the economic development of underdeveloped countries that did not need complex organizations and high capital technology as much as they needed intermediate and appropriate technology.

In addition to the theories mentioned above, which could be defined as "extreme", since the 1980s various studies have formulated a third theory that identifies SMEs as stable and independent entities having distinct and typical characteristics, structures and managerial mechanisms (Churchill and Lewis 1983).

It appears misleading to consider SMEs as "immobile" in present-day economic and social contexts, where globalization and rapid technological development render competition more and more aggressive as the interaction between economic actors becomes increasingly articulate and turbulent.

Virtuous SMEs, capable of facing the continuous challenges of the market and conquering their own enclave, are not static entities in an ever-evolving world. On the contrary, they are organizations that identify and follow paths of growth and affirmation while maintaining their reduced size.

SMEs account for 95 % of companies, provide 60–70 % of employment opportunities and generate a large portion of new work posts in the economies of OECD countries.

Studies show that the development of SMEs is linked tightly to economic growth. For example, Beck et al. (2005) reveal the robust positive relation between the two. According to Ayyagari et al. (2007), in high-income countries SMEs contribute, on average, up to 50 % of the gross national product (GNP).

SMEs possess specific strong and weak points that require appropriate policies. With the appearance of new technologies and globalization, the importance of many activities of economies of scale has decreased, while the potential capability of small businesses has risen.

However, many of the problems that SMEs traditionally face – lack of funds, difficulty in the use of technology (optimization), limited managerial skills, scarce productivity, normative confinements – have worsened in a globalized, dynamic and technology dominated environment.

On one hand, large companies reduce and commission various activities; on the other, the relevance of SMEs to the economy is expanding. In addition, the competition linked to the rise of these businesses heavily influences the increase in productivity and the consequent economic growth.

This process implies a great mobility of work posts, which is, itself, a fundamental aspect of the competitive process and structural change. Less than half of small start-ups survive for more than five years, and only a small number is able to become part of the group of companies that are leaders in innovation.

2.2   European Commission Definition of SMEs

There are multiple definitions of SMEs. However, rarely do these definitions differentiate between micro (artisan), small and medium-sized enterprises, thus creating more than a little confusion.

The notion of SMEs has been an object of study for the European Commission since the beginning of the 1990s.

In a single market with no internal boundaries, it becomes essential that pro-SME policies have a common definition for reasons of consistency and efficiency. A single definition also limits the incidence of distortion in competition, given the evident interaction between the requirements of SMEs and the opportunity for the organizations that satisfy these requirements to access community and national benefits to promote and assist their development.

In 1996, the Commission adopted Recommendation 96/280/CE, April 3, 1996, which established the first common definition of SMEs. This definition has been extensively applied in a variety of contexts, both community and national. Nevertheless, the definition has also shown various weaknesses, leaving space for both interpretive difficulties and the elusive practices of a few, mostly large enterprise groups, regardless of the traceability to the concept of an SME comprising the elements of a single company.

Given such weaknesses, the European Commission modified the critiques and parameters of the definition of SMEs in Recommendation 2003/361/CE May 2003, which replaced its predecessor Recommendation 96/280/CE, April 3, 1996.

The new definition entered into force on January 1, 2005; it is applied to all policies, programs and measures relating to SMEs put into effect by the Commission.

The new definition is the result of in-depth discussions between the Commission, the Member States, business organizations and experts, and even two consultations carried out on the Internet.

The changes introduced reflect the economic developments that have taken place since 1996 and a growing awareness of the specific obstacles that SMEs find themselves facing.

The document is particularly important in the light of the fact that the new regulation will directly influence all future actions by the community legislator. Particularly, it will play a significant role in the tricky subject of forms of aid to states, the next structural funds program, and the rules of accounts and budgets of all European businesses.

The new definition is more appropriate for the various categories of SMEs, affording greater consideration to the different liaisons between companies. Furthermore, the definition helps to promote innovation and favors partnerships while ensuring that public programs concentrate only on companies truly in need of aid. The Recommendation essentially extends the concept of enterprise to all entities that exercise an economic activity regardless of its juridical form. Such an extension addresses some interpretative doubts relative to the nature of enterprise for those businesses that carry out an artisan activity, or individual or family-run activities.

Recommendation 2003/361/CE states that a business may qualify as small or medium-sized if it meets the criteria regarding autonomy, staffing levels and financial turnover.

Autonomy: An enterprise is defined "autonomous" if it is neither associated with nor linked to another business – that is, if it does not control (or is not controlled by) other companies.

Staffing levels:

- A micro enterprise should have fewer than 10 employees;
- A small enterprise should have fewer than 50 employees;
- A medium-sized enterprise should have fewer than 250 employees.

Financial turnover:

- A micro enterprise should have an annual turnover or a total annual balance (which corresponds to the total of the company's assets) of less than €2 million;
- A small enterprise should have an annual turnover or a total annual balance of less than €10 million;
- A medium-sized enterprise should have an annual turnover or a total annual balance less than €43 million.

In summary: in micro, small and medium-sized enterprises, the criteria regarding staffing levels and annual turnover are cumulative, in the sense that both must coexist.

The criteria governing the definition of "actual" employees are essential in determining into which category an SME fits. This criterion depends on whether personnel is full-time, part-time or seasonal, and includes the following categories:

- employees;
- the people that work for the company – i.e. employees that, according to national legislation, are considered as the other employees of the company;
- owners and management;
- partners who conduct a regular activity within the company and that benefit from the financial advantages that derive therefrom.

Not considered as part of the work force are those who benefit from an apprenticeship contract or students with internship contracts. In addition, no record is made of the duration of maternity or family leave.

With regard to the financial status of a business, the annual turnover is determined by deducting all relevant outgoings from the sum obtained during the year of reference for the sale of products and for services rendered. Turnover does not include tax on additional value (IVA [Impuesto al Valor Agregado]/VAT [Value Added Tax]) or other indirect taxes. Another relevant change concerns the new notion of independence; only an independent enterprise can qualify as an SME: no other company may control more than 25% of an SME, either directly or indirectly. This is particularly important because it is defined more precisely and because it includes partnerships in the concept of independence. It was not clear how partnerships would be viewed prior to the establishment of the new definition.

2.3   US Small Business Administration Definition of SMEs

In the United States, the definition of SMEs varies according to the sector in which a company operates. The US Small Business Administration (SBA) determines the variable thresholds, which generally include the following parameters:

- fewer than 500 employees; or
- an annual turnover of less than US$5 million.

Depending on the sector, the range for employees may vary from 50 to 1500 and the turnover could vary anywhere between US$750 thousand and US$38.5 million.

2.4   Other Definitions of SMEs

On an international level, multilateral institutions do not share a specific definition of an SME. As evidenced in Table 2.1, the maximum number of employees can vary between 50 and 300. If one analyzes profit, this varies between US$3 million and US$15 million.

2.5   The OECD Study

Based on an analysis conducted on OECD information concerning the various definitions of an SME (with exclusive reference to the parameter of the employees), 33 out of 34 participating countries (Australia excluded) yielded the following results: 24 countries use the European Community definition (i.e. all EU countries in addition to Mexico, Switzerland and Turkey). The remaining seven countries (Canada, Colombia, South Korea, Israel, New Zealand, Russia, Thailand) use their own national definitions, each of which differs from the others (see Table 2.1).

In short, the definition of SMEs proposed by the EU primarily uses the criteria of quantity (employees, turnover, assets). In the USA, on the other hand, what is essential in defining SMEs is the number of employees, with the exception of non-productive sectors.

2.6   The SMEs Business Environment in Europe

The EU-28 is represented by countries which have adhered to a unique economic and political partnership, based on 28 countries with a combined population of 507 million inhabitants in 2014 (Croatia joined the EU as of July 1, 2013) which account for most of the continent (see Table 2.2).

Table 2.1 SME definitions

Country	Micro ent.	Small ent.	Medium ent.	Large ent.
Canada	–	0–99	100–499	>500
Colombia	0–10	11–50	51–200	>500
South Korea	0–9	10–99	100–299	>500
Israel	0–4	05–20	21–100	>500
New Zealand	0–9	10–49	50–99	>500
Russia	0–15	16–100	101–250	>500
Thailand	–	0–50	50–200	>500

Source: Our elaboration on OECD data

Table 2.2 Eurostat population change

Country	2013	2014
Belgium	11,161.6	11,204.0
Bulgaria	7,284.6	7,245.7
Czech Republic	10,516.1	10,512.4
Denmark	5,602.6	5,627.2
Germany	80,523.7	80,780.0
Estonia	1,320.2	1,315.8
Ireland	4,591.1	4,604.0
Greece	11,062.5	10,992.6
Spain	46,727.9	46,507.8
France	65,578.8	65,856.6
Croatia	4,262.1	4,246.7
Italy	59,685.2	60,782.7
Cyprus	865.9	858.0
Latvia	2,023.8	2,001.5
Lithuania	2,971.9	2,943.5
Luxembourg	537.0	549.7
Hungary	9,908.8	9,879.0
Malta	421.4	425.4
Netherlands	16,779.6	16,829.3
Austria	8,451.9	8,507.8
Poland	38,533.3	38,495.7
Portugal	10,487.3	10,427.3
Romania	20,020.1	19,942.6
Slovenia	2,058.8	2,061.1
Slovakia	5,410.8	5,415.9
Finland	5,426.7	5,451.3
Sweden	9,555.9	9,644.9
United Kingdom	63,905.3	64,308.3
EU 28	505.0,675.0	507.0,416.6

Source: Our elaboration on Eurostat population change (1,000 population).

The list of member countries and their respective gross domestic product (GDP) at market prices from 2008 to 2013 is presented in Table 2.3.

In the EU, SMEs comprise the majority of businesses, and are a primary employment resource and a stimulus for development. In 2014, SMEs in the EU-28 area totaled approximately 21.3 million, with 886 million workers and with an added value of €3.5 trillion. Tables 2.4, 2.5 and 2.6) show, respectively, the number of companies, number of employees and added value present in the EU-28 zone from 2008 to 2014.

Table 2.3 GDP at market prices

Country		2013	2012	2011	2010	2009	2008
Belgium	B	395,262.1	388,254.3	379,990.6	365,747.0	349,702.7	355,065.5
Bulgaria	BG	41,047.9	40,926.7	40,103.1	36,764.3	36,078.4	36,450.2
Czech Republic	CZ	157,284.8	160,947.8	163,579.1	156,369.7	148,357.4	160,961.5
Denmark	DK	252,938.9	250,786.4	246,074.7	241,516.9	230,231.3	241,087.3
Germany	DE	2,809,480.0	2,749,900.0	2,699,100.0	2,576,220.0	2,456,660.0	2,558,020.0
Estonia	EE	18,738.8	17,636.7	16,403.8	14,709.1	14,138.2	16,511.0
Ireland	IE	174,791.3	172,754.7	171,042.3	164,931.2	168,114.0	186,870.2
Greece	EL	182,438.0	194,204.0	207,752.0	226,210.0	237,431.0	242,096.0
Spain	ES	1,049,181.0	1,055,158.0	1,075,147.0	1,080,913.0	1,079,034.0	1,116,207.0
France	FR	2,113,687.0	2,091,059.0	2,059,284.0	1,998,481.0	1,939,071.0	1,995,850.0
Croatia	HR	43,561.5	43,933.7	44,708.6	45,004.3	45,090.7	48,129.8
Italy	IT	1,618,904.0	1,628,004.0	1,638,857.0	1,605,694.0	1,573,655.0	1,632,933.0
Cyprus	CY	18,118.9	19,411.1	19,486.7	19,062.9	18,423.1	18,768.8
Latvia	LV	23,265.0	22,217.0	20,197.0	18,015.1	18,816.1	24,403.2
Lithuania	LT	34,955.6	33,314.0	31,247.3	28,001.3	26,934.8	32,696.3
Luxembourg	LU	45,288.1	43,812.0	42,410.4	39,370.8	36,093.9	37,522.5
Hungary	HU	100,536.5	98,699.4	100,350.9	97,814.8	93,317.7	107,150.1
Malta	MT	7,543.9	7,212.8	6,893.2	6,599.5	6,138.6	6,128.7
Netherlands	NL	642,851.0	640,644.0	642,929.0	631,512.0	617,650.0	635,794.0
Austria	AT	322,594.6	317,213.1	308,675.0	294,207.9	286,188.4	291,930.4
Poland	PL	395,962.4	386,143.3	377,028.1	359,816.0	314,689.4	363,691.8
Portugal	PT	171,211.0	169,668.2	176,166.6	179,929.8	175,448.2	178,872.6
Romania	RO	144,282.2	133,806.1	133,305.9	126,746.4	120,409.2	142,396.3
Slovenia	SI	36,144.0	36,006.0	36,868.4	36,219.6	36,166.2	37,951.2
Slovakia	SK	73,593.2	72,184.7	70,159.8	67,204.0	63,798.9	65,679.0
Finland	FI	201,341.0	199,069.0	196,869.0	187,100.0	181,029.0	193,317.1
Sweden	SE	436,342.4	423,340.7	404,945.5	369,076.6	309,678.7	352,317.1
United King.	UK	2,017,193.8	2,041,491.2	1,863,940.9	1,816,615.0	1,663,573.3	1,907,212.3
EU 28		13,529,099.6	13,437,764.0	13,173,516.9	12,789,850.6	12,245,901.0	12,986,406.7

Source: Our elaboration on Eurostat gross domestic product at market prices (€million).

Table 2.4 EU-28 number of enterprises

Number of enterprises						
	Micro (%)	Small (%)	Medium (%)	SMEs (%)	Large (%)	Total
2014	19,676,714	1,403,820	233,051	21,313,585	45,457	21,359,042
	92.1 %	6.6 %	1.1 %	99.8 %	0.2 %	
2013	19,025,518	1,362,643	225,952	20,614,113	44,021	20,685,134
	92.1 %	6.6 %	1.1 %	99.8 %	0.2 %	
2012	18,783,480	1,349,730	222,628	20,355,838	43,454	20,399,292
	92.1 %	6.6 %	1.1 %	99.8 %	0.2 %	
2011	19,138,446	1,359,983	222,022	20,720,451	43,159	20,763,610
	92.2 %	6.5 %	1.1 %	99.8 %	0.2 %	
2010	19,364,827	1,328,203	219,086	20,912,116	42,014	20,954,131
	92.4 %	6.3 %	1.0 %	99.8 %	0.2 %	
2009	18,407,598	1,335,615	223,021	19,966,234	42,440	20,008,674
	92.0 %	6.7 %	1.1 %	99.8 %	0.2 %	
2008	18,655,757	1,374,163	225,884	20,255,804	44,242	20,300,046
	91.9 %	6.8 %	1.1 %	99.8 %	0.2 %	

Source: Our elaboration on Eurostat, National Statistical Offices, DIW econ, London Economics.

At first glance, it is possible to deduce from Tables 2.4, 2.5 and 2.6 that the most numerous type of SME is the micro enterprise, which makes up 90 % of the total of companies. In addition, micro enterprises account for approximately 28 % of personnel employed in all enterprises and generate 21 % of added value produced by all companies.

The added value generated by SMEs in the EU-28 has returned to its level prior to the financial crisis that began in 2008 and, in the period 2013–2014, grew by 2.8 %. Similarly, the number of people in employment registered an increase of 0.16 %, while the number of SMEs diminished by 0.23 %. However, changing the trend of the previous period (2012–2013), the number of businesses dropped by 0.90 %. Table 2.7 summarizes these data.

2.7   A Comparison between the EU-28, Japan and the USA

Having presented the EU-28 data, we are able to conduct a brief analysis in order to compare European SMEs to those of Japan and the United States. The comparison is also significant in light of the fact that the

Table 2.5 EU-28 number of employees

Number of persons employed

	Micro (%)	Small (%)	Medium (%)	SMEs (%)	Large (%)	Total
2014	38,369,835	27,134,078	23,125,668	88,629,583	44,394,691	133,024,3273
	28.8 %	20.4 %	17.4 %	66.6 %	33.4 %	
2013	37,618,702	26,712,322	22,761,274	87,092,299	43,634,097	130,726,395
	28.8 %	20.4 %	17.4 %	66.6 %	33.4 %	
2012	37,494,458	26,704,352	22,615,906	86,814,717	43,787,013	130,601,730
	28.7 %	20.4 %	17.3 %	66.5 %	33.5 %	
2011	37,881,704	26,906,990	22,638,152	87,426,846	43,597,457	131,024,303
	28.9 %	20.5 %	17.3 %	66.7 %	33.3 %	
2010	38,292,646	26,778,437	22,457,527	87,528,611	42,865,548	130,394,158
	29.4 %	20.5 %	17.2 %	67.1 %	32.9 %	
2009	38,243,087	26,879,684	22,523,479	87,646,250	42,641,337	130,287,587
	29.4 %	20.6 %	17.3 %	67.3 %	32.7 %	
2008	38,251,850	27,017,378	23,054,380	88,323,609	44,316,564	132,640,173
	28.8 %	20.4 %	17.4 %	66.6 %	33.4 %	

Source: Our elaboration on Eurostat, National Statistical Offices, DIW econ, London Economics.

Table 2.6 EU-28 gross value added

Gross value added (€million)					
	Micro (%)	Small (%)	Medium (%)	SMEs (%)	Large (%)	Total
2014	1,304,396	1,116,462	1,115,659	3,536,517	2,578,162	6,114,679
	21.3 %	18.3 %	18.2 %	57.8 %	42.2 %	
2013	1,259,454	1,084,150	1,086,381	3,429,985	2,502,964	5,932,949
	21.2 %	18.3 %	18.3 %	57.8 %	42.2 %	
2012	1,242,724	1,076,388	1,076,270	3,395,383	2,495,926	5,891,309
	21.1 %	18.3 %	18.3 %	57.6 %	42.4 %	
2011	1,256,654	1,089,632	1,093,321	3,439,607	2,504,494	5,944,101
	21.1 %	18.3 %	18.4 %	57.9 %	42.1 %	
2010	1,240,700	1,061,324	1,072,394	3,374,418	2,509,176	5,883,594
	21.1 %	18.0 %	18.2 %	57.4 %	42.6 %	
2009	1,180,545	1,036,295	1,017,258	3,234,099	2,287,314	5,521,412
	21.4 %	18.8 %	18.4 %	58.6 %	41.4 %	
2008	1,321,166	1,131,028	1,113,063	3,565,257	2,550,714	6,115,971
	21.1 %	18.5 %	18.2 %	58.3 %	41.7 %	

Source: Our elaboration on Eurostat, National Statistical Offices, DIW econ, London Economics.

Table 2.7 Annual growth in SME performance indicators 2012–2014

Size class	Indicator	% change 2012–2013	% change 2013–2014
Micro	Enterprises	−0.93	−0.28
	Value added	1.57	2.46
	Employment	−0.98	−0.25
Small	Enterprises	−0.42	0.33
	Value added	0.99	2.87
	Employment	−0.21	0.34
Medium	Enterprises	−0.50	0.45
	Value added	0.72	3.14
	Employment	−0.07	0.62
Large	Enterprises	−0.40	−0.49
	Value added	−0.03	2.39
	Employment	0.05	−0.08
SMEs	Enterprises	−0.90	−0.23
	Value added	1.12	2.80
	Employment	−0.51	0.16
Total	Enterprises	−0.90	−0.23
	Value added	0.63	2.63
	Employment	−0.33	0.08

Source: Our elaboration on Eurostat, National Statistical Offices, DIW econ, London Economics.

economies of these countries are quite similar. In short, there are 20.6 million non-financial SMEs in the EU-28 with approximately 87 million employees, 18.2 million with 487 million employees in the USA and around 3.9 million with 33.5 million employees in Japan.

If the number of companies were to be determined by the GDP, it is possible to see that the EU-28 and USA are much closer than one would think in terms of the number of businesses (1.65 and 1.63 per million of GDP, respectively). Japan on the other hand, has only 0.85 of businesses per million of GDP. If, however, the number of employees is considered over GDP, the result differs; Japan has the highest number of employees per million of GDP (7.24) compared with, respectively, 6.80 and 4.36 employees per million of GDP of the EU-28 and USA.

2.8   A Brief Analysis of Sector Trends in the Period 2008–2013

According to the Eurostat classification, the major sectors are:

- Manufacturing;
- Construction;
- Retail and wholesale;
- Accommodation/food;
- Business services;
- Others.

The EU-28 SME construction sector, which represents 11 % of added value for SMEs and 12 % of the workforce within the businesses, experienced a strong decline in 2008–2013. In 2013, added value was 21.7 % lower than it had been in 2008, employment had dropped by 18 % and the number of businesses dropped by 10.1 %.

The manufacturing sector is performing below its levels in 2008, with a drop in added value of 2.9 % in 2013 compared with 2008. Employment had decreased by 9.9 % and the number of businesses had dropped by 5.3 %. Today, the manufacturing sector provides employment for more than 17 million people and generates 21 % of added value to SMEs in Europe.

The added value of the SMEs in the retail and wholesale sector rose by 3.1 %, while employment and the number of businesses remained the same in 2008–2013. This sector alone accounts for 26 % of the SME workforce and represents 22 % of added value produced by SMEs in the EU.

Conversely, the SME business services sector grew significantly between 2008 and 2013, with a rise in added value of 7 %, a 5.4 % increase in employment and 10.2 % growth in the number of businesses during that period.

Business services produce approximately 13 % of added value for SMEs and employ approximately 9 million people (11 %).

Last, but definitely not least, the accommodation/food sector shows the strongest growth (10.4 % added value and 6.0 % employment) among the five specific sectors illustrated in the present work, as can be seen in Figs. 2.1, 2.2 and 2.3.

2.9   The Major Problems Confronting European SMEs

After presenting the framework of the quantitative nature of SMEs, we should mention the European Commission study, *Survey on the Access to Finance of Small and Medium-sized Enterprises (SAFE)*, 2013. The study

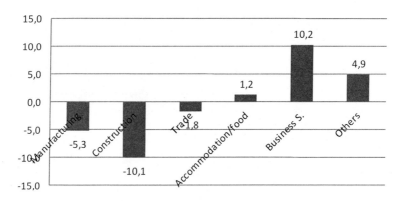

Fig. 2.1 Number of enterprises 2008–2013 percentage change (*Source*: Our elaboration on Eurostat data.)

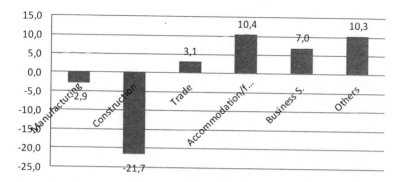

Fig. 2.2 Value added 2008–2013 percentage change (*Source*: Our elaboration on Eurostat data.)

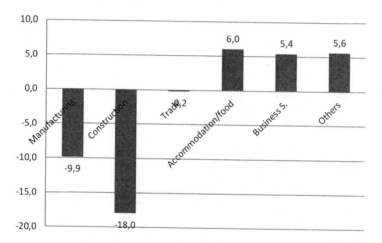

Fig. 2.3 Employment 2008–2013 percentage change (*Source*: Our elaboration on Eurostat data.)

was conducted on 37 European countries including the 28 Member States (EU) and 17 Eurozone countries and had previously been undertaken in 2009 and 2011. Table 2.8 presents a summary of the most persistent problems that European SMEs find themselves facing.

The main issue tackled by European SMEs appears to be the "search for clients", followed by the issue of access to funding. The latter appears stable over time, while the problem of market shares is subject to a slight

Table 2.8 Persistent problems reported by SMEs

Rank	SME problems	2013 (%)	2011 (%)	2009 (%)
1	Finding customers	22	24	19
2	Access to finance	15	15	10
3	Availability of skilled staff or experienced managers	14	14	5
4	Regulation	14	8	4
5	Competition	14	15	8
6	Cost of production of labor	13	12	5
7	Other	7	10	10
8	No Answer	0	1	3

Source: Our elaboration on the access to finance of small and medium-sized enterprises (SAFE) data.

2 % decrease compared with 2011. The difficulties in terms of the apparent similar percentage are the necessity of having skilled managers, aspects tied to standards (this last element has increased considerably since 2011) and competition. Last, but equally important, is the issue of labor costs. The focus will now have to be on how to access the various sources of funding. We shall not discuss these issues here, as they are not strictly pertinent to the purpose of our study.

In terms of impact, regardless of the fact that governments have increased support measures favoring SMEs throughout the financial crisis, SMEs in most countries apparently have not yet witnessed improvement (at least considering the results of the research).

Although various public aid measures are in place to facilitate SME access to funding, ensuring this access for SMEs is still difficult.

With regard to access to various sources of funding, Table 2.9 illustrates the variations in the general SME Access to Finance (SMAF) Index[1] for Member States in the period 2007–2013. In total, 24 countries showed an improvement in their access to financial circles throughout the entire period analyzed. In particular, Latvia, Lithuania, Estonia, France and Ireland experienced significant difficulty regarding funding. The Member States which registered deterioration in their SMAF Index

---

[1] The SMAF Index provides an indication of the changes in circumstances experienced by SMEs regarding access to funds over time in the EU and its Member States. The Index is calculated using the year 2007 = 100 as the base, allowing the comparison between different states over time. The 2007 reference base deliberately sets a boundary prior to the financial crisis.

Table 2.9 SMAF index (EU = 100, 2007) per country

	2007	2008	2009	2010	2011	2012	2013
Austria	112.0	110.0	116.8	121.4	122.8	122.0	123.0
Belgium	106.0	103.4	106.4	105.5	106.3	109.0	111.0
Bulgaria	91.0	90.2	90.6	91.2	90.8	95.0	98.0
Cyprus	106.0	105.8	105.5	105.9	94.9	95.0	82.0
Czech Republic	99.0	98.4	101.6	105.3	107.1	108.0	109.0
Germany	110.0	110.4	113.5	114.9	114.8	123.0	119.0
Denmark	105.0	103.4	104.5	105.9	106.4	107.0	110.0
Estonia	94.0	94.5	97.3	94.6	99.1	103.0	112.0
Greece	93.0	93.9	98.3	93.6	81.8	79.0	78.0
Spain	86.0	83.8	80.8	89.9	100.3	96.0	101.0
Finland	107.0	108.6	114.8	124.4	122.3	120.0	122.0
France	110.0	110.1	117.1	124.0	120.7	121.0	126.0
Croatia	98.0	96.5	99.5	106.9	112.2	115.0	112.0
Hungary	81.0	78.2	74.6	86.4	91.4	95.0	95.0
Ireland	96.0	95.5	103.1	104.3	106.0	107.0	111.0
Italy	102.0	101.4	107.5	111.0	105.8	96.0	107.0
Lithuania	92.0	90.4	92.4	100.2	103.9	110.0	116.0
Luxembourg	106.0	107.5	111.1	105.7	105.1	107.0	121.0
Latvia	83.0	84.0	77.3	97.2	110.3	111.0	109.0
Malta	105.0	103.2	106.0	108.1	109.5	110.0	106.0
Netherlands	103.0	101.6	108.6	112.7	114.1	117.0	117.0
Poland	100.0	96.6	98.6	101.4	103.2	103.0	108.0
Portugal	95.0	95.1	97.4	99.2	92.2	87.0	97.0
Romania	90.0	87.0	84.5	92.0	92.9	95.0	85.0
Sweden	117.0	117.9	119.8	119.5	112.0	113.0	114.0
Slovenia	103.0	101.5	104.4	107.9	109.9	112.0	114.0
Slovak Republic	107.0	106.7	111.7	110.1	105.5	107.0	112.0
United Kingdom	102.0	104.7	112.4	110.9	107.3	106.0	112.0
European Union	100.0	99.3	102.0	105.4	105.3	106.0	108.0
Eurozone	103.0	102.0	105.9	107.8	106.5	107.0	109.0

Source: Our elaboration of EU Commission-SMEs access to finance index data

score compared with their original position in 2007 were Cyprus, Greece and Romania. The only countries to have a constant index value superior to 110 were Sweden, Germany, France and Austria. It is important to point out that although Sweden registered a deterioration, it remained one of the strongest states in terms of access to funds, with scores superior to the EU-28 average throughout the entire 2007–2008 period.

The SMAF debt finance sub-index is composed of indicators based on the use of diverse sources of debt funding, the perception of SMEs on sources of funding through loans, and true interest rate data on debt. Analysis of the SMAF sub-index reveals that the value of the index applied to the EU-28 Member States has increased by nine points since 2007. The result slightly improves for countries in the Eurozone. Luxemburg, France and Austria represent the countries with the highest sub-index values, while Greece, Cyprus and Romania find a less favorable framework for debt financing. (See Table 2.10.)

If, on the other hand, we consider the "funding as a form of personal assets" sub-index (taking as a reference the volume of investments and the

Table 2.10 SMAF debt finance sub-index (EU = 100, 2007) per country

	2007	2008	2009	2010	2011	2012	2013
Austria	115	114	121	127	126	127	125
Belgium	104	102	105	107	107	109	114
Bulgaria	93	90	90	91	91	94	97
Cyprus	107	106	106	106	93	93	79
Czech Republic	101	100	102	109	113	114	113
Germany	111	111	116	118	117	127	125
Denmark	102	100	103	105	104	101	107
Estonia	94	94	97	96	101	102	108
Greece	95	95	99	95	81	79	77
Spain	85	81	79	91	103	98	104
Finland	102	102	111	123	121	118	121
France	110	109	116	125	122	123	128
Croatia	97	95	99	108	113	115	112
Hungary	79	76	73	87	91	94	93
Ireland	94	93	100	101	102	102	107
Italy	106	104	110	115	109	98	109
Lithuania	92	90	92	102	105	109	116
Luxembourg	107	106	114	110	110	111	128
Latvia	82	83	74	96	111	112	111
Malta	105	102	106	108	109	110	106
Netherlands	100	99	105	112	114	117	115
Poland	102	98	101	106	108	107	111
Portugal	93	91	97	98	92	84	94
Romania	90	87	84	93	93	96	84
Sweden	112	111	119	118	109	110	113
Slovenia	103	101	103	107	110	112	114
Slovak Republic	109	109	115	114	109	110	113
United Kingdom	97	98	108	108	104	104	113
European Union	100	98	102	106	106	106	109
Eurozone	102	101	106	109	107	107	110

Source: Our elaboration EU Commission-SMEs access to finance index data.

number of offers/beneficiaries), Ireland, Estonia, Denmark, Holland and Finland perform best, while Luxembourg, Greece and Spain, according to this sub-index, have fewer opportunities to access sources of funding based on equity. The EU-28 sub-index value is 103, thus indicating a slight improvement since 2007. Sixteen countries have improved their performance, according to the sub-index of personal asset based financing in the period 2007–2013. (See Table 2.11.)

Table 2.11 SMAF-equity finance sub-index (EU = 100, 2007)

	2007	2008	2009	2010	2011	2012	2013
Austria	88	85	91	87	99	95	105
Belgium	113	108	113	93	99	102	92
Bulgaria	77	88	90	88	87	98	104
Cyprus	99	101	101	99	102	103	98
Czech Republic	86	88	94	83	73	71	82
Germany	99	105	96	95	100	97	86
Denmark	120	121	111	108	117	134	125
Estonia	92	93	94	85	83	106	130
Greece	79	85	89	82	81	80	78
Spain	88	94	88	83	80	79	81
Finland	133	141	132	127	125	126	123
France	110	112	121	114	113	111	114
Croatia	100	101	101	99	102	110	107
Hungary	88	88	78	81	92	102	98
Ireland	102	108	116	118	124	131	130
Italy	81	83	88	88	84	86	94
Lithuania	90	90	91	90	92	115	115
Luxembourg	98	110	89	79	75	81	77
Latvia	89	89	90	101	102	100	97
Malta	103	105	105	104	108	106	102
Netherlands	120	114	125	112	109	111	123
Poland	83	85	80	74	74	73	88
Portugal	107	117	99	101	89	97	110
Romania	85	86	84	83	87	87	84
Sweden	138	151	119	123	123	127	117
Slovenia	100	100	109	110	108	107	110
Slovak Republic	89	89	90	85	85	83	103
United Kingdom	129	137	131	124	121	118	102
European Union	100	103	100	97	98	101	103
Eurozone	100	103	103	98	98	100	104

Source: Our elaboration EU Commission-SMEs access to finance index data

In the 2013 European Commission study *Survey on the Access to Finance of Small and Medium-sized Enterprises (SAFE)*, the Analytical Report shows the results of the research on the extent of the utilization of the various forms of financing available for companies. According to the study, internal funds were a principle source of funding for 26 % of EU SMEs in 2013. Additional sources of funding continued to be widely used by SMEs: in particular, current bank accounts (39 %), leasing/renting, purchasing/factoring (35 %), commercial credit (32 %), and bank loans (32 %). Approximately 1 in 7 (15 %) SMEs resorted to other loans from linked companies and/or stockholders, 13 % used subsidized bank loans, 5 % used their own assets and a few (2 %) resorted to subordinated loans. (See Table 2.12.)

In relation to the issue of access to funds, the relationship between the indebtedness of micro, small and medium-sized enterprises of European SMEs must be underlined. The relationship indicates a company's asset structure, in addition to providing a good idea of the financial lever employed. A low percentage implies that a company is less dependent on

Table 2.12 SME forms of funding

Internal and external financing SMEs	Used (%)	Did not use but have experience with instrument (%)	Instrument is not applicable to firm (%)	Na (%)
Bank overdraft, credit line or credit card overdraft	39	21	39	1
Leasing or hire-purchase or factoring	35	26	40	0
Trade credit	32	13	55	1
Bank loan	32	37	31	0
Retained earnings or sale of assets (internal funds)	26	19	54	1
Other loan	15	17	67	1
Grants or subsidized bank loan	13	27	59	1
Equity	5	12	82	1
Debt securities issued	2	5	92	1
Subordinated loans, participation loans or similar financing instruments	2	5	92	1

Source: Our elaboration of *Survey on the Access to Finance of Small and Medium-sized Enterprises (SAFE)*, Analytical Report 2013 data.

loaned money. In general, the higher the percentage of borrowed funding, the higher the risk to which a company is exposed. When, therefore, the relationship is high, a business has a higher debt than its assets. This infers that the company will be subject to higher obligations with regard to the reimbursement of capital and interest, which may become a significant cash outflow.

It ought not to be forgotten that a high leverage level may have a considerable impact on taxation: the higher the level, the higher the interest costs; this impacts the income statement, thus bringing about a decrease in income taxation. A contained level of indebtedness may also reveal that a company has the opportunity to make responsible use of the financial lever as an instrument of business growth, rather than taking advantage of the situation.

Data are reported in Table 2.13.

Table 2.13 SME leverage

SMEs debt ratio			
Country	Medium (%)	Small (%)	Micro (%)
Italy	70.30	76.50	76.80
France	64.90	61.30	61.10
Austria	64.20	61.30	57.00
Croatia	63.00	67.00	68.00
Greece	62.30	57.90	55.70
Slovenia	61.90	63.30	60.60
Sweden	61.80	59.70	59.80
Belgium	61.50	63.10	48.30
Germany	61.50	63.20	62.60
Netherlands	61.10	62.70	54.10
Finland	60.00	60.00	54.30
Spain	58.70	59.40	62.60
Romania	58.30	62.20	61.40
United Kingdom	57.70	55.80	49.60
Luxembourg	57.40	55.60	59.20
Bulgaria	52.80	53.50	48.30
Lithuania	51.10	52.80	55.10
Poland	51.10	50.90	49.50
Ireland	50.90	47.50	49.60
Estonia	48.20	48.00	43.00

Source: Our elaboration of SME taxation in Europe, 2015, EU Commission data.

Table 2.13 is organized on a descending scale of the highest level of indebtedness in relation to medium-sized businesses (column 2);it transpires that this is Italy, with 70.3 %. This "achievement" is also relates to Italian small and micro businesses. At the opposite end of the scale, Estonia has the lowest level of indebtedness, approximately 48.2 % in relation to the country's medium-sized businesses. It can be deduced that, on average, companies operating in these countries finance an average of 50 % or more of their activity through equity.

2.10 SMEs in EU: A Comparison Analysis of France, Germany, Italy, the Netherlands, Spain, Sweden and the United Kingdom

The focus of this section is the manufacturing sector, which accounts for over 99 % of SMEs. Under analysis are the countries that make up 70 % of EU-28 GDP:

- France;
- Germany;
- Italy;
- The Netherlands;
- Spain;
- Sweden;
- United Kingdom.

Although the countries selected belong to the EU, there is a strong heterogeneity in their economic, social and institutional contexts:

- France – a country with a large centralized state;
- Germany – a country leader in industry;
- Italy and Spain – two Mediterranean countries,;
- Sweden – a country whose economic policies engender a specific industrial setting;

Table 2.14 GDP trends

Country	2008	2009	2010	2011	2012	2013	2014
France	0.20	−2.90	2.00	2.10	0.20	0.70	0.20
Germany	1.10	−5.60	4.10	3.70	0.40	0.30	1.60
Italy	−1.00	−5.50	1.70	0.60	−2.80	−1.70	−0.40
Netherlands	1.70	−3.80	1.40	1.70	−1.10	−0.50	1.00
Spain	1.10	−3.60	0.00	−0.60	−2.10	−1.20	1.40
Sweden	−0.60	−5.20	6.00	2.70	−0.30	1.30	2.30
United Kingdom	−0.30	−4.30	1.90	1.60	0.70	1.70	3.00

Source: Our elaboration on OECD data.

- United Kingdom – an important, yet anomalous, organization; and
- The Netherlands – a country that may be small in size but that has a very high degree of openness towards internationalization.

This chapter presents a rather harsh consideration of the period 2008–2014 for Europe; first, it suffered the effects of the collapse of Lehman Brothers and, subsequently, the crisis of the sovereign debt. Table 2.14 presents the actual GDP trends of selected states during that period.

Table 2.15 details the number of companies operating in the manufacturing sector and Table 2.16 reflects the percentage of SMEs in relation to the total number of manufacturing companies. SMEs represent a very high proportion of the manufacturing sector – over 99 %.

It is interesting to observe that Italy has the highest number of small and medium-sized businesses. In 2008–2011, this figure was almost double the number of SMEs in Germany, Spain, France and the United Kingdom.

In respect of the number of businesses, Spain has suffered the highest loss in terms of percentage in the period 2008–2014 period (–19.10 %), followed by Italy (–14.30 %) and the United Kingdom (–7.12 %). Conversely, as shown in Fig. 2.4, several countries presented a positive result over the same period: France (+8.02 %), Sweden (+10.06 %), Germany (+12.76 %), and the Netherlands (+19.10 %).

Growth is tied to the development of commercial and financial globalization, which, in addition to rapid technological developments, has significantly broadened opportunities for SMEs. The fragmentation of

Table **2.15** Number of SMEs in manufacturing sector

Country	2008	2009	2010	2011	2012	2013	2014
France	210,074	205,449	210,665	248,743	217,949	220,911	226,925
Germany	191,269	175,878	205,417	203,620	203,620	208,070	215,676
Italy	458,332	437,765	425,471	419,391	383,481	384,086	392,794
Netherlands	43,034	45,187	50,361	47,922	47,519	47,821	49,047
Spain	206,556	191,106	187,921	182,252	163,643	163,885	167,107
Sweden	53,964	53,610	54,157	54,280	53,208	56,627	59,392
United Kingdom	130,162	126,936	122,664	121,206	120,419	117,052	120,896
EU-28	2,107,790	2,025,811	2,108,095	2,124,188	2,055,866	2,071,162	2,134,390

Source: Our elaboration on Eurostat, National Statistical Offices, DIW econ, London Economics.

Table 2.16 SMEs in manufacturing sector (%)

Country	2008 (%)	2009 (%)	2010 (%)	2011 (%)	2012 (%)	2013 (%)	2014 (%)
France	99.3	99.2	99.3	99.3	99.3	99.3	99.3
Germany	97.9	97.8	98.1	98.0	98.0	98.0	98.0
Italy	99.7	99.7	99.7	99.7	99.7	99.7	99.7
Netherlands	99.1	99.2	99.3	99.2	99.2	99.2	99.2
Spain	99.5	99.5	99.6	99.6	99.5	99.5	99.5
Sweden	99.3	99.3	99.4	99.4	99.3	99.3	99.3
United Kingdom	98.7	98.8	98.9	98.9	98.8	98.7	98.7
EU-28	99.2	99.2	99.3	99.2	99.2	99.2	99.2

Source: Our elaboration on Eurostat, National Statistical Offices, DIW econ, London Economics.

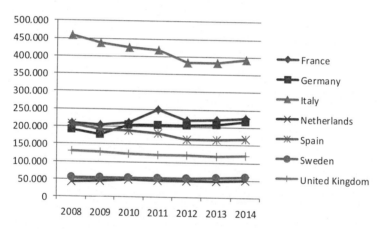

Fig. 2.4 Number of SMEs per country (Source: Our elaboration on Eurostat, National Statistical Offices, DIW econ, London Economics.)

the increasingly decentralized and outsourced productive processes of large companies facilitates the emergence and development of small organizations in new and often distant markets, where they carry out complex and sophisticated activities. In this scenario, SMEs seem to have an organizational structure particularly appropriate in a globalized framework because they are able to unite specialized productivity, good technical competence and maximum organizational flexibility. A thorough understanding of these processes requires an in-depth analysis of the make-up of the SME sector. This sector not only has a strong presence of micro enterprises, but also characterized by the heterogeneity of the individual countries. Table 2.17 presents the percentage of workers employed according to classification by size of business (2014 data) in the manufacturing sector.

Italy has the highest percentage of workers employed in micro enterprises (46.0 %) while, conversely, the country has the lowest percentage of workers employed in large enterprises (20.2 %) (see Fig. 2.5). The UK is in the reverse position, where the lowest proportion of workers are employed in micro enterprises (18.3 %), while large companies employ almost 48 % of the countries work. Figure 2.5 presents these data.

Table 2.17 Distribution by employee and size

2014				
Country	0–9 (%)	10–49 (%)	50–249 (%)	250+ (%)
France	29.4	19.2	15.2	36.2
Germany	18.6	23.2	20.6	37.7
Italy	46.0	21.5	12.4	20.2
Netherlands	28.7	20.0	0.2	33.1
Spain	39.5	21.0	13.8	25.6
Sweden	26.2	–	21.2	35.0
United Kingdom	18.3	18.0	16.0	47.7
EU-27	28.8	20.4	17.4	33.4

Source: Eurostat, National Statistical Offices, DIW econ, London Economics.

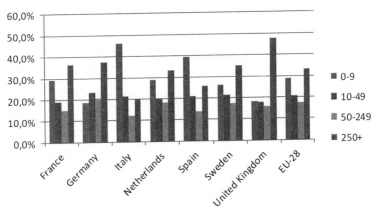

Fig. 2.5 Percentage of workers in micro enterprises (*Source*: Eurostat, National Statistical Offices, DIW econ, London Economics.)

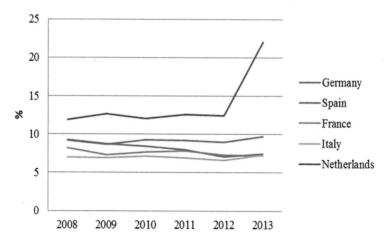

Fig. 2.6 EBITDA/net turnover (*Source*: Our elaboration of BACH data.)

The performance of SMEs in the countries under study here, taking as a reference point the EBITDA/Net Turnover index (which represents the amount of revenue generated per € of turnover, is presented in Fig. 2.6, which reflects the trends of the Index from 2008 to 2013.

Figure 2.6 presents data, by country, in relation to the revenue per € of turnover achieved by SMEs. If 2013, the last year for which data is available, is taken as a reference point, the highest average earnings were achieved in the Netherlands (22.06 %) and Germany (9.74 %). SMEs in Italy, France and Spain all converged on a value of approximately 7 % in 2013.

As to the profitability of SMEs, analyzing the trends in return on equity (ROE) for 2008–2013, it is possible to make a distinction between two groups of countries. The first group is composed of France, Germany and the Netherlands, the second comprises Italy and Spain.

Figure 2.7 shows how the difference between these two groups was evident throughout 2013. The difference between these two groups of countries averages around 8 %.

SMEs are also specific in their funding structure. For external financing, SMEs resort to banks more often than large companies do; however, the risk of their not obtaining funds is greater. As previously pointed out, the SMEs in the countries under study show an evident disequilibrium between internal funds (equity) and external funding (see Fig. 2.8).

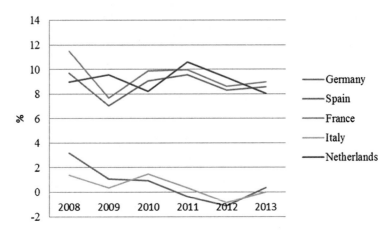

Fig. 2.7   Return on equity (ROE) (*Source*: Our elaboration of BACH data.)

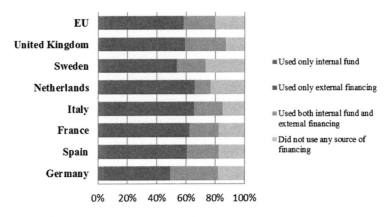

Fig. 2.8   Financing structure of SMEs (*Source*: Our elaboration of *Survey on the Access to Finance of Small and Medium-sized Enterprises (SAFE)*, Analytical Report 2013.)

Let us now examine a few indicators in relation to funding structure. The first indicator is the Asset/Equity ratio, which is an indicator of the financial leverage of a company. The indicator in question has been determined for SMEs in France, Germany, Italy, Netherlands and Spain.

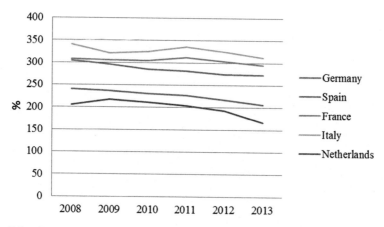

Fig. 2.9 Assets to equity ratio (*Source*: Our elaboration of BACH data.)

As demonstrated in Fig. 2.9, for all countries under study in 2008–2013, the index trend registered a slight decrease. Italy and France were the countries where SMEs had higher leverage. The most virtuous SMEs were those found in the Netherlands. Another important indicator is the ratio between EBITDA[2] (earnings before interest, taxes, depreciation and amortization) and financial charges. Similar indices express the ability of the business to provide adequate cover for the financial costs tied to administrative and financial policies. Given that the EBITDA is calculated net of operative funding provisions and gross of depreciation, it is representative of the flow of circulating capital deriving from operational management (see Fig. 2.10).

The index registers a general increase with the exception of Dutch SMEs, which reached, on average, a maximum value compared with SMEs in other countries. The Netherlands achieved a figure equal to 691 % in 2011, which then decreased to 643 % in 2013. During the same period, following a static trend, French SMEs reached, on average, the highest value equal to 661 % (compared with SMEs in the other countries). Italian and Spanish SMEs show a performance gap compared with the SMEs of other countries, although more contained than the other indicators previously analyzed.

---

[2] EBITDA or Gross Operating Margin.

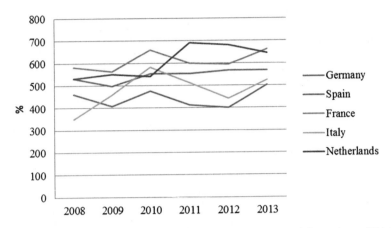

Fig. 2.10   EBITDA/interest of financial debt (*Source*: Our elaboration of BACH data.)

In interpreting the data on the shares of loans relative to SMEs, it is important to emphasize that large companies are usually less dependent on bank financing than are SMEs and that they benefit from the ability to obtain financing directly through the market. SMEs usually have far fewer funding sources available and thus are more vulnerable to the changing conditions of the credit market.

Therefore, in theory, a rise in the quota of loans to SMEs may be attributed to their more favorable access to bank credit compared with large companies. This however, may also be a result of large companies making greater use of non-banking financial instruments.

An increase in the number of loans granted to SMEs may be a reflection of financial and strategic trends and opportunities put into action by large companies, rather than easier access to funding for SMEs. This seems to be the case for Italy, Spain and the United Kingdom. Spain is the country with the highest amount of funding distributed to SMEs: a value that increased from 40 % to 34 % between 2007 and 2013. In the United Kingdom, the increase in the amount of loans given to SMEs over the period does not necessarily indicate an easier access to debt, as the overall volume on loans decreased (OECD, Financing SMEs and Entrepreneurs 2015)[3] (see Fig. 2.11). By contrast, Dutch

---

[3] Data for Germany are not presented in the OECD study.

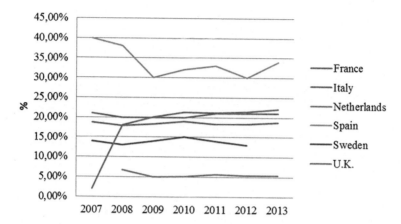

Fig. 2.11 Business loans, SMEs as a percentage of total business loans (*Source*: Our elaboration of OECD, financing SMEs and entrepreneurs 2015 data. *Data for the Netherlands available only for 2008; **Data for Sweden are not available for 2013.)

SMEs showed the lowest values, decreasing from 7 % to 5 % in the period 2008–2013.

From the point of view of risk management undertaken by commercial banks, it is understandable that banks adopt a more selective approach in credit supply during a period of recession in order to preserve the quality of assets on their financial statements. In general, though, the restrictive credit measures are a difficulty SMEs must face, as banking institutions consider SMEs to be a higher insolvency risk, as opposed to large companies. The banking institutions are also wary of SMEs due to their being unable to transition easily from bank credit to other forms of external funding.

Figure 2.12 below illustrates the trend of the cost of money maintained by SMEs in the 2007–2013 period.

For the majority of countries during the period 2007–2010, SMEs found themselves having to face harsher, more restrictive credit conditions compared with large companies. These difficulties, as demonstrated in Fig. 2.11, have taken the form of higher interest rates, shorter terms and more requests for guarantees. Figure 2.11 should be read and analyzed in conjunction with Fig. 2.12, in which the average spreads between interest rates applied to large companies and those applied to SMEs are underlined (see Fig. 2.13).

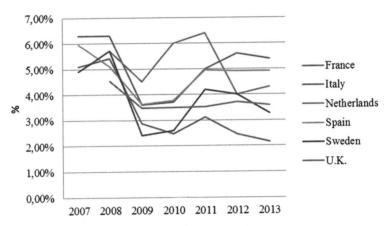

Fig. 2.12 Interest rate, average SMEs rate (*Source*: Our elaboration of OECD, financing SMEs and entrepreneurs 2015 data. *Netherlands and UK data not available for the year 2007.)

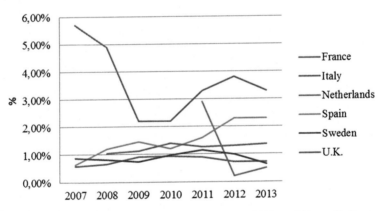

Fig. 2.13 Interest rate spread (between average SME and large % firm rate) (*Source*: Our elaboration of OECD, financing SMEs and entrepreneurs 2015 data. *Netherlands and UK data are not available for the years 2007–2010; **UK data is not available for 2007.)

Two facts should be mentioned in order to illustrate this point. First, SMEs tend to face higher costs for bank funding. A simple comparison between small loans (typical of SMEs) and larger loans (typical of larger companies) demonstrates that, in the countries under study, SMEs paid an average of 1.60 % additional base rate; there were higher peaks in Italy and Spain, where spreads in 2007–2013 reached values of 3.6 % and 1.53 %, respectively.

Listed below are a few considerations regarding access to finance according to the Small Business Act for Europe (SBA)[4] document:

- Rejected requests for funding and unacceptable financing offers (percentage of funding requested by SMEs);
- Access to public financial support, including guarantees (percentage of those interviewed that referred to an impoverishment);
- Availability of banks in granting a loan (percentage of those interviewed that referred to an impoverishment);
- Funding costs for loans with reduced payment compared with high payment (%);
- Total time employed to be paid (days);
- Loss of unpayable credit (percentage of overall turnover);
- Investments in risk capital (percentage of GDP);
- Index of legal rights strength.

See Table 2.18 for the data for the countries under study.)

As demonstrated in Table 2.18, particular attention should be paid to the elevated percentage of the rejection of loans requested by SMEs. SMEs in the most important Eurozone countries (with the exception of Ireland, where access to funding is difficult regardless of size) regularly face more obstacles to funding than large businesses. There are structural reasons why this occurs: SMEs are less readily identifiable; their business capability is often difficult to evaluate because their financial statements are less detailed; and, usually, SMEs generally have a brief credit history. In addition, there are higher fixed costs of evaluation and monitoring. These circumstances translate into higher transaction costs – in particular, those deriving from asymmetrical information.

---

[4] The Small Business Act for Europe (SBA) is the EU's flagship initiative to support small and medium-sized enterprises (SMEs); it includes a series of policy measures organized around ten principles ranging from entrepreneurship to internationalization and the creation of an administration attentive to the needs of SMEs.

Table 2.18 SMEs access to finance

	France	Germany	Italy	Netherl.	Spain	Sweden	United King.	EU avrg.
Rejected loan applications and loan offers (% of loan applications by SMEs)	13.600	2.500	16.700	38.600	19.200	12.000	21.900	14.400
Access to public financial support including guarantees (% of respondents who indicated a deterioration)	31.500	5.900	17.300	22.500	39.600	4.800	11.900	17.300
Willingness of banks to provide a loan (% of respondents who indicated a deterioration)	34.100	10.400	40.500	39.200	36.900	10.200	17.700	24.600
Relative difference in interest rate levels between loans up to €1 million and loans over €1 million	15.020	39.590	33.490	44.160	23.820	19.880	29.550	23.820
Total duration to be paid (no. of days)	52.000	31.330	113.330	38.670	99.330	31.670	38.330	50.760
Lost payments (% of total turnover)	2.000	2.000	2.700	2.600	2.700	2.000	3.700	3.830
Venture capital investments – early stage (% of GDP)	0.032	0.021	0.004	0.027	0.009	0.053	0.038	0.040
Strength of legal rights (0–10)	7.000	7.000	3.000	5.000	6.000	8.000	10.000	6.820

Source: Our elaboration of SBA Fact Sheets database.

In periods of economic recession, it is inevitable that the sources of credit for small businesses tend to drain more rapidly than those destined to large companies, thus hindering SME activity and investment to a greater extent.

The situation described above is what occurred during the Eurozone crisis. The merit of SME financial health and credit deteriorated to a greater degree than those of large companies, and the prolonged period of economic weakness has had a further negative impact on SME issues of information asymmetry.

3

European Funding of SMEs through Securitization: An Introduction

The weakness of bank credit in the Eurozone reflects both a drop in business demand for funding and a more restrictive availability of funding from banks. However, in countries that have suffered to a greater extent due to the economic crisis, the criteria related to obtaining credit distribution have also been negatively affected by the increased risk involved in funding entrepreneurs and the number of deteriorated loans on bank balance sheets: various steps have been taken in response to this situation.

A first, fundamental response was the increased requirements regarding banks holding adequate capital. This process is still under way, solicited in some countries by supervisory authorities.

A second response was the reduction of deteriorated loans, which weigh on bank balance sheets, by yielding such exposure to specialized operators, as well as through interventions aimed to rationalize the management of deteriorated credit through dedicated structures. Similar structures allow banks to pursue efficiency earnings in the management of deteriorated credit (non-performing loans: NPLs) and an increased transparency in their evaluation. Special mention must be made of supervisory action, as in 2015 Banque Centrale Européenne (BCE) (European Central Bank: ECB) *Asset Quality Review*, as it favors improvement in both transparency and

© The Author(s) 2017
G. Oricchio et al., *SME Funding*,
DOI 10.1057/978-1-137-58608-7_3

dependability of bank financial statements. The re-launch of bank credit is the specific objective pursued by targeted long-term refinancing operations (TLTROs). The BCE announced the first series of TLROs on June 5, 2014, and a second series (TLTRO-II) on March 10, 2016. The purpose of TLTROs is to provide an incentive to banks to issue loans to companies, tying the concession of BCE cash to the credit actually issued. On a longer-term basis, bank credit may benefit from the development of securitization transactions. The three principle options aimed to support and improve financing conditions for SMEs are:

- direct loans from public institutions such as the Banque européenne d'investissement (BEI) (European Investment Bank: EIB), or public guarantees for loans issued by commercial banks;
- a higher degree of securitization for loans to SMEs through pledged assets and the acquisition of assets by the BCE;
- long-term financing issued by the BCE and an interest rate linked to the expansion of total loans; one option does not exclude another and may be applied at the same time.

In the field of SME financing, in addition to traditional methods we find[1]:

- asset-based finance: asset-based lending, factoring, purchase order finance, warehouse receipts and leasing;
- alternative debt: corporate bonds, securitized debt, covered bonds, private placements and crowd funding debt;
- hybrid instruments: subordinated loans/bonds, silent participation, participating loans, profit participation rights, convertible bonds, bonds with warrants and mezzanine finance;
- equity instruments: private equity, venture capital, business angel, specialized platform for public listing of SMEs and crowd funding (equity).

---

[1] For a more detailed analysis of the listed methods, see OECD, *New approaches to SME and entrepreneurship financing: Broadening the range of instruments*, OECD, 2015.

We will now focus our attention on the aspects of securitization in relation to SMEs.

3.1   Securitization Models: A Brief Overview

Securitization operations have developed considerably in the last 30 years. Securitization is how a bank outsources one or more phases in the credit process: from funding to risk-taking in relation to loans requiring concise securitization. This evolution has implied a complete transformation of the banking model: a shift from the "Originate to Hold" (OtH) model to that of "Originate to Distribute" (OtD). The OtD model transfers the risk, potentially, to a multitude of investors. This action increases the degree of interdependence between banks and the capital market, allowing a shared risk, on the one hand, and, on the other, a heightened expansion and amplification of the risk itself.

In general terms, securitization is an operation that allows a body (bank, business, public entity) acting as the originator of a loan to:

1. transfer non-cash and non-negotiable financial or non-financial activities to the market in exchange for cash (classic securitization);
2. simply transfer the risk (concise securitization).

Figure 3.1 clarifies the base concept of the operation well: the originator of a loan is motivated to improve the liquidity of its assets and reduce its exposure to risk. In the capital market, there are investors willing to

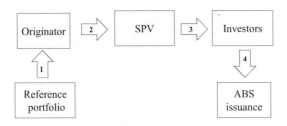

Fig. 3.1 Typical securitization flow chart

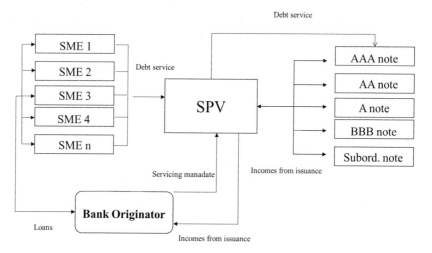

Fig. 3.2 SME securitization structure

subscribe to bonds issued by special purpose vehicles (SPV: a legal entity created to fulfill narrow, specific or temporary objectives), providing the SPV with the necessary funds to buy the assets sold by the originator. The bonds will thus have a financial profile that the expected cash flow from the purchased asset will cover. The profitability and risk of this bond are a function of the tranching performed during issuance. There are diverse classes of bond, differentiated according to seniority – that is, the priority given to the issuing of cash flow generated by the asset (Fig. 3.1).

Figure 3.2 illustrates the "base structure" of a securitization operation on credit flow to SMEs. The originator (bank) selects a package of loans comparable in amount, expiration and reimbursement plan: this represents the core of the operation. The SPV specifically constitutes places in the market with different rating levels that range from investment grade to high yield that represent the first barrier capable of absorbing possible defaults in the loan portfolio.

With the income from the bonds subscribed to by investors, the SPV buys the package of loans from the originator, acquiring the patrimonial rights so that the relative cash flow becomes usable to cover the debt originated by the banknotes in circulation. The fact that the originator (bank) usually carries out the function of a servicer ensures that the liaisons with clientele are not subject to specific negative impacts.

For the sake of simplicity, in the framework presented below, other bodies are not present. Examples of such bodies are rating agencies, the servicer bank and, especially, those entities that carry out a role relating to guarantees (in many cases there are public and para-public forms of guarantee).

The advantage for the originator (bank), which can improve funding that, alone, is of primary relevance, lies in the opportunity to widen the offer of credit to the SME market.

An aspect of market development is the articulation of operations based on large technical typologies. Asset-based securities (ABSs) are a versatile form of security and are divided into a range of segments (see Fig. 3.3). Thus, there is a segment of the market which assesses mortgage loans; another large sector, more relevant to ABS in the strict sense, includes different forms of credit (credit cards, leasing, etc.), in addition to assets that are not strictly financial, such as insurance and royalties. So-called collateral debt obligation (CDO) represents another large field and, in turn, comprises collateralized loan obligation (CLO) and collateralized bond obligation (CBO). Collateral debt obligation has grown significantly from 1996 and is often highlighted as a category of operations involved in the 2007–2008 financial crisis.

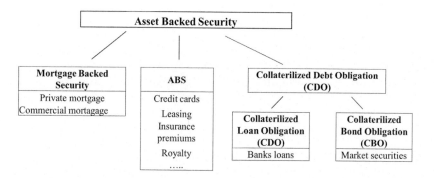

Fig. 3.3 ABS classification

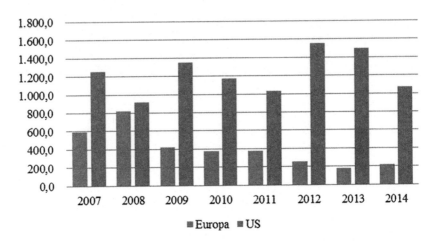

Fig. 3.4 European and US securization issuance (euro billions) (Source: Our elaboration of AFME 2015 data)

3.2 Securitization in Europe and the USA: A Comparison

In terms of issuances, the securitization market registered a constant rise until 2007, although inferior in volume compared with the USA. In 2008, in conjunction with the explosion of the financial crisis, the volume of issuances was still strong (€800 billion). From 2009 to 2013, issuances dropped significantly (€180 billion in 2013). An approximately 40 % drop has taken place in issuances since 2009. In 2014, there was an increase of issuances, bringing the value to approximately €216 billion. In the meantime, the USA has witnessed broader signs of resilience in securitization activities during 2009–2013, registering a decline in 2014, approximately €1000 billion (−28 % compared with 2013) (Fig. 3.4).

3.3 Securitization in Europe according to Country and Typology

Briefly presented below are securitization data and composition pertaining to a limited number of European countries according to various typologies.

The principle type of securitization, according to AFME, comprises asset-backed securities:

- Collateralized debt obligation (CDO);
- Commercial mortgage-backed security (CBMS);
- Residential mortgage-backed security (RMBS);
- Securities backed by small and medium-sized enterprises (SME);
- Whole business securitization (WBS).

Figure 3.5 presents the sum of the volume of securitization (expressed in € billions) of Belgium, France, Germany, Greece, Ireland, Italy, Holland, Portugal and Spain for the period 2008–2014.

Figure 3.6 presents the percentage of the six different types of securitization in operation in Europe in 2014 (representing a value of approximately €216 billion).

Finally, we present the sum of securitization according to typology and country for the first quarter of 2015 and the last quarter of 2014 in Table 3.1.

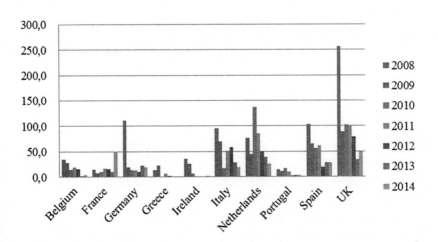

Fig. 3.5 Issuance by country of collateral (€ billions) (Source: Our elaboration of AFME 2015 data.)

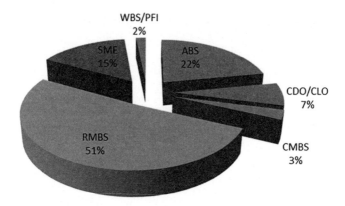

Fig. 3.6 European issuance by collateral (%) (Source: Our elaboration of AFME 2015 data.)

3.4   Securitization in Europe for SMEs

We can consider the economies of Europe and the USA as comparable. Europe, however, has a smaller pool of available funds compared with the USA. The number of activities in which to invest in Europe total just half of the number the USA can offer: €30,000 billion of activities compared with the €49,000 billion of the USA. A similar picture applies to financial activities invested in the stock market: the share capital quotes in Europe (€10,000 billion) is equivalent to approximately half the share capital quoted in the USA (€19,000 billion). The comparison with the USA demonstrates that the structure and the sources of funding are a key problem for Europe. Most financing in Europe is provided by regulated entities, such as banks and insurance companies; in the United States, there is a higher degree of diversification and flexibility in financing sources.

On the US market, private pension plans, investment fund managers and other categories of investor (angel investors, hedge funds, private equity and risk capital) offer a greater proportion of financing to companies compared with Europe. However, as illustrated in Table 3.2, in certain sectors – that is, those affecting SMEs – there seems to be greater funding in Europe as opposed to in the United States.

Table 3.1 Securitization in Europe, outstanding stock in 2015Q1–2014Q2 (€ billions)

Country	ABS		CDO/CLO		CMBS		RMBS		SME		WBS/PFI		TOTAL
	15-Q1	14-Q4	15-Q1	14-Q4	15-Q1	14-Q4	15-Q1	14-Q4	15-Q1	14-Q4	15-Q1	14-Q4	15-Q1
Austria	0.27	0.27			0.20	0.20	1.70	1.70					3.40
Belgium	0.04	0.02			0.16	0.17	51.48	55.81	18.10	18.48			143.86
Finland	0.63	0.72									0.50	0.50	1.00
France	19.28	19.83			0.50	0.52	49.75	50.48	0.32	1.02	0.54	0.55	102.66
Germany	40.50	40.87	0.85	1.07	6.71	7.46	19.31	20.16	1.71	1.89	0.05	0.05	43.17
Greece	12.46	12.68	1.75	1.75	0.24	0.24	3.47	3.66	6.33	6.73			20.19
Ireland	0.33	0.33	0.08	0.10			35.33	36.16					71.49
Italy	44.87	47.43	1.72	1.78	9.53	9.65	74.80	78.26	22.33	23.95	0.33	0.33	199.99
Netherlands	2.26	2.62	0.50	0.53	2.11	2.22	233.48	239.77	8.13	9.56			490.95
Portugal	3.37	3.50					25.67	26.05	6.59	5.59			63.90
Spain	21.98	23.05	0.43	0.46	0.20	0.22	119.53	122.57	28.09	30.06	0.01	0.02	300.28
UK	38.78	38.38	2.49	9.60	52.67	54.17	195.52	217.85	7.96	8.72	70.13	71.53	571.72
Europe Tot.	184.77	189.70	7.82	15.29	72.32	74.84	810.04	852.48	99.56	106.00	71.55	72.98	2012.61

Source: Our elaboration of AFME 2015 data – Securitization in Europe, outstanding stock in 2015Q1–2014Q2 (€ billions).

Table 3.2 Stock of funds available and flow of new financing

	Stock at end of 2013				Flow of new financing 2013		
	Banks	Non-banks	Government	Total	Banks	Non-banks	Government
US (€ billion)	494	688	54	1236	286	258	27
EU (€ billion)	1543	332	132	2007	748	112	66

Source: Our elaboration of the Association for Financial Markets in Europe (AFME)/Boston Consulting Group (BCG), *Bridging the growth gap*, 2015 data.

The total stock of funds available in Europe for SMEs amounts to €2000 billion compared with €1200 billion available in the USA.

The term "Banks" refers to the set of:

• Loans
• Securities loans
• Bonds/equity.

The term "Non-banks" refers to the set of:

• Mutual funds
• Segregated mandates
• Pension funds
• Insurance
• Sovereign wealth funds (SWFs)
• Private equity funds
• Venture capital funds
• Family and friends
• Crowd funding
• Angel investing.

The term "Government" refers to the set of:

• Government guarantees and sponsored loans.

Regardless of the importance the sector holds (of course, not in huge terms of volume as demonstrated in Table 2.17, due to its specific function), just a small proportion of the amount of funds is employed in the securitization of SMEs. The principle reason for this apparent contradiction relates to the financial gap that weighs heavily on this category of business; this expresses itself, essentially, as the risk of insufficient capital, an absence of stable sources and a high likelihood of default. The utilization of the instruments listed above would not only be advantageous to originators (collection of liquidity and risk transfer), but could also be beneficial for SMEs. The effect of growth in the credit capacity of banks could mean an increase in the volume of loans to SMEs. At the same time, the more advantageous conditions involved in the costs of funding would act as stimuli for the supply of loans to SMEs offering interest rates that were more competitive.

Because SMEs are small businesses and because collecting information on their projects is expensive, they have limited access to capital markets. In this context, securitization offers the holders of large European savings funds – that is, insurance companies and pension funds – the opportunity to direct resources to SMEs. From this point of view, the efforts made by the *Prime Collateralized Securities* (PCS) Initiative deserve support.[2]

The PCS has defined the common criteria of normalization, quality, simplicity and transparency with the aim of improving the depth of the market and liquidity for ABSs. The PCS also includes specific measures in relation to ABSs and SMEs. Prudential reforms may even contribute to the relaunching of securitization.

A fundamental initiative in this direction is found in the insurance sector: the Solvency II Directive. This initiative proposes the alignment of the patrimonial requirements with the risks that insurance companies have actually taken on in their investment activity. The present Solvency II Directive came into force on January 1, 2016.

---

[2] The Prime Collateralized Securities Initiative (PCS) is an independent, not-for-profit initiative set up to re-enforce the asset-backed securities market in Europe as a key to generating robust and sustainable economic growth for the region. At the heart of the PCS Initiative is the PCS Label, which is designed to enhance and promote good practice, and is awarded to specific asset-backed securities.

3.5   European Union Reform of Stock Markets

On September 30, 2015, the European Commission began a project to free funds in favor of European businesses and to stimulate growth within the EU through the creation of a single stock market. The unification of stock markets involves all 28 EU Member States being in concordance and the integration of the EU Bank (which is concerned with the Euro area), and is closely connected with and supports the objectives of the "Junker Plan" on strategic investments. Inserted in the framework of the Green Paper of February 18, 2015, the program proposed by the EU represents the most important European integration project promoted by the new Commission and by the new European Parliament Legislation.

Companies, however, still rely heavily on banks: companies draw upon stock markets seldom and to a lesser extent (as previously mentioned). The purpose of the Commission's project is to remove the obstacles in cross-border EU investments that prevent companies from accessing alternative forms of funding. The Commission has thus committed to the preparation, by 2019, of the constitutive elements that form the foundation of stock markets. The Commission's task is to ensure that these elements are well-organized, integrated and involve all Member States in order that the entire economy may benefit from the advantages offered by stock markets and financial entities other than banks.

A fully functional unified stock market could offer many opportunities for growth. According to European Commission estimates, if EU risk capital markets were to have the degree of importance of those of the Unites States during the period 2008–2013, European companies could obtain supplementary financing amounting to approximately €90 billion. The unification of stock markets could also facilitate access to funds for businesses that are incapable of reaching investors, thus directing funds in the most efficient way possible. With regard to the Green Paper of February 18, 2015, the Commission has acceded to a three-month consultation the result of which will be fundamental in defining a road map capable of contributing to the unblocking of funds from entities other than banks in order to allow start-ups to prosper and to support further expansion of larger companies. The Green Paper differentiates between two groups of measures: those that are already mature and therefore require immediate action; and those that are more complex and require more time to mature. Among the latter, the Green Paper includes measures of legislative reform that should regulate revenue, bankruptcy, stock markets, pension funds, corporate governance and consumer protection.

There are various key points in relation to the group of measures requiring immediate action:

- Development of proposals in favor of high-quality securitizations and the decongestion of bank balance sheets in order to foster and implement lending capacity. An EU initiative assessing the subject of securitization (simple, transparent and standardized securitization, STS) should have the effect of improving the standardization of products thus securing thorough procedural regulations, legal certainty and full comparability of securitization instruments. This would allow, in particular, an increase in transparency, consistency and the fundamental information available to investors not only to the benefit of the SME sector, but also beneficial to the promotion of an increase in liquidity. The process would therefore simplify the issuing of securitized products, which would allow institutional investors to exercise due diligence with regard to products that meet their needs, terms of asset diversification, profitability and term horizon.
- Re-examination of the prospectus of the plan to support companies, especially small businesses, in obtaining funding and in finding cross-border investors. A prospectus is a disclosure document used by companies in order to attract investments. If, on the one hand, these documents aid investors in the decision-making process concerning investments; on the other, they are often lengthy documents containing detailed information that involve companies in administrative costs and fees. In addition, it is not always easy for investors to orient themselves in relation to the vast amount of information provided.
- Commence activities to improve the availability of information concerning the credit status of SMEs in order to facilitate investors willing to invest in these businesses. In Europe, the majority of SMEs resort to banks to obtain funding; on average, approximately 13 % of their

requests are rejected. Often, the rejection is due solely to the fact that the risk profiles of these businesses do not meet the requirements set by banks, even though these requests are economically sustainable. Banks could be encouraged to provide detailed information to SMEs that have had loan requests rejected and help make them aware of alternative forms of funding available. In the field of disclosure, International Financial Reporting Standards (IFRS) have assumed a fundamental role in promoting an appropriate and standardized language within the EU that fosters easier access to global capital markets for large EU firms quoted on the Stock Exchange. Nonetheless, a full application of IFRS to smaller companies – in particular, to those seeking participation in trading venues – would result in an increase of supplementary costs. A high-quality, simplified international accounting standard appropriate for quoted companies could, in some trading venues, constitute a step forward in terms of transparency and comparability and, if applied proportionally, could make companies more attractive to cross-border investors.

- Collaboration with the sector to put a private pan-European placement system into effect in order to encourage direct investment in smaller companies. December, 10 2016, the European Commission published a Green Paper on retail financial services and insurance in order to obtain opinions on how to increase competition and cross-border offers of retail financial products. In addition, in 2018 an all-encompassing evaluation of European markets for retail investment products is expected. The purpose of the evaluation is to identify the different ways retail investors can access products that are appropriate in terms of cost efficiency and equity. Moreover, the evaluation will also examine how to benefit fully from the new possibilities offered by online services and from financial technology (also known as "FinTech").

- Support resorting to new European long-term investment funds in order to channel investments in favor of infrastructures and other long-term investments – that is, European long-term investment funds (ELTIF), created at the end of 2014. In order to facilitate long-term funding for infrastructural investment, the Commission has presented, along with an action plan, a revision of calibrations in Solvency II to guarantee that insurance companies are subject to prudential treatment that better reflects the risk factor of investments in infrastructure and ELTIF. Additionally, the Commission is to complete the revision of the regulations concerning asset requirements. Also, when judged necessary, the Commission is to modify the risk calibration applicable to infrastructural investments for the banking sector. Jonathan Hill, former European Commissioner for Financial Stability, Financial Services and Capital Markets Union presenting a series of measures aimed to establish a Capital Markets Union concluded as follows: "the European Union's commitment to a single market to capital dates back to the Treaty of Rome. Now is the time to drive it forward; to unlock the single market's potential; and deliver more competitiveness, more jobs and more growth across Europe".

4

Corporate and SME Credit Rating Models

4.1 PD Corporate SME Model Development

This section describes the main activities underlying the developmental steps of a model for the estimation of the PD (see Fig. 4.1). Our focus is mainly on the customer segment of corporate small and medium-sized enterprises (corporate SMEs). We refer the reader to Sect. 6.4 for a description of the main validation tests; these should be performed after the model estimation and before its final functional specification and passage to the production phase.

4.1.1 Step 1: Perimeter of Applicability and Definitions

Whatever the future application of the model to be developed, to establish a firm foundation for the entire process, it is important to pay great attention in the initial phase (Step 1) to the regulatory and operative reference framework, and to the definition of the event to be forecast: the default probability (see Table 4.1).

© The Author(s) 2017
G. Oricchio et al., *SME Funding*,
DOI 10.1057/978-1-137-58608-7_4

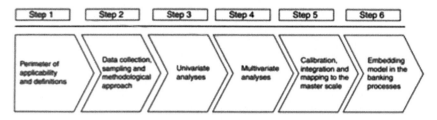

Fig. 4.1 Main steps in developing a rating model

Table 4.1 Main steps in developing a rating model

Step 1: Perimeter of applicability and definitions
Identification of the segment of interest (perimeter of applicability)
Definition of the event to be forecast (the default)
Establishment of the working team
Analysis of the internal and external regulatory framework
Analysis of processes, IT procedures and data to support the credit unit data availability
Analysis of the portfolio
Definition of the modality for dealing with outliers and exceptions
Comparison and discussion with the business and credit experts

The main objective of the model is the estimation of the probability of default within a determined temporal horizon (typically, one year) to classify customers in a portfolio according to their degree of risk.

The central role in the design of a rating model is the definition of default, which allows (future) insolvent customers (defined as the "bads" within the estimation samples) to be distinguished from solvent customers (the "goods"). The definition of default has to be set sufficiently far in advance (far enough from the onset of a problematic situation) to permit the identification of a default before it is too late to take corrective action and, in the meantime, sufficiently close to the moment of default to make an effective distinction between bads and goods.

The default definition used in model development should also be consistent with that used elsewhere in the bank and in line with the default definition required by the regulator. The default definition provided by the New Capital Accord includes bad debts, sub-standard loans, restructured exposures, and past due and overdrawn positions (see Basel Committee 2006).

To develop an effective rating tool, it is essential to establish a heterogeneous working group, characterized by a range of quantitative technical skills (mathematical, statistical and computer science) for:

- descriptive and inferential analysis;
- model design, the architecture of the rating system, the analysis of the origin of existing credit, and monitoring processes;
- the management of databases and implementation of the IT environment for the estimation and validation processes;
- and qualitative skills (economical and juridical) for:

  - the analysis of the enterprises' financial situation and balance sheet data;
  - the assessment of scenario and sector components; and
  - an in-depth knowledge of the bank's internal norms, and national and international rules.

Further requirements are solid experience in the field of the estimation and validation of rating systems, sufficient seniority and knowledge of the main internal processes of a banking group.

The working group should first analyze:

- the internal regulatory framework (of the bank or the banking group) and the external regulatory framework (supervisory regulations, and domestic and international guidelines);
- the credit process underlying the origination of the credit and monitoring of the corporate SME counterparts; and
- the IT procedures that support this process.

The working group should then analyze the corporate SME segment using the most recent data available (for example, up to December 31 of the previous year) with respect to the main classification variables (industry sector, geographic area, company size, and so on) both in terms of position and volumes (that is, credit limit and outstanding debts).

The portfolio analysis represents a central activity within the estimation process: the segment data analyzed in the recent portfolio should be the main reference for the working group in relation to:

- the editing of the data request finalized to the construction of the estimation and model validation samples;
- the definition of existing fields for the indicators; and
- the management of outliers, exceptions and preliminary factor transformations and normalizations, in order to reduce the impact of outliers and to make the multi-factor regression analysis more efficient and factor weights easier to interpret.

4.1.2 Step 2a: Data Collection and Sampling

After analyzing the availability, length of historical series and the quality of the databases underlying the credit processes, the next step is to edit the designated "long list" of potential predictors of default. This list is based on the academic literature, as well as on the input from the experiences of relationship managers and personnel from the credit department of the bank: the so-called "experts" of the working group (see the first activity of Step 2 in Table 4.2). In order to carry out a proper statistic-economic analysis, the indicators included in the initial long list should be grouped into areas and informative categories, obtaining the definition of as many long lists as the number of areas

Table 4.2 Developing a rating model: main activities of Step 2

Step 2: Data collection, sampling and methodological approach
Editing of indicator long list(s)
Comparison with the credit experts and possible enlargement or restriction of the proposed long list(s)
Definition and formulation of the data request
Preliminary explorative data analysis
Data cleaning
Construction of model estimation and validation samples
Validation of representativeness and stability of the identified samples with respect to the recent portfolio
Selection of the methodological approach

of information considered. Typical information areas to be analyzed in the development of an estimation model for probability of default for the corporate SME segment are financial, internal behavioral, external behavioral and qualitative.

The risk indicators belonging to each of the four inquiry areas will be grouped successively into categories for analysis; this is to facilitate the economic interpretation of the subsequent statistical evidence and to verify that, during the reduction that the area's initial long lists will undergo, all the informative categories will be adequately represented.

Table 4.3 presents examples of indicators belonging to the financial area, grouped into information categories.

After finalizing the indicators' long lists and extracting all necessary data, a thorough analysis of the databases must be performed, paying particular attention to:

- the possible presence of duplicated positions for the same analysis key;
- the consistency of elementary variables;
- their economic coherence, both in terms of content and number of expected observations per period (month);
- the variation of indicator values; and
- their stability over time, also with respect to their relative risk by subsegments of analysis (industry sector, geographic area, company size, and so on).

After carefully carrying out data cleaning, the next step is estimation sample extraction and model validation, ensuring:

- sufficient cardinality and sample depth;
- the correct identification of goods and bads, both in the development and in the model validation samples;
- an adequate proportion of bads and goods, which permits an adequate representation of the event to be forecast within the estimation samples; and
- the stability/representativeness of the samples with respect to the reference portfolio.

Table 4.3 Financial indicators grouped by categories: an illustrative example

Category	Indicator
Size	Capital employed; Cash.
	Equity; Fixed assets; Inventory; Net margin; Net sales.
	Operating cash flow; Profit or loss; Provision funds; Total assets; Turnover.
	Value added
Profitability	(Gross margin)/(Capital employed)
	(Net margin)/Equity
	(Net margin)/(Total assets)
	(Operating cash flow)/Sales
	(Profit after interest expenses)/(Capital employed)
	(Profit before interest expenses)/Sales
	(Profit or loss)/(Total assets)
Debt service capacity	(Commercial debt)/Turnover
	(Financial debt)/(Gross margin)
	(Financial debt)/Turnover (Fiscal debt)/Turnover
	(Gross margin)/(Current liabilities)
	(Interest expenses)/(Total debts)
	(Long-term debt)/Turnover
	(Net margin)/(Interest expenses)
	(Net margin)/(Long-term debt)
	(Operating cash flow)/(Total debts)
	(Profit after tax)/(Financial debt)
	[(Short + Long term debt)−Cash]/Equity (Total debt)/Turnover
Liquidity	Accounts receivable Cash/Turnover Cash/Equity
	Cash/(Total current liabilities) Cash/(Total debt)
	(Current liabilities)/Sales
	(Debt to suppliers)/(Raw materials) Inventory/Turnover Revaluation/Sales
	(Total credits)/Turnover
	(Total credits)/(Capital employed)
	(Total credits)/(Total assets)
	(Total credits)/(Total current liabilities)
	(Total credits)/(Total debt)
	(Total current assets)/(Total current liabilities)
	Working capital
	(Working capital)/(Net sales)
	(Working capital)/Turnover

(continued)

Table 4.3 (continued)

Category	Indicator
Gearing	(Book equity)/(Total assets)
	(Capital employed)/(Fixed assets)
	(Current liabilities)/(Total assets)
	Equity/(Long-term debt)
	Equity/(Total assets)
	Equity/(Fixed assets)
	[Equity–(Issued shares)]/(Total assets)
	(Issued shares)/(Total assets)
	(Issued shares)/(Total liabilities)
	(Long term debt)/(Fixed assets)
	(Short + Long-term bank debt)/(Book equity)
	(Total debt)/Equity
	(Total debt)/(Total assets)
Activity	(Direct cost)/(Total assets)
	(Direct cost)/Turnover (Labor cost)/Sales
	(Operating cash flow)/(Interest expenses)
	(Provision reserves)/Turnover
	(Raw materials)/(Commercial debt)
	Sales/(Fixed assets)
	Sales/(Total assets)
Stability	Change in capital employed
	Change in current assets
	Change in fixed assets Change in cash
	Change in [(Financial debt)/(Gross margin)]
	Change in long-term debt
	Change in [(Net margin)/(Interest expenses)]
	Change in [(Operating cash flow)/(Sales)]
	Change in return on investment (ROI)
	Change in [Sales/(Fixed assets)] Change in turnover
	Change in total assets

Generally, for the construction of the estimation samples of a rating model, all the positions that went into default in the observation horizon (bad customers) and a sub-set of the positions that never went into default in the observation horizon (good customers) are adopted. In certain cases, the samples could be balanced – that is, the same number of bads and goods.

One possible sampling methodology is the random extraction of positions, without repetition, stratified with respect to the representative

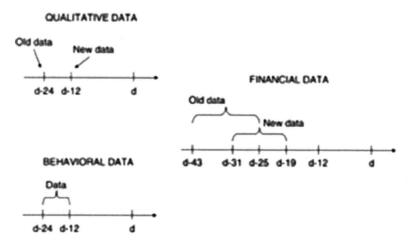

Fig. 4.2   Information-gathering rules: an illustrative example

variables and to the year of default, with constant sampling probability (simple sampling) within layers. Of the extracted samples, one must verify carefully the completeness of information and the existing fields (ranges) observed in the recent portfolio. The possible infeasibility of one of the above conditions requires the re-extraction of the sample.

The linking of information (financial, behavioral and qualitative) to the sample positions must be performed in a manner coherent with the effective availability of the information (updating time, source, and so on). This allows for the construction of the indicators defined in the long lists to be carried out early enough to respect the time of default, both for the single bad position and for the corresponding (twin) good positions in the sample.

A possible information-linking rule is depicted in Fig. 4.2.

If "d" denotes the instant (month) of entrance into default of a generic bad position, the period of data observation of the bad position and of the corresponding good one varies between:

- "d-12" and "d-24" for the information of a qualitative nature – to evaluate the possible variation of this kind of information across the interval of 12 months;

- "d-12" and "d-24" for the behavioral information – to build relevant derived indicators such as quarterly, semi-annual and annual averages/variations;
- "d-19" and "d-43" for the financial variables – to simulate the effective availability of at least two balance sheets in the production phase.

Once a preliminary sample analysis has been performed (quality, numeracy and observation depth), it is possible to design the model structure and define the best methodological approach to be followed during the model development.

4.1.3 Step 2b: Model Structure

The most widespread rating model structure is modular, with the number of modules equal to the number of information areas that feed the model – in this case, four: one financial module, two behavioral modules and a qualitative module. Each module, according to the chosen methodology, produces as output a score that expresses, in numerical terms, the credit merit of the counterpart, depending on the type of information computed: the accounting data (financial module); the borrower behavior with the bank (internal behavioral module), or with the banking system (external behavioral module); and the qualitative judgment expressed by the relationship manager (qualitative module).

Depending on the practical availability of data (financial, behavioral and qualitative), it is possible to develop models on a statistical basis (in the presence of sufficient robust data) or an expert basis (judgmental).

As shown in Fig. 4.3, the score produced by a module developed on a statistical base is transformed, successively, into a default probability that is expressed on a scale from 0 (minimal risk) to 1 (maximum risk) to the likelihood that, during a period of 12 months, the borrower will become insolvent, according to the default definition adopted. The (modular) PDs obtained separately are then integrated, according to an algebraic formula, in a unique default probability, associated successively with a rating class of the bank's master scale.

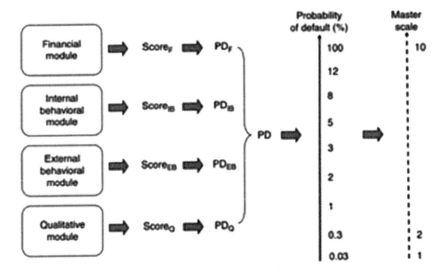

Fig. 4.3 Main steps in the development of statistical models

The score produced by the modules developed on a judgmental basis (inside the upper dotted line in Fig. 4.4) is generally not transformed into a default probability but, rather, is used to correct – upward (upgrading) or downward (downgrading) – the rating class assigned by the statistical component of the model (inside the lower dotted line shown in Fig. 4.4).

Finally, in the presence of modules and components developed only on an expert basis, the judgmental score can be employed to correct (upward or downward) the rating class corresponding to the default probability assigned (ex ante) to the portfolio segment, following the analysis of its current and historical default rates in the medium to longer term (see Fig. 4.5).

4.1.4 Step 2c: Methodological Approach

As far the methodological approach is concerned, for the segments characterized by databases that are sufficiently broad and stable and that have an adequate number of defaults (called a "high default portfolio"), it is

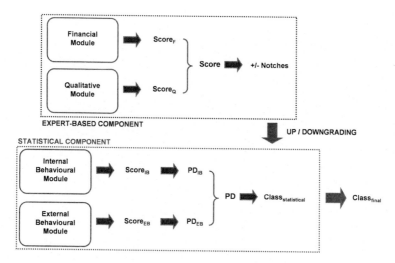

Fig. 4.4   Main steps in the development of statistical/expert-based models

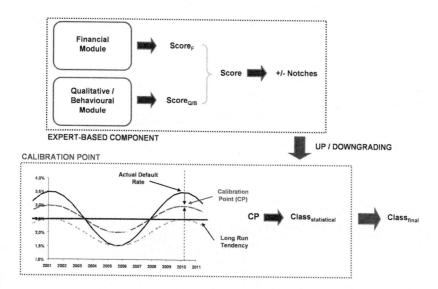

Fig. 4.5   Main steps in the development of purely expert-based models

possible to adopt a statistical approach for the assessment of qualitative information in cases supported by judgmental techniques .

The most frequently adopted statistical technique for the corporate SME segment is logistic regression: alternative techniques are discriminant analysis; probit models; and the more recent inductive models of a heuristic nature, such as genetic algorithms and neural networks.

For insights regarding the listed approaches, see Resti and Sironi (2007). Next, we describe the development of a default probability estimation model based on the logit method.

4.1.5 Statistical Methodology

In the literature, it is recognized that logistic regression is one of the best methodologies for the estimation of a function capable of linking the probability of the possession of a dichotomous attribute (in this case, bad = 1; good = 0) to a set of explicative variables (financial, behavioral or qualitative).

The logistic regression represents a specific case of regression analysis: the dependent variable, Y, is dichotomous, its distribution is binomial and the estimation of Y, varying from 0 to 1, assumes the meaning of a probability: $P\{Y = 1 \mid x\} = \pi(x)$ that is:

$$Y = \begin{cases} 1, & \text{with probability } \pi(x) \\ 0, & \text{with probability } 1 - \pi(x) \end{cases}$$

The logistic regression function has the form:

$$\text{logit}(\pi(x)) = \beta_i + \sum_{i=1}^{n} \beta_i \cdot x_i = x \cdot \beta$$

where logit $(\pi(x))$ denotes the natural logarithm of the ratio of the probability of "success" (that is, the probability that the analyzed position defaults in the 12 months successive to the evaluation) and the probability of "no success" (solvent) given the vector **x** of n predictive variables (for example, the vector **x** could contain behavioral variables of the customer):

$$\text{logit}\big(\pi\left(x\right)\big) = \ln\left[\frac{\pi\left(x\right)}{1 - \pi\left(x\right)}\right]$$

As $\pi(\mathbf{x})$ denotes the probability that Y is 1, conditional to the explicative variables **x**, the probability of Y can be expressed as a logistic function:

$$\pi\left(x\right) = \frac{e^{x} \cdot \beta}{1 + e^{x \cdot \beta}}$$

The choice of the logit to describe the function that links the probability of Y to the combination of predictive variables is determined by the observation that the probability gets gradually close to the limits "0" and "1", describing an "S" shape (called a "sigmoid").

While it is not a unique function that permits the modeling of the probability of a phenomenon, the logit is privileged with respect to the others as it represents a transformation of the ratio of two complementary probabilities (a quantity known as "odd"); that is, the *ratio* of the number of successes over each failure of the examined phenomenon.

4.1.5.1 Expert-based Methodology

The modules developed according to an expert approach are generally inspired by a multi-attribute value theory such as the Analytical Hierarchical Process™ (AHP) proposed by Saaty at the end of the 1970s. The AHP method allows the modeling of a decision problem by means of a hierarchy of levels (see Fig. 4.6) and by the conversion of qualitative and quantitative information in a uniform manner by means of the concept of relative importance in a finite set of alternatives.

The choice of a hierarchical approach for the definition of the expert-based components is often preferred to alternative techniques; this is for reasons of conceptual and implementable simplicity, methodological

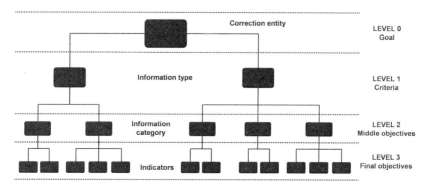

Fig. 4.6 Schematic view of the proposed hierarchy

transparency and the possibility of performing fine-tuning on all the parts of the structure, also in an independent manner.

Following a top-down approach, the main objective of the analysis – that is, the determination of the quantity of the improvement/worsening of the counterparty risk estimated by the statistical component of the model – is decomposed according to a hierarchy of sub-objectives at lower levels of the hierarchy specifically for the segment to which the borrower belongs.

Such decomposition allows us to design a sort of "conceptual map" of the expert-based component and, at the same time, to formalize the basic hierarchical structure.

Following this method, it is possible to define the mathematical formalization of one or more (expert-based) modules of a rating model in parallel with the definition of the conceptual map(s), with these main objectives:

- to establish the criteria to be used for dealing with differing information, according to its type (continuous or categorical) to ensure the correct transformation of indicators into model variables;
- to assure the uniqueness of the variables' value range;
- to define the criteria for dealing with missing values;
- to identify the model variables to which to assign a weight;
- to establish the criteria for the computation of weights to manage possible diversity in the "discriminant capability" of some risk indicators.

At the highest level of the hierarchy, the total risk function is computed – the score (integrated if it results from more than one module) which determines the size of the correction of the statistical rating class – whose value depends on the nodes at the lower hierarchy level.

The hierarchy proposed consists of four levels.

- "Level 0" (or the "starting level") contains the main objective (or "goal") of the evaluation: the risk expert-based score to be assigned to the examined positions.
- "Level 1", containing the evaluation criteria (financial and/or qualitative) that specify the content and meaning of the goal: the Level 1 criteria are divided into more specific objectives.
- The objectives of "Level 2" (the categories of information to be analyzed which, in case of a qualitative module, can be: demand/offer in the reference market; competitive position of the company; proprietary structure/account quality; and so on) that are themselves subdivided in Level 3.
- The single terminal objectives of "Level 3" of the hierarchy, originated from single module variables.

A value is assigned to each modality of the variables that feed the expert-based component – continuous for continuous variables and discrete for categorical variables in the interval – for example, from 0 (maximum risk) to 10 (minimum risk).

To each objective of the structure, a "local weight" is assigned ranging from 0 to 1, which determines the relative importance with reference to the objective of the higher level.

The importance of each terminal objective in relation to the goal is determined by the "hierarchy composition rule":

- the local weights assigned to the different terminal objectives are multiplied by the value of the corresponding variables;
- the values so computed are summed up to obtain the values of the objectives of the higher level; and moving from the bottom to the top, the weighted sums of the variables, first, and then the categories/types of information lead to the determination of the score (integrated,

where more than one module is present) of the expert-based model component.

4.1.6 Step 3: Univariate Analysis

The aim of the univariate analysis is to investigate the link between the single variable (financial, behavioral, qualitative) and the default, and the consequent reduction of the factors' long lists to medium lists that are logically and methodologically sound, removing factors that do not perform well or that show a high percentage of missing values (see Table 4.4).

The univariate analysis follows the preliminary explorative sample analysis (data quality and representativeness) and after the rebuilding of the factor algebra (by association with all the sample observations the indicators defined in the long lists).

The aims of the univariate analysis – performed separately for each informative category of the single areas of enquiry – are:

Table 4.4 Developing a rating model: main activities of Step 3

Step 3: Univariate analyses
Univariate statistical analysis (for continuous variables) and analysis of the distribution (for categorical variables) of the single indicators of the long lists
Analysis of the economic meaning of indicators and analysis of their relation to the default
Definition of the modality to deal with missing values
Management of missing data, outliers and exceptions
Exclusion of the variables characterized by a rate of missing data higher than a predetermined threshold (vertical missing analysis)
Exclusion of observations characterized by missing information greater than a predetermined threshold (horizontal missing analysis)
Analysis of the discriminant power of the stand-alone indicators
Transformation and normalization of indicators at univariate level
Definition of the medium lists of indicators made for a single inquiry area by the transformed variables, which result, at the end of the transformation, in being more predictive than the others
Verification, on the validation sample, of the stability of the chosen transformations and of the predictivity of the medium lists' variables
Comparison with the credit experts and possible enlargement/reduction of the individuated medium lists

- to analyze the distribution (in classes or quantiles according to the type) of all the variables in their fields of existence;
- to verify the economic soundness of the factors; and their proper relationship with the default.

As an example, in Figs. 4.7, 4.8 and 4.9 three variables are characterized by identical distributions for a range of values (shaded bars), but by three different relations with the risk (default rate of the population in the eight ranges, shown by the curve on the graph). Figure 4.7 shows a trend growing with the risk, Fig. 4.8 shows a decreasing trend and Fig. 4.9 illustrates uncertainty.

In the first two cases, if the trend with respect to the risk is confirmed by the economic interpretation of the indicators under consideration, the two variables will be included in the factors' medium list(s) to be analyzed, at multivariate level, in Step 4.

The variable represented in Fig. 4.9 will be excluded from the successive analysis process because of its undetermined relation with respect to the event to be forecast – the default.

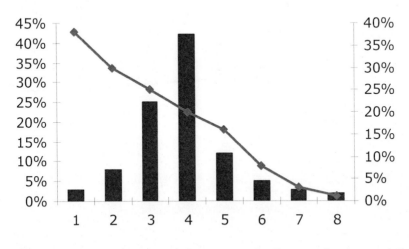

Fig. 4.7 Example of a variable growing monotonically with the risk

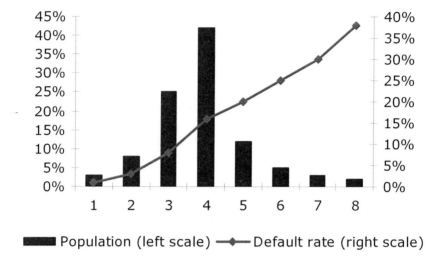

Fig. 4.8 Example of a variable decreasing monotonically with the risk

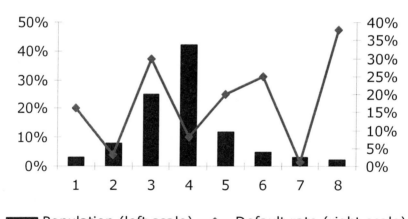

Fig. 4.9 Example of an uncertain relation with the risk

It is necessary to work out the analysis of distribution and its relation with the default, both before and after the preprocessing of data. This is intended to eliminate problems such as missing data, outliers and exceptions (for example, "0/0", "missing/0" and so on).

There are a number of ways to manage missing data: elimination of the indicators not available for a significant percentage of observations (vertical missing data), substitution of the missing data with predefined values, or the elimination of observations for which a significant number of indicators from the long lists are not available (horizontal missing data).

A common approach to the management of outliers is to define their data variability in order to assess their economic and statistical feasibility ranges and the consequent substitution of values outside the range of pre-fixed thresholds. Definition of these feasibility ranges requires special attention; if the ranges are too narrow, this could lead to models the fit of which is biased by an arbitrary variance reduction of the input data.

As with the missing data and the outliers, the exceptions also require specific treatment.

In the construction of variables derived across time horizons of three, six, twelve months and so on – as minimum, maximum, correlation, coefficient of variation and so forth – it is necessary to define the minimum thresholds for the presence of information; below such thresholds, the value obtained for the indicator should be considered to be missing.

Generally, for indicators built on a number of n months, it is it may be necessary to have at least $n + 1$ information if n is odd, or n if n is even.

There are two other important activities related to univariate analysis: the management of the "U-shaped" factors; and their transformation, inside the feasibility interval, to emphasize their relation with the default.

The first of these two analyses, performed separately on each factor of the long lists, is devoted to identifying the possible "U" relation – which must also be confirmed by the economic analysis – between the range of values assumed by the indicator and the default rate (see Fig. 4.10, upper chart).

The analysis is carried out by dividing the interval of assumed values into quantiles, from which the default rate is computed.

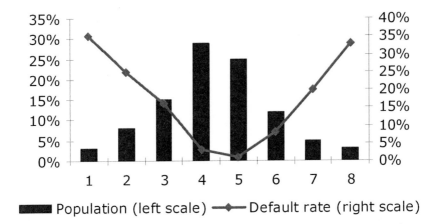

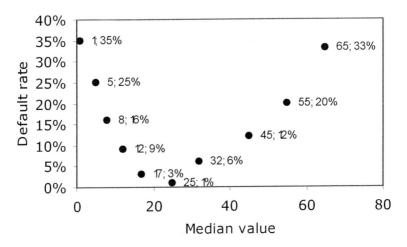

Fig. 4.10 Example of a "U-shaped" factor

The median value of each quantile and the corresponding default rate are identified, respectively, on the x and y axes of the Cartesian plane, allowing the graphical representation of the relation of each indicator with the default (see Fig. 4.10, lower chart).

In the event of a "U-shaped" pattern, once the point $(x_0; y_0)$ of the derivative sign change has been set – that is, the minimum of the function, ideally a parabola with the two branches going upward – it is possible to identify the best preliminary transformation that ensures a cross near the point $(x_0; y_0)$ and, simultaneously, to minimize the deviation between the interpolating curve and the observed values.

At the end of such transformation, the most significant factors of the long lists will show a monotonous trend (increasing or decreasing, according to their economic meaning) with respect to the default. They may also be subjected to a final phase of (deterministic) transformation and normalization to reduce the impact of outliers, and to make the multifactor regression analysis more efficient and the factor weights easier to interpret.

As an example, for continuous variables, one can identify, for each indicator, the value interval $[x_l; x_u]$, where a significant portion of observations falls (equal, e.g., to 75–80 %) and, at the same time, the monotonic relation with the default event appears with specific evidence.

Then, the upper and lower bounds are denoted, respectively, as xu and xl – and it is possible, by means of a deterministic transformation (e.g. logit) to enhance the discriminatory capability of the single factor in the interval $[xl; xu]$ and flatten it outside the interval, where the relation with the default is less important. Following this transformation, the analysis of the ordering capability of individual indicators at univariate level is carried out using a discriminatory power test on both the developing sample and the validation sample.

By setting the minimum level of acceptability for the discriminatory power tests required for the variables belonging to the same types of information (financial, behavioral or qualitative) and by assessing the coherence of the indicators' behavior (values and relation to the default) with respect to their economic significance, it becomes possible to select from the corresponding long list the three sub-sets of factors (financial, behavioral and qualitative) that are:

- most predictive of the default event;
- intuitive from the economic point of view; and
- capable of ensuring coverage of the main risk categories, which the panel of experts considers to be the determinants in the evaluation of creditworthiness.

Such sub-sets of indicators are usually referred to as the "medium" list. It is very important to eliminate factors with low predictive power before initiating the multifactor analyses: including a factor with no ability to differentiate between bad and good clients creates unwanted noise and increases the risk of over-fitting the model to the sample data.

4.1.7 Step 4: Multivariate Analysis

The aim of the multivariate analysis is to determine the optimal variable selection and weight of each indicator (see the main activities in Table 4.5). First, a further reduction of indicators is carried out, to eliminate from the medium lists those that are highly correlated with other, more predictive indicators.

In this phase of the analysis, the indicators are compared at multivariate level inside the informative categories to which they belong, applying techniques such as cluster analysis and logistic regression inside the identified clusters.

In this way, the single short lists of indicators can be defined, one for each information category analyzed (see Table 4.6).

Table 4.5 Developing a rating model: main activities of Step 4

Step 4: Multivariate analyses

Correlation analysis separated by information category and area

Cluster analysis by information category and area

Identification of the short lists, containing the most predictive and least correlated variables of each information category

Comparison with the credit experts and verification of the coverage of the main risk drivers

Integration of variables' category according to the selected techniques: purely statistic (e.g. logit analysis), statistical-judgmental or purely judgmental

Definition of one or more alternative modules for each information area

Assessment, on the validation sample, of the statistical robustness and discriminatory power of the identified modules

Comparison with the credit experts for the selection of the best module for each information area that satisfies the criteria of coverage of relevant risk variables and statistical robustness

Table 4.6 From the long list to the final model indicators

Information area	Single modules					Integrated model
	Long list	Medium list	Short list	Input to the regression analysis	Final list	Model indicators
Financial	Financial long list (unique to all the information categories of the financial area	Financial medium list (unique to all the information categories of the financial area, obtained after the univariate analyses)	Short list of "size" Short list of "profitability" Short list of "debt service capacity" Short list of "stability" / One of each information category of the financial area, obtained after the multivariate analyses performed on each information category	Unique list of financial indicators, obtained after the multivariate analyses performed on the merging of the short lists of the area	Variables selected after the final regression analysis performed on the financial area	Set of all the variables feeding the developed modules
Internal behavioral	Internal behavioral long list (unique to all the information categories of the internal behavioral area)	Internal behavioral medium list (unique to all the information categories of the internal behavioral area, obtained after the univariate analyses)	One of each information category of the internal behavioral area, obtained after the multivariate analyses performed on each information category	Unique list of internal behavioral indicators, obtained after the multivariate analyses performed on the merging of the short lists of the area	Variables selected after the final regression analysis performed on the internal behavioral area	

(continued)

Table 4.6 (continued)

Information area	Single modules					Integrated model
	Long list	Medium list	Short list	Input to the regression analysis	Final list	Model indicators
External behavioral	External behavioral long list (unique to all the information categories of the internal behavioral area)	External behavioral medium list (unique to all the information categories of the internal behavioral area, obtained after the univariate analyses)	One of each information category of the external behavioral area, obtained after the multivariate analyses performed on each information category	Unique list of external behavioral indicators, obtained after the multivariate analyses performed on the merging of the short lists of the area	Variables selected after the final regression analysis performed on the external behavioral area	
Qualitative	Qualitative long list (unique to all the information categories of the internal behavioral area)	Qualitative medium list (unique to all the information categories of the internal behavioral area, obtained after the univariate analyses)	One of each information category of the qualitative area, obtained after the multivariate analyses performed on each information category	Unique list of qualitative indicators, obtained after the multivariate analyses performed on the merging of the short lists of the area	Variables selected after the final regression analysis performed on the qualitative area	

Successively, the short lists of the same enquiry area are merged, obtaining, in this case, four lists of variables to be tested jointly through the logistic regression analysis performed by:

- applying the step-by-step selection technique – without setting the maximum number of predictors;
- according to the cluster analysis identified in the hierarchical manner – where each class (cluster) of variables belongs to a larger cluster, which is again contained in a larger one and so on until the cluster that contains the whole set of analyzed factors is reached; and
- relying on identification through logical-economic considerations, starting with the short list, the sub-set of "best" variables – in relation to their economic interpretation, capability of covering the main risk categories, forecasting power and in relation to the correlation matrix – to be provided as input to the regression analysis for the enquiry area.

The final list of factors of each module is chosen from among the optimal candidates and constructed using both statistical and experience-based criteria. The factor weights of the single module and significance level of each factor are then calculated through a statistical regression (typically, a logistic regression). In general, for each area of analysis, there are several modules that are near optimal and present only minor differences in terms of performances: to select a final model, it is necessary to consult the bank experts, to make sure that all the above-mentioned criteria have been satisfied.

Four illustrative modules are presented in Tables 4.7, 4.8, 4.9, 4.10: (financial, external behavioral, internal behavioral, and qualitative); these could potentially be employed in the evaluation of the creditworthiness of corporate SME counterparties. (Table 4.11)

The coefficients of the first three modules, estimated by means of logistic regression, are expressed as percentages.

Indeed, setting the existing monotonic relation between the logistic function:

Table 4.7 Financial module: an illustrative example

Code	Description	Weight (%)
D1	Gross margin/Interest expenses	9.6
D2	Interest expenses/Turnover	23.8
G1	(Equity–Book equity–Intangible assets)/(Total assets–Intangible assets)	9.2
G2	(Long-term debt + Total current liabilities)/Total assets	14.6
L1	Cash/Total assets	6.2
L2	(Total current assets–Inventory)/(Total current liabilities–Advanced payments by clients)	10.2
P1	Gross margin/Total assets	13.8
ST1	Turnover {t}/Turnover {t–1}–1	12.6

Table 4.8 External behavioral module: an illustrative example

Code	Description	Weight (%)
EB1	Six months' average of the ratio: Withdrawn facilities outstanding toward the banking system (evaluating bank excluded)/Withdrawn facilities limit toward the banking system (evaluating bank excluded)/	83.5
EB2	Three months' average of: Unauthorized drawn toward the banking system (evaluating bank excluded)	16.5

Table 4.9 Internal behavioral module: an illustrative example

Code	Description	Weight (%)
IB1	Six months' average of the ratio: Average balance/Withdrawn facilities limit	41.5
IB2	Three months' average of the ratio: Withdrawn facilities outstanding/ Withdrawn facilities limit	58.5

Table 4.10 Qualitative module: an illustrative example

Code	Description	Weight (%)
Q1	For how many years has the company been a customer of the bank?	5.56
Q2	What percentage of assets/investments is not linked strategically to the company's business?	5.56
Q3	Has the company's top management developed a business plan?	5.56
Q4	If a business plan has been developed, has the proposed strategy been implemented?	5.56
Q5	Has the company been involved in any extraordinary operations (mergers, acquisitions, divisions and so on) with negative effects?	5.56
Q6	Overall, how have you evaluated the management with reference to the level of knowledge, experience, skills and competences?	5.56
Q7	Is the future of the company dependent on a few key managers?	5.56
Q8	Is there an investor (or a group of investors) holding a share of the company's stock sufficient to influence the company's strategies?	5.56
Q9	What is the evaluation of the market in which the company operates?	5.56
Q10	What is the expected production trend for the current year?	5.56
Q11	What is the quality of the company's market references?	5.56
Q12	Does the company's official financial forecast appear realistic?	5.56
Q13	What is the quality of the official financial information that the company communicates to the market?	5.56
Q14	What is the company's geographical business concentration?	5.56
Q15	To what extent is the company's business diversified?	5.56
Q16	What is the level of liquidity of the company's inventories?	5.56
Q17	What is the quality of the company's customers?	5.56
Q18	Has the company required deferred payments to the bank (interests, capital)	5.56

Table 4.11 Developing a rating model: main activities of Step 5

Step 5: Calibration, integration and mapping to the master scale
Estimate of the average default probability (calibration point) against which to calibrate the output of every module
Integrate the different modules
Comparison with the credit experts' opinion for the verification of the correct weight of each information area (module) inside the integrated model
Definition of the master scale
Mapping of the calibrated default probability into the master scale
Identification of the events that determine the assignment of positions to the administrated rating classes, independently of the model risk forecast
Complete validation of the selected model
Possible tuning of the model following the outcomes of the validation activity
Documentation of the model estimation process to ensure the complete replicability of obtained results

$$\pi(x) = \frac{e^{x \cdot \beta}}{1 + e^{x \cdot \beta}}$$

and the exponential function argument:

$$x \cdot \beta = \beta_0 + \sum_{i=1}^{n} \beta_i \cdot x_i$$

it is possible to compute the weights p_1, p_2, $\dots$, p_n of the n variables of each module as:

$$p_i = \frac{\beta_i}{\sum_{i=1}^{n} \beta_1}$$

with

$$\sum_{i=1}^{n} p_{1=1}$$

and

$$0 \leq p_i \leq 1 \ for \ any$$
$$i = 1,\ldots,n$$

and postpone, to the following phase of calibration, the transformation of the risk score into a default probability.

Put differently, the weights assigned to the variables (questions) of the qualitative module have been assigned in a directly judgmental way, as an alternative to the proposed multi-attribute value theory method.

4.1.8 Step 5: Calibration, Integration and Mapping to the Master Scale

The output of the logistic regressions assumes values in the interval [0; 1] and could be interpreted as a default probability. Yet, the regression output is correctly "calibrated" when bank's risk manager estimates the average probability on the perimeter under consideration close to the one-year forecast default rate (the so-called "calibration point") and not by the average frequency of the default of the sample.

The calibration process, which allows the transformation of the logistic regression output in a default probability to 12 months, can be represented in the steps shown in Table 4.11:

- estimation of the calibration point (*CP*), which represents the level of average PD considered coherent with the portfolio under examination;
- computation of the default rate of the sample used for the calibration DR^{sample};
- sub-division of the sample in n quantiles, ordered with respect to the regression output (the score);
- computation of the median score associate with each quantile $(i = 1, \ldots, n)$;
- computation of the default rate relative to each quantile, $DR_i(i = 1, \ldots, n)$;

• re-apportionment of the default rate of each quantile with respect to the *CP*, by applying Bayes theorem:

$$DR_i^{\text{calibrated}} = \frac{DR_i \cdot \dfrac{AP}{DR^{\text{sample}}}}{DR_i \cdot \dfrac{AP}{DR^{\text{sample}}} + \left(1 - DR\right) \cdot \dfrac{\left(1 - AP\right)}{1 - DR^{\text{sample}}}}$$

where $DR^{\text{calibrated}}$ denotes the re-apportioned default rate of the *i* quantile, constrained to the interval [0; 1]; and

• the estimation of the (*a*) and (*b*) parameters which specify the exponential curve equation that relates to the score and the (re-apportioned) default rate observed in the quantiles:

$$\ln\left(DR_i^{\text{calibrated}}\right) = \alpha \cdot s_i + b$$

so obtaining the punctual (granular) values of default probability for each sample position contained in the interval [0; 1], and such that the average PD estimated on the whole sample will be equal to the calibration point.

The re-calibrated (and standardized) output of every module can eventually be integrated using both statistical methodologies (if a sufficiently large sample is available on which all the model indicators are computed; see Table 4.6), and internal bank experience alone. Table 4.12 presents

Table 4.12 Module integration weights

Type of customer	Financial PD (%)	Internal behavioral PD (%)	External behavioral PD (%)	Qualitative PD (%)
New (without internal behavioral information)	38.00	–	57.00	5.00
Old (with internal behavioral information)	33.25	28.50	33.25	5.00

examples of integration weights for the default probabilities estimated (and calibrated) separately for every module.

It is a reasonable suggestion initially to assign a limited weight to the qualitative module (in this case, 5 %) and to increase it progressively after comparing the judgment assigned by the relationship managers (by means of a questionnaire) with the quantitative model components (financial, external and internal behavior) and testing their correctness.

The integrated default probability is then associated with a rating class; that is, to one (and only one) of the ordered and disjoint sets that determines the partition of the possible values that the probability can assume.

The table on the left-hand side of Fig. 4.11, representing the so-called "master scale" of a generic rating system, illustrates the method for associating a default probability with a corresponding rating class.

For the definition of the master scale, the numerosity and amplitude of the rating classes should be set so that the scale:

- divides the portfolio customers into a sufficient number of risk classes;
- avoids excessive concentrations (both in terms of the number of positions and outstanding debts) in single rating classes; and
- allows a direct comparison with the final assessment (rating class) expressed, with the same counterparties, and the main external agencies and banking groups adopting a comparable master scale both in terms of average PDs and default definition.

Risk	Rating class	Medium PD	Minimum PD	Maximum PD
Low risk	1	0,01%	0,00%	0,02%
	2	0,04%	0,02%	0,07%
	3	0,13%	0,07%	0,22%
	4	0,39%	0,22%	0,52%
Medium risk	5	0,70%	0,52%	0,90%
	6	1,17%	0,90%	2,02%
	7	3,51%	2,02%	6,08%
High risk	8	10,55%	6,08%	18,29%
	9	31,73%	18,29%	48,78%
	10	75,00%	48,78%	100,00%

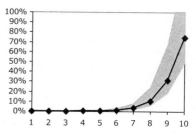

Fig. 4.11   An illustrative master scale

Risk	Rating class	Medium PD	Population distribution
Low risk	1	0,01%	3%
	2	0,04%	8%
	3	0,13%	15%
	4	0,39%	25%
Medium risk	5	0,70%	20%
	6	1,17%	14%
	7	3,51%	6%
High risk	8	10,55%	5%
	9	31,73%	3%
	10	75,00%	1%

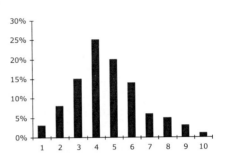

Fig. 4.12   Rating class distribution

Figure 4.12 shows, for the purposes of illustration, a possible portfolio distribution analyzed by rating class.

The risk judgment expressed by the integrated model can be corrected (in general, worsening the outcome) in the presence of events/behavior that represent eminent risk to the counterparty or its risk group. Corrections following policy rules or discriminatory events, even if they do not modify the default probability estimated by the algorithm, increase the attention level of the counterparty during the origination phase. This may lead the counterparty to assign its credit evaluation to higher power delegation, and, in the monitoring phase, the counterparty may move to a dedicated management unit. Before releasing the model into production, it is necessary to submit it to a thorough validation, correcting/integrating it and documenting the whole estimation process to ensure that the nature of the results is replicable.

4.1.9   Step 6: Embedding the Model in the Banking Processes

The model release happens, generally, by means of a preliminary prototype development, which allows us to test the calibration impact on bank credits and commercial policies (see Table 4.13).

As stated in Table 4.13, among the main uses of a rating model within the banking processes are:

Table 4.13 Developing a rating model: main activities of Step 6

Step 6: embedding model in the banking process
Estimated model prototype development
Definition of the risk parameter weights to identify delegation powers
Embedding of risk parameters inside the credit management process
Embedding of risk parameters inside pricing policies
Optimization of the risk/return profile of the bank's capital requirement computation

- the definition of delegation powers in relation to the expected loss associated with the single risk position;
- the definition of the pricing for the required facility;
- the cost of risk computation; and
- the optimization of the risk/return profile of the bank.

Some of these will be detailed in later chapters of this book.

4.2   PD Corporate SME Sub-segment Models

In relation to the practical availability of data (financial, behavioral and qualitative), it is possible to estimate the different modules of a PD model either on a statistical basis (in the presence of sufficiently robust data) or on an expert basis. Also, in the presence of company samples that fall into the good/bad type, representative of the bank's portfolio and statistically robust, expert evaluation always plays a part, both in the selection of final financial and behavioral modules, and in the development of the qualitative module (Tables 4.14, 4.15, 4.16).

Table 4.14 Start-up model: an illustrative financial module

Category	Code	Weight (%)	Indicator
Gearing	G1	30	Equity/Initial investment
Profitability	P1	20	Initial investment/EBITDA steady
Debt service capacity	D1	30	(Financial debts – Subordinate debts to partners)/(Book equity + Subordinate debts to partners)
	D2	20	(Financial debts + Interests outflow)/EBITDA steady

Table 4.15 Consortia model: an illustrative financial module

Category	Code	Weight (%)	Indicator
Size	SZ1	5	Net sales
Debt service capacity	D1	5	(Financial debts – Subordinate debts to partners with residual life of less than five years)/ (Equity + Subordinate debts to partners with residual life of less than five years)
	D2	15	(Net margin + Tangible depreciations and amortizations)/Interest expenses
	D3	15	Interest expenses/Net sales
Liquidity	L1	5	Cash/Total assets
	L2	10	(Total current assets – Inventories)/(Total current liabilities – Advanced payments by clients)
Gearing	G1	10	(Equity – Intangible fixed assets)/(Total assets – Intangible fixed assets)
	G2	15	(Equity – Issued shares)/Total Assets
Stability	ST1	10	Net sales {t}/Net sales
	ST2	10	{t − 1} − 1 Capital employed {t}/Capital employed {t − 1} − 1

Table 4.16 Financial company model: an illustrative financial module

Category	Code	Weight (%)	Indicator
Profitability	P1	8	(Extraordinary profit or loss + Revaluations)/ Total assets
	P2	8	(Profit or loss)/Equity
Debt service capacity	D1	15	Financial liabilities/Equity
Gearing	G1	24	Equity/Total assets
	G2	15	(Equity – Intangible fixed assets)/Financial liabilities
Activity	A1	15	Credit risk provision funds/(Extraordinary profit or loss + Revaluations)
	A2	15	Operating costs/Operating incomes

In the absence of robust databases, the expert-based component simply assumes a more relevant role in the framework of the definition of the whole structure of the model.

In particular, models composed from expert-based modules refer to customer sub-segments characterized by portfolios that are:

- rarefied in terms of counterparts (for example, insurance companies); or

- constituted by a reduced number of defaults (non-profit organizations); or
- lacking a historical database of clearly codified balance sheets (non-profit organizations) or sufficiently reliable.

The release of models with expert-based modules also aims to make known the rating discipline in terms of number of positions/default rates for portfolios/sub-segments that are less relevant than others.

This contributes to the settling down of a data collection process on a systematic base on these bank portfolios.

As soon as a reliable database is available for these modules, it will be possible to start the "objectivization" phase of weights and variables following statistical techniques.

4.2.1   Statistical Expert-based Models

Possible models constituted both by statistical components and by expert-based modules are devoted to the evaluation of corporate SME counterparties belonging, for example, to the following segments: farmers, start-ups, consortia and financial companies.

In the case of farmers, the expert-based component could be represented by the qualitative module; in the remaining three models (devoted to start-ups, consortia and financial companies), one could assume that the expert-based score would be the result of the weighted average of the scores produced by the financial and qualitative modules.

The following two sub-sections present a brief description of the process of derivation of the financial and qualitative expert-based modules, as illustrated earlier in the chapter.

As explained in Figure 4.3, such modules/components will be allowed to modify, in a limited manner (in terms of notches), the behavioral (or behavioral and financial) evaluation expressed by the model's statistical component.

4.2.1.1   Qualitative Modules

In the definition of the qualitative modules of the models devoted to the evaluation of farmers, start-ups, consortia and financial companies, all the variables suggested by the expert are generally inserted into the final components, with a weight variable from 0 to 1 in relation to its recognized importance to the insolvency forecast capability.

The weights indicated by the experts are differentiated according to their "vintage", assuming that, for "new" customers, no answer could be found for certain questions (variables): in a first approximation, the relative weights could simply be redistributed proportionally over the remaining questions.

The score assigned to each indicator included in the interval [0; 1] must be obtained according to the examined variable type:

- for indicators similar to continuous variables, a score can be assigned by means of linear regression, analogous to what was undertaken for the variables of a financial nature; or
- for indicators of a categorical type, the expert team must identify the possible outcomes and set the relative risk score.

Tables 4.17, 4.18, 4.19 and 4.20 describe the structure of four possible quantitative modules for the evaluation of, respectively, farmers, start-ups, consortia and financial corporate SMEs.

4.2.1.2   Integration of the Statistical and Expert-based Components

As mentioned earlier in the chapter, the rating class of a counterparty in the sub-segments of farmers, start-ups, consortia and financial companies, estimated by means of the statistical component of the corresponding rating model, can be corrected upward or downward, according to the score level assigned to the same counter party from the expert-based component.

As every variable of the expert-based component has a value between 0 and 1, as well as other possible intermediate expert-based scores, according to the hierarchical structure, the final score will also be included in the interval [0; 1].

Having sub-divided the score variation range into seven risk sub-intervals, the magnitude of correction upward or downward of the

Table 4.17 Farmers model: an illustrative qualitative module

Category	Variable	Weight new customer (%)	Weight old customer (%)
Competitive position/ business image	Company life-cycle and growth perspectives	9	8
	Existence of trade agreements for purchasing raw materials (seeds, fertilizers and so on)	13	11
	Existence of trade agreements for sale of final products	13	11
	Product quality	13	11
	Does the company benefit from government contributions?	4	4
	Is the company subject to government obligations which limit production capabilities?	4	4
	Does the company respond positively to requirements to benefit from interbanking insurance funds?	10	8
Business characteristics/ credit portfolio	Geographical concentration of sales	9	8
	Is there any procedure to manage and monitor the credit risk of trade activities?	4	4
Management/ sponsor characteristics/ business plan/ property	For how many years has the entrepreneur operated in the sector?	9	8
	Entrepreneur's reputation	4	4
	Ethical behavior of the entrepreneur	4	4
	Entrepreneur's attitude to safety and environmental issues	4	4
Relation with the bank	Bank manager's opinion of the fiduciary relationship with the customer (for old customers only)	–	11

rating class, estimated statistically, could be defined, agreeing with the expert team, as shown in Table 4.21, or be further differentiated in relation to the rating class estimated by means of the model's statistical component.

Table 4.18 Start-up model: an illustrative qualitative module

Category	Variable	Weight (%)
Sector characteristics	Existence of entry barriers	5
	Growth perspectives of the sector	5
	Risk level of the sector	8
	Niche differentiation	5
	Costs leadership	5
	Level of competition	3
Management/Sponsor characteristics/Business plan/Property	Capital and economic strength of the entrepreneur (of the partners)	5
	Enterpreneur's (partners') reputation	3
	For how many years has the entrepreneur (partners) operated in the sector?	5
	Ethical behavior of the entrepreneur (of the partners)	3
	Enterpreneur's (partners') attitude to safety and environmental issues	3
	Management capability to produce a business plan	8
	Completeness and level of detail of the business plan	8
	Business plan's objective reachability	5
	Stress analysis	5
Business characteristics/ Credit portfolio	Percentage of medium/long-term loans for which the interest rate risk is hedged	5
	Existence of trade agreements which stabilize the costs	5
	Existence of trade agreements which stabilize the sales	5
	Has enterprise already obtained the concessions to make the investments?	5
	Is there any procedure to manage and monitor the credit risk of trade activities?	4

Following such a correction, it is possible to associate the counterparties belonging to particular corporate SME sub-segments, such as farmers, start-ups, consortia, financial companies, with a final rating class and a default probability to be employed for both regulatory and management purposes (delegation powers, remuneration and pricing).

Table 4.19 Consortium model: an illustrative qualitative module

Category	Variable	Weight new customer (%)	Weight old customer (%)
Business characteristics/ credit portfolio	Level of standardization of products/services offered	13	10
	Production differentiation level and geographical sales concentration	18	16
	Production growth forecasts with respect to the previous year	7	6
	Is there any procedure to manage and monitor the credit risk of trade activities?	7	6
Management/ Sponsor characteristics/ Business plan/ Property	For how many years has the consortium operated in the sector?	13	10
	Consortium's reputation	7	6
	Ethical behavior of the consortium	7	6
	Capital and economic strength of the consortium	7	6
	Consortium's attitude to safety and environmental issues	7	6
	Management's capability to produce a business plan	7	6
	Business plan's objective reachability	7	6
Relation with the bank	Bank manager's opinion of the fiduciary relationship (for old consortia only)	–	16

4.2.2   Pure Expert-based Models

Pure expert-based models are, for example, those that can be developed for the corporate SME counterparties in the sub-segments of insurance companies, holding companies and non-profit organizations.

As illustrated in Fig. 4.5, the model structure is still modular: the financial module and the qualitative/behavioral module compute, separately, two scores that express in numerical terms the creditworthiness of the counterparty.

Table 4.20 Financial company model: an illustrative qualitative module

Category	Variable	Weight new customer (%)	Weight old customer (%)
Relation with the bank	Bank manager's opinion on the fiduciary relationship (for old customers only)	–	12
Management/Sponsor characteristics/Business plan/Property	For how many years has the management operated in the sector?	8	8
	Management's reputation	5	4
	Ethical behavior of the management	5	4
	Operational risk management	5	4
	Existence of internal control bodies/procedures	5	4
	Management's capability to produce a business plan	5	4
	Business plan's objective reachability	9	8
	Level of completeness/ reliability of official financial information (balances, quarterly/ semi-annual reports, financial plans)	8	8
Business characteristics/ Credit portfolio	Geographical differentiation level of the credit portfolio	5	4
	Sector differentiation level of the credit portfolio	8	8
Competitive position/ Business image	Company's competitive position in the domestic market	13	12
	Company's market share	9	8
	Differentiation and diffusion level of distribution channels	5	4
	Diversification level of offered products/services	5	4
Risk management	Effectiveness of risk management strategies	5	4

Table 4.21 Expert-based correction entity

Score	Up/downgrading
0	+3
[1;2]	+2
[3;4]	+1
5	0
[6;7]	−1
[8;9]	−2
10	−3

The scores generated by the two modules are combined, adopting a weighted average, in a final score variable between 0 (maximum risk) and 10 (minimum risk), expressing the size of upward correction (upgrading) or downward correction (downgrading) to be applied to the rating corresponding to the average risk of the segment under examination, possibly corrected in a through-the-cycle perspective (the calibration point).

For the correction, one can refer to a structure similar to that proposed in Table 4.21.

4.2.2.1 Financial Modules

Tables 4.22, 4.23 and 4.24 summarize the structure of three possible financial modules for the evaluation, respectively, of insurance companies, holding companies and non-profit organizations.

4.2.2.2 Qualitative/Behavioral Modules

Tables 4.25, 4.26 and 4.27 describe the structures of three possible qualitative/behavioral models for the evaluation of insurance companies, holding companies and non-profit organizations, respectively.

4.2.2.3 Integration of Pure Expert-based Modules

As anticipated at the beginning of this section, the scores generated separately by the financial and qualitative/behavioral modules are integrated according to a weighted average (convex combination) in a final score variable, which is also in the interval [0; 10].

Table 4.22 Insurance companies model: an illustrative financial module

Category	Code	Weight (%)	Indicator
Size	SZ1	30	Operative result
	SZ2	20	Ln (Total assets)
Profitability	P1	10	(Profit or loss)/Equity
	P2	10	Loss ratio + (Administrative costs/Profit before taxes)
	P3	10	Profit before taxes/Net premium
Gearing	G1	20	Net technical reserves/Equity

Table 4.23 Holding companies model: an illustrative financial module

Category	Code	Weight (%)	Indicator
Profitability	P1	17	Dividends and income from investments/ Fixed assets in investments
Debt service	D1	17	Cash/Equity
Capacity	D2	17	(Financial income + Revaluations)/(Interest expenses + Depreciation)
Gearing	G1	24	(Financial liabilities − Cash)/Investment value
Activity	A1	8	Depreciation/Income from investment
	A2	17	Depreciation/Fixed assets in investments

Table 4.24 Organizations model: an illustrative financial module

Category	Code	Weight (%)	Indicator
Profitability	P1	18	Loss/Equity
Debt service	D1	10	Interest expenses/Turnover
capacity	D2	18	(Net financial debts - Sub. debt to affiliates)/ (Equity + Sub. debt to affiliates)
Liquidity	L1	18	Liquidity/Financial debts
Gearing	G1	18	(Fixed assets market value + Liquidity)/ Financial debts
	G2	18	Financial debts/Total assets

Table 4.28 proposes possible integration weights for the two modules, differentiated for types of counterpart (insurance companies, holding companies and non-profit organizations).

The integrated score, when divided, for example, into the seven classes presented in Table 4.20, can be used to establish whether the risk of the single counterparty is greater or smaller than the average of a sub-segment, and to assign to these a specific default probability.

Table 4.25 Insurance companies model: an illustrative qualitative/behavioral module

Category	Indicator	Weight new customer (%)				Weight old customer (%)			
		Listed company		Non-listed company		Listed company		Non-listed company	
		With parent company	Without parent company	With parent company	Without parent company	With parent company	Without parent company	With parent company	Without parent company
Relation with the bank	Bank manager's opinion on the fiduciary relationship with the customer (customer)	6				8	10	9	11
	Bank (banking group) percentage of overall activity (bank limit/banking system limit)	7	7	7	8	6	8	6	7
	Undrawn credit amount (Limit-Outstanding limit)/Limit versus Banking system	9	11	10	14	8	10	9	11
Competitive position/	Company market share (damage+ life)	9	10	10	14	7	10	9	11
Business image	Diversification level of products/ services	3	4	3	4	3	3	3	4
	Differentiation and diffusion level of distribution channels	3	4	3	4	3	3	3	4
Business characteristics/ Credit portfolio	Prudential parameters of investment policy	6	7	7	8	6	7	6	7

(continued)

Table 4.25 (continued)

Category	Indicator	Weight new customer (%)				Weight old customer (%)			
		Listed company		Non-listed company		Listed company		Non-listed company	
		With parent company	Without parent company	With parent company	Without parent company	With parent company	Without parent company	With parent company	Without parent company
Management/ sponsor characteristics/ business plan/ Property	Management capability to produce a business plan	3	4	3	4	3	3	3	4
	Business plan objective reachability	3	4	3	4	3	3	3	4
	Level of completeness/ reliability of the official financial information (Balances, quarterly/ semi-annual reports, financial plans)	3	4	3	4	3	3	3	4
	For how many years has the management operated in the sector?	6	7	7	8	6	7	6	7
	Management reputation	3	4	3	4	3	3	3	4
	Ethical behavior of the management	3	4	3	4	3	3	3	4
	Operational risk management	3	4	3	4	3	3	3	4
	Existence of internal control bodies/procedures	6	7	7	8	6	7	6	7
Risk management	Effectiveness of risk management strategies	7	7	8	8	6	8	7	7

Market stock trend	Stock growth rate in the previous year	3	4	3	3
	Stock growth rate in the previous year with respect to the main competitors	3	4	3	3
	Analysts' assessment in recent equity researches	3	4	3	3
Relationship with the parent company	Strategic importance of the parent company	9	10	7	9
		9	10	7	9
	Capital and economic strength of the parent company	9	10	7	9

Table 4.26 Holding companies model: an illustrative qualitative/behavioral module

Category	Indicator	Weight new customer (%)	Weight old customer (%)
Business characteristics/ Credit portfolio	Geographical diversification level of the investment portfolio	7	7
	Sector diversification level of the investment portfolio	7	7
	Liquidity of the investment portfolio	11	10
	Volatility of the subsidiaries' economic results	7	7
	Percentage of holding investments in the overall portfolio	11	10
Management/ sponsor characteristics/ business plan/ Property	Management's capability to produce business plan	7	7
	Business plan's objective reachability	7	8
	Level of completeness/reliability of the official financial information (balances, quarterly/semi-annual reports, financial plans)	4	3
	For how many years has the management operated in the sector?	7	8
	Management reputation	4	3
	Ethical behavior of the management	4	3
	Operations risk management	4	3
	Existence of internal control bodies/procedures	4	3
Risk management	Effectiveness of risk management strategies	4	3

Table 4.27 Example of default data

Year	Number of companies at start of year	Defaults per year	Cumulative defaults
1	100	1	1
2	99	2	3
3	97	3	6
4	94	4	10
5	90	5	15

Table 4.28 Mapping of suggested master scale to S&P grades

Suggested master scale grade	S&P equivalent grade	S&P grade used
1	AAA	AAA
2	AA+	AA+
3	AA	AA
4	AA–	AA–
5	A+	A+
6	A	A
7	A–	A–
8	BBB+	BBB+
9	BBB	BBB
10	BBB–	BBB–
11	BB+	BB+
12	BB+/BB	BB+
13	BB	BB
14	BB/BB–	BB
15	BB–	BB–
16	BB–/B+	BB–
17	B+	B+
18	B+/B	B+
19	B	B
20	B/B–	B
21	B–	B–
22	CCC	CCC

4.3   Term Structure of Probability of Default

The effects of grade migration over a period of time create a term structure of PDs. For example, an AAA-rated borrower cannot improve in rating over time and so, on average, is likely to deteriorate. However, a CCC-credit rated borrower, if it survives, can only improve.

4.3.1 Observed Term Structures

Figure 4.13 shows the term structure observed for Standard & Poor's (S&P) rated companies. It can be seen from this figure that higher-quality credits tend to deteriorate over time and lower-quality credits improve.

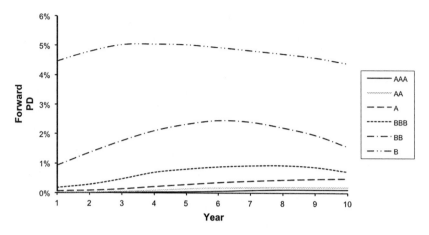

Fig. 4.13 Observed term structure of S&P rated companies (based on one-year forward PD) (Source: Internal Rating Model Development Handbook – Capitalia Banking Group)

4.3.2 Marginal, Forward, and Cumulative Probability of Default

The PDs for each year shown in Fig. 4.10 are *forward* PDs; they are the PDs that would be expected that year expressed as a percentage of companies that have survived. The number of companies that survive can be determined from the *cumulative* default rate. To illustrate these concepts, consider the simple example in Table 4.27.

Consider three different questions. What is the probability that:

1. a company will default over a four-year period?
2. a company in year four will default over the next year?
3. a company will default in the fourth year of a facility?

The answers require different combinations of the numbers presented in Table 4.27:

1. Of 100 companies, 10 default in the first four years: 10 %.
2. The *Cumulative Default Rate* in year four is 10 %.

3. Of the 94 companies that survived until year four, 4 will default in year four: 4.2 % is the *Forward Default Rate* in year four.
4. Of the 100 companies, 4 that have been granted loans default in the fourth year of their life: 4.0 % is the *Marginal Default Rate* in year four.

The pricing model requires both the cumulative PD and forward PD for the discounted cash flow calculation. The cumulative PD is required to determine the probability of which revenues and costs are incurred in any given year (that is, to account for survivorship) and the forward PD is required to calculate expected loss and regulatory capital.

4.3.3 Mapping PD Ratings to Observed Term Structures

Once the marginal PDs have been calculated (Fig. 4.14), it is then possible to calculate the forward PDs using the following equation:

$$PD_{\text{forward,year } n} = \frac{PD_{\text{marginal,year } n}}{1 - \displaystyle\sum_{\text{year}=0}^{n} PD_{\text{marginal}}}$$

As not all grades of the suggested 22-point grade system master scale can be mapped directly onto the S&P grade system (as some of them are intermediate grades), the simplified mapping shown in Table 4.28 can be used to determine the forward PDs. The result based on the suggested 22-point rating system master scale is shown in Table 4.29.

4.4   Transition Matrix State – Dependent

In the previous sections, an analysis was used that was indifferent to the phases of the economic cycle. This section approaches the production of European transition matrices based on the different phases of the cycle

Marginal PD Year n+1		1 Year Migration Matrix		Marginal PD Year n

$$\begin{bmatrix} AAA \\ AA+ \\ AA \\ AA- \\ A+ \\ A \\ A- \\ BBB+ \\ BBB \\ BBB- \\ BB+ \\ BB \\ BB- \\ B+ \\ B- \\ CCC \end{bmatrix} = \begin{bmatrix} AAA \ldots CCC & \\ \text{AAA} & \\ \text{AA+} & \\ \text{AA} & \\ \text{AA-} & \\ \text{A+} & \\ \text{A} & \\ \text{A-} & \\ \text{BBB+} & \ldots \quad \ldots \quad \ldots \quad \ldots \quad \ldots \\ \text{BBB} & \\ \text{BBB-} & \\ \text{BB+} & \\ \text{BB} & \\ \text{BB-} & \\ \text{B+} & \\ \text{B-} & \\ \text{CCC} & \end{bmatrix} \times \begin{bmatrix} \text{AAA} \\ \text{AA+} \\ \text{AA} \\ \text{AA-} \\ \text{A+} \\ \text{A} \\ \text{A-} \\ \text{BBB+} \\ \text{BBB} \\ \text{BBB-} \\ \text{BB+} \\ \text{BB} \\ \text{BB-} \\ \text{B+} \\ \text{B-} \\ \text{CCC} \end{bmatrix}$$

Fig. 4.14 Calculating marginal PD from the migration matrix

itself. The type of transition matrix states of the economy dependent on each business segment are summarized in Table 4.30. The average downgrading and upgrading probability states of the economy dependent on all of the business segments are shown in Table 4.31.

Downgrading probabilities are, on average, increasing from recovery to hard landing.

Upgrading probabilities decrease from recovery (higher probabilities) to hard landing.

Tables 4.32, 4.33, 4.34 and 4.35 show state-dependent transition matrices for large corporates, corporates, SME corporates and SME retail.

4.5 Validation of Internal Credit Rating Models

A credit rating system undergoes a "validation process". This consists of a formal set of activities, instruments and procedures aimed at ensuring that the design of a model is conceptually sound; that its implementa-

Table 4.29 Forward PD for suggested master scale with 22-point ratings (illustrative, (%))

	Year									
	1	2	3	4	5	6	7	8	9	10
1	0.010	0.014	0.018	0.022	0.028	0.035	0.042	0.051	0.061	0.072
2	0.020	0.023	0.028	0.033	0.040	0.049	0.059	0.070	0.082	0.096
3	0.030	0.034	0.039	0.047	0.057	0.068	0.082	0.096	0.111	0.127
4	0.040	0.045	0.054	0.065	0.080	0.096	0.114	0.133	0.152	0.171
5	0.050	0.060	0.075	0.094	0.115	0.139	0.163	0.187	0.210	0.232
6	0.070	0.087	0.111	0.140	0.171	0.203	0.234	0.264	0.291	0.315
7	0.090	0.125	0.167	0.212	0.258	0.301	0.340	0.374	0.404	0.429
8	0.130	0.195	0.264	0.330	0.391	0.445	0.491	0.528	0.558	0.580
9	0.220	0.330	0.430	0.519	0.594	0.655	0.702	0.737	0.760	0.774
10	0.390	0.542	0.678	0.792	0.880	0.943	0.985	1.009	1.018	1.015
11	0.670	0.904	1.086	1.216	1.302	1.352	1.371	1.368	1.349	1.317
12	0.670	0.904	1.086	1.216	1.302	1.352	1.371	1.368	1.349	1.317
13	1.170	1.480	1.690	1.816	1.875	1.884	1.856	1.804	1.737	1.660
14	1.170	1.480	1.690	1.816	1.875	1.884	1.856	1.804	1.737	1.660
15	2.030	2.419	2.619	2.685	2.661	2.579	2.462	2.328	2.186	2.045
16	2.030	2.419	2.619	2.685	2.661	2.579	2.462	2.328	2.186	2.045
17	3.510	3.869	3.941	3.840	3.643	3.399	3.139	2.882	2.638	2.413
18	3.510	3.869	3.941	3.840	3.643	3.399	3.139	2.882	2.638	2.413
19	6.080	6.114	5.797	5.322	4.798	4.285	3.811	3.388	3.018	2.697
20	6.080	6.114	5.797	5.322	4.798	4.285	3.811	3.388	3.018	2.697
21	10.540	9.404	8.134	6.924	5.860	4.964	4.226	3.625	3.136	2.737
22	18.270	13.862	10.447	7.934	6.132	4.843	3.914	3.231	2.718	2.324

Source: Internal Rating Model Development Handbook – Capitalia Banking Group

Table 4.30 List of transition matrix states of the economy dependent on each business segment

	Recovery	Overheat	Hard landing	Soft landing
Large corporate	√	√	√	√
Corporate	√	√	√	√
SME corporate	√	√	√	√
SME retail	√	√	√	√

Table 4.31 Transition probabilities in terms of stability, downgrading and upgrading (%)

	Recovery	Overheat	Hard landing	Soft landing
Stability	77.17	75.13	73.80	75.97
Downgrading	13.46	18.59	19.12	15.97
Upgrading	14.55	13.69	12.53	13.79

tion is accurate and consistent with the theory; and to assess the accuracy of the estimates of all material risk components and the regular operation, predictive power and overall performance of the internal rating system.

A model validation process will be triggered whenever a new model is developed, or when any significant changes are made to one that has been previously approved. Models are also subject to periodic reviews, which aim to reassess the adequacy of their performance over time (e.g. the verification of the validity of their assumptions under different market conditions; investigation of mismatches between realized and model-predicted values; and comparisons with competitors' best practice).

Hence, model validation must be seen as an ongoing process: at least once a year, banks have to verify the reliability of the results generated by the rating system on an ongoing, iterative basis and also its continued consistency with regulatory requirements, operational needs and changes in the reference market.[2]

The rating system validation process is complementary to the developmental process (see Fig. 4.15).

The initial validation, before a model's implementation, aims to consolidate all new models; the ongoing validation ensures the reliability and robustness of the regulatory parameters over time.

Table 4.32 Large corporate transition matrices

	AAA	AA+	AA	AA-	A+	A	A-	BBB+	BBB	BBB-	BB+	BB	BB-	B+	B	B-	CCC	Default
AAA	83.9	3.3	6.2	1.7	2.5	1.7	0.8	0.0	0.0	0.0	0.0	0.0	0.0	0.0	0.0	0.0	0.0	0.0
AA+	2.0	92.1	3.3	2.6	0.0	0.0	0.0	0.0	0.0	0.0	0.0	0.0	0.0	0.0	0.0	0.0	0.0	0.0
AA	0.0	1.1	82.2	11.2	4.5	0.0	0.7	0.4	0.0	0.0	0.0	0.0	0.0	0.0	0.0	0.0	0.0	0.0
AA-	0.2	0.2	2.4	80.5	12.7	3.0	0.8	0.0	0.2	0.0	0.0	0.0	0.0	0.0	0.0	0.0	0.0	0.0
A+	0.1	0.1	0.0	2.4	87.6	7.4	1.3	1.1	0.0	0.0	0.1	0.0	0.0	0.0	0.0	0.0	0.0	0.0
A	0.0	0.0	0.1	0.3	3.2	82.7	9.8	2.9	0.9	0.0	0.4	0.0	0.0	0.0	0.0	0.0	0.0	0.0
A-	0.0	0.2	0.0	0.0	1.3	8.8	78.9	7.1	2.3	0.9	0.3	0.1	0.0	0.0	0.0	0.0	0.0	0.0
BBB+	0.0	0.0	0.1	0.0	0.0	1.1	7.7	79.4	8.1	2.6	1.6	0.1	0.1	0.3	0.0	0.0	0.0	0.0
BBB	0.0	0.0	0.0	0.1	0.1	0.4	1.6	6.2	80.8	7.5	5.0	0.4	0.5	0.6	0.1	0.1	0.0	0.0
BBB-	0.0	0.0	0.0	0.0	0.6	0.0	0.8	2.4	9.5	75.7	1.6	3.1	1.6	0.1	0.7	0.4	0.1	0.0
BB+	0.0	0.0	0.0	0.0	0.2	0.4	0.4	0.7	2.0	9.0	73.5	6.8	4.5	1.6	0.9	0.2	0.0	0.4
BB	0.0	0.0	0.0	0.0	0.2	0.1	0.2	0.9	0.9	2.9	12.0	70.2	5.6	1.1	2.9	1.3	1.3	0.0
BB-	0.0	0.0	0.0	0.0	0.0	0.4	0.1	0.0	0.4	0.3	1.8	8.8	73.9	5.1	6.1	1.6	0.4	1.3
B+	0.1	0.0	0.0	0.0	0.1	0.1	0.1	0.1	0.6	0.1	0.1	3.0	8.8	72.9	5.1	4.7	1.6	2.2
B	0.0	0.0	0.0	0.0	0.0	0.4	0.2	0.0	0.0	0.0	0.4	1.3	2.9	9.4	67.7	9.6	5.4	3.1
B-	0.0	0.0	0.2	0.0	0.0	0.0	0.0	0.2	0.2	0.2	0.0	0.6	0.6	5.8	7.3	65.2	9.6	10.0
CCC	0.0	0.0	0.0	0.0	0.0	0.0	0.0	0.0	0.0	0.0	0.6	0.0	0.6	0.6	1.5	6.8	68.5	21.4

Large corporate – overheat (%)

	AAA	AA+	AA	AA-	A+	A	A-	BBB+	BBB	BBB-	BB+	BB	BB-	B+	B	B-	CCC	Default
AAA	86.6	3.9	8.7	0.0	0.0	0.8	0.0	0.0	0.0	0.0	0.0	0.0	0.0	0.0	0.0	0.0	0.0	0.0
AA+	2.6	77.6	2.0	17.1	0.7	0.0	0.0	0.0	0.0	0.0	0.0	0.0	0.0	0.0	0.0	0.0	0.0	0.0
AA	1.8	4.3	79.1	11.0	1.2	2.5	0.0	0.0	0.0	0.0	0.0	0.0	0.0	0.0	0.0	0.0	0.0	0.0
AA-	0.0	0.0	0.0	86.4	6.5	4.3	1.0	0.5	0.0	0.0	0.0	0.0	0.0	0.0	0.0	0.0	0.0	0.0
A+	0.0	0.0	0.4	3.2	81.1	9.8	3.6	1.6	0.0	0.2	0.0	0.0	0.2	0.0	0.3	0.0	0.0	0.0
A	0.4	0.0	0.1	0.4	3.2	81.8	7.1	4.5	1.0	0.1	0.3	0.0	0.7	0.0	0.0	0.0	0.0	0.0
A-	0.0	0.0	0.0	0.2	1.3	5.6	75.5	9.7	4.5	1.6	0.5	0.3	0.3	0.2	0.0	0.0	0.0	0.3
BBB+	0.0	0.0	0.0	0.2	0.2	0.3	4.4	75.7	9.6	4.7	2.3	0.6	0.0	0.9	0.2	0.6	0.3	0.2

(continued)

Table 4.32 (continued)

	AAA	AA+	AA	AA-	A+	A	A-	BBB+	BBB	BBB-	BB+	BB	BB-	B+	B	B-	CCC	Default
BBB	0.1	0.3	0.0	0.0	0.3	0.3	1.1	5.6	76.9	9.7	1.4	1.3	0.6	0.4	0.5	0.0	1.0	0.5
BBB-	0.2	0.0	0.0	0.0	0.0	0.5	0.2	0.8	8.3	74.2	7.5	2.4	2.4	1.0	0.5	0.3	0.8	0.8
BB+	0.2	0.0	0.0	0.0	0.2	0.7	0.0	0.5	2.3	9.7	68.1	7.6	4.2	2.3	0.2	1.6	0.7	1.6
BB	0.0	0.0	0.3	0.3	0.0	0.3	0.0	0.0	0.0	2.2	9.4	70.2	8.3	4.1	2.8	0.6	0.8	0.8
BB-	0.0	0.0	0.0	0.0	0.0	0.0	0.2	0.6	0.2	0.8	2.4	8.5	73.2	5.4	4.6	1.4	1.3	1.4
B+	0.0	0.0	0.0	0.0	0.0	0.0	0.1	0.5	0.3	0.0	1.0	2.5	6.3	72.1	8.7	4.5	2.5	2.2
B	0.0	0.0	0.0	0.0	0.0	0.0	0.2	0.5	0.0	0.5	0.2	0.3	1.9	9.1	68.4	8.8	5.3	5.0
B-	0.0	0.0	0.0	0.0	0.0	0.0	0.2	0.0	0.4	0.0	0.4	0.2	1.5	2.7	11.0	64.2	13.5	5.8
CCC	0.0	0.0	0.0	0.0	0.0	0.2	0.0	0.0	0.0	0.4	0.2	0.4	0.4	1.2	2.8	8.7	69.8	15.8
Large corporate – hard landing (%)																		
AAA	93.2	1.0	5.2	0.5	0.0	0.0	0.0	0.0	0.0	0.0	0.0	0.0	0.0	0.0	0.0	0.0	0.0	0.0
AA+	2.0	77.6	6.8	13.6	0.0	0.0	0.0	0.0	0.0	0.0	0.0	0.0	0.0	0.0	0.0	0.0	0.0	0.0
AA	1.5	3.0	79.0	11.4	2.6	1.8	0.4	0.0	0.4	0.0	0.0	0.0	0.0	0.0	0.0	0.0	0.0	0.0
AA-	0.2	1.3	1.6	83.1	7.8	2.9	1.8	0.4	0.0	0.2	0.2	0.0	0.4	0.0	0.0	0.0	0.0	0.0
A+	0.0	0.2	0.5	4.0	81.9	9.7	3.4	0.3	0.0	0.0	0.0	0.0	0.0	0.0	0.0	0.0	0.0	0.0
A	0.2	0.0	0.3	2.8	4.2	76.8	10.9	2.2	1.2	0.3	0.3	0.2	0.0	0.0	0.2	0.0	0.1	0.2
A-	0.1	0.3	0.3	0.6	0.8	5.5	74.8	9.8	4.4	1.4	0.3	0.3	0.6	0.4	0.3	0.1	0.1	0.0
BBB+	0.0	0.3	0.1	0.0	0.0	1.6	4.3	76.9	10.6	3.7	0.7	0.9	0.3	0.1	0.0	0.0	0.1	0.4
BBB	0.1	0.1	0.0	0.4	0.3	0.5	2.4	5.4	75.4	10.6	2.3	1.0	0.4	0.1	0.5	0.4	0.0	0.0
BBB-	0.0	0.0	0.0	0.2	0.0	0.5	1.2	2.6	9.6	69.9	5.2	3.4	3.3	1.9	0.3	0.0	0.9	1.0
BB+	0.0	0.0	0.0	0.0	0.0	0.2	1.9	0.8	1.9	8.8	71.0	3.5	5.6	1.9	2.1	1.2	0.0	1.2
BB	0.0	0.0	0.0	0.0	0.0	0.0	0.0	0.2	0.7	2.7	7.5	67.9	9.0	2.3	5.4	1.8	0.9	1.6
BB-	0.0	0.0	0.0	0.0	0.0	0.2	0.0	0.0	0.1	1.0	2.8	3.9	70.2	3.2	8.2	4.2	1.4	5.0
B+	0.0	0.0	0.1	0.0	0.2	0.0	0.0	0.1	0.0	0.7	0.7	1.5	4.0	69.4	5.8	7.9	3.4	6.1
B	0.0	0.0	0.0	0.0	0.0	0.0	0.1	0.4	0.3	0.0	0.5	0.5	1.7	4.3	67.9	6.8	7.0	10.3
B-	0.0	0.0	0.2	0.0	0.2	0.0	0.2	0.0	0.0	0.2	0.0	0.4	0.5	2.1	2.3	62.3	12.8	18.9
CCC	0.0	0.0	0.0	0.0	0.0	0.0	0.0	0.0	0.0	0.0	0.0	0.0	0.0	0.5	0.0	2.5	67.7	29.3

Large corporate – soft landing (%)

	AAA	AA+	AA	AA–	A+	A	A–	BBB+	BBB	BBB–	BB+	BB	BB–	B+	B	B–	CCC	D
AAA	91.7	3.6	2.3	1.0	1.0	0.3	0.0	0.0	0.0	0.0	0.0	0.0	0.0	0.0	0.0	0.0	0.0	0.0
AA+	2.4	83.2	5.6	2.8	3.6	0.8	0.4	0.8	0.0	0.0	0.4	0.0	0.0	0.0	0.0	0.0	0.0	0.0
AA	0.5	4.6	81.7	4.9	4.1	2.0	1.7	0.0	0.0	0.0	0.0	0.0	0.2	0.0	0.0	0.0	0.0	0.0
AA–	0.1	0.7	3.6	81.5	6.1	5.5	1.2	0.4	0.1	0.4	0.0	0.1	0.0	0.0	0.0	0.0	0.0	0.0
A+	0.1	0.1	0.7	5.2	81.4	6.1	2.6	0.7	0.7	0.3	0.8	0.8	0.2	0.3	0.0	0.0	0.0	0.0
A	0.0	0.1	0.3	0.5	4.5	84.5	5.3	2.2	1.5	0.5	0.1	0.1	0.2	0.1	0.1	0.0	0.1	0.0
A–	0.0	0.0	0.1	0.0	1.5	7.9	78.5	5.9	2.5	2.4	0.4	0.3	0.1	0.2	0.1	0.2	0.0	0.0
BBB+	0.1	0.0	0.0	0.1	0.3	3.3	6.8	78.7	5.8	2.6	1.2	0.0	0.4	0.5	0.1	0.0	0.0	0.0
BBB	0.0	0.2	0.0	0.1	0.0	1.2	3.1	6.6	80.5	4.9	1.7	0.2	0.5	0.5	0.4	0.2	0.0	0.0
BBB–	0.0	0.0	0.0	0.0	0.0	0.7	0.5	3.7	9.2	75.1	6.7	1.9	0.9	0.5	0.2	0.3	0.1	0.3
BB+	0.0	0.0	0.0	0.1	0.1	0.0	0.7	0.9	5.0	9.2	70.1	6.1	3.9	1.0	1.6	1.0	0.6	0.2
BB	0.0	0.0	0.0	0.0	0.0	0.1	0.1	0.7	0.8	2.8	9.1	67.9	9.6	2.9	3.3	1.4	0.6	0.6
BB–	0.0	0.1	0.0	0.0	0.1	0.1	0.2	0.5	0.2	0.6	3.0	4.7	68.5	10.5	5.9	3.0	0.8	1.8
B+	0.0	0.0	0.0	0.1	0.1	0.0	0.2	0.0	0.2	0.0	0.5	2.5	7.1	67.9	12.3	4.2	1.9	3.1
B	0.0	0.0	0.0	0.0	0.0	0.1	0.0	0.1	0.0	0.1	0.3	0.8	2.4	7.9	65.8	10.7	6.5	5.3
B–	0.0	0.0	0.0	0.0	0.0	0.0	0.0	0.3	0.0	0.0	0.0	0.4	1.0	4.5	7.6	66.7	11.4	8.0
CCC	0.0	0.0	0.0	0.0	0.0	0.0	0.0	0.0	0.2	0.2	0.2	0.0	0.7	1.1	2.3	4.5	74.8	15.9

Table 4.33 Corporate transition matrices

	AA	AA-	A+	A	A-	BBB+	BBB	BBB-	BB+	BB	BB-	B+	B	B-	CCC	Default
Corporate – recovery (%)																
AA	54.9	35.8	8.0	0.0	1.3	0.0	0.0	0.0	0.0	0.0	0.0	0.0	0.0	0.0	0.0	0.0
AA-	18.1	26.8	39.0	7.5	3.2	0.0	5.4	0.0	0.0	0.0	0.0	0.0	0.0	0.0	0.0	0.0
A+	0.0	11.3	35.8	31.0	6.6	15.3	0.0	0.0	0.0	0.0	0.0	0.0	0.0	0.0	0.0	0.0
A	2.2	6.5	14.4	21.9	31.1	16.4	4.8	0.0	2.6	0.0	0.0	0.0	0.0	0.0	0.0	0.0
A-	0.0	0.0	9.6	22.8	23.6	25.8	13.4	2.7	2.2	0.0	0.0	0.0	0.0	0.0	0.0	0.0
BBB+	0.0	0.0	0.0	3.6	21.5	28.2	33.3	11.8	1.2	0.0	0.2	0.1	0.0	0.0	0.0	0.0
BBB	0.0	0.6	0.0	1.1	3.4	16.4	28.1	30.9	12.0	6.5	0.8	0.2	0.0	0.0	0.0	0.0
BBB-	0.0	0.0	0.0	0.0	3.0	4.9	22.9	31.4	18.7	13.2	5.2	0.2	0.5	0.1	0.0	0.0
BB+	0.0	0.0	0.1	0.0	0.3	1.6	2.6	18.1	40.6	23.1	8.7	3.3	0.3	0.0	0.0	1.3
BB	0.0	0.0	0.0	0.1	0.4	0.8	2.5	7.3	34.3	37.6	12.9	2.6	1.3	0.3	0.1	0.0
BB-	0.0	0.0	0.0	0.0	0.0	0.0	1.0	0.8	5.6	44.2	33.9	7.5	4.7	0.2	0.0	2.0
B+	0.0	0.0	0.0	0.0	0.0	0.0	1.4	0.0	1.2	13.4	35.1	35.5	5.8	3.1	0.1	4.2
B	0.0	0.0	0.0	0.0	0.0	0.0	0.0	0.0	3.2	8.2	16.4	31.7	28.6	5.7	1.4	4.8
B-	0.0	0.0	0.0	0.0	0.0	0.0	0.0	0.0	0.0	4.7	4.9	24.7	34.4	13.0	2.9	15.5
CCC	0.0	0.0	0.0	0.0	0.0	0.0	0.0	0.0	0.0	0.0	5.4	9.8	23.0	30.3	15.4	16.1
Corporate – overheat (%)																
AA	54.2	36.3	2.2	7.2	0.0	0.0	0.0	0.0	0.0	0.0	0.0	0.0	0.0	0.0	0.0	0.0
AA-	11.5	37.0	25.7	13.8	4.9	7.1	0.0	0.0	0.0	0.0	0.0	0.0	0.0	0.0	0.0	0.0
A+	5.2	11.1	24.0	29.8	13.7	16.0	0.0	0.3	0.0	0.0	0.0	0.0	0.0	0.0	0.0	0.0
A	2.7	8.0	13.2	19.9	20.9	23.2	4.6	1.1	6.5	0.0	0.0	0.0	0.0	0.0	0.0	0.0
A-	0.0	0.0	8.2	12.5	19.3	29.9	22.1	3.9	2.6	0.5	0.0	0.3	0.0	0.0	0.0	0.0
BBB+	0.0	0.0	2.1	0.9	10.7	23.7	34.8	18.9	8.6	0.0	0.0	0.1	0.0	0.0	0.0	0.0
BBB	0.0	0.0	0.0	0.6	2.1	12.4	22.4	33.7	8.9	18.9	0.9	0.1	0.0	0.0	0.0	0.0
BBB-	0.0	0.0	0.0	0.5	0.6	1.6	19.5	29.8	27.4	10.1	7.8	1.1	0.3	0.1	0.0	1.2
BB+	0.0	0.0	0.1	0.0	0.0	1.0	2.9	18.4	35.3	24.3	7.6	4.4	0.1	0.1	0.3	5.5
BB	0.0	0.0	0.0	0.1	0.0	0.0	0.0	5.4	26.1	36.7	18.6	9.3	1.2	0.1	0.0	2.5

	AA	AA−	A+	A	A−	BBB+	BBB	BBB−	BB+	BB	BB−	B+	B	B−	CCC	D
BB−	0.0	0.0	0.0	0.0	0.0	0.2	0.4	2.2	7.2	42.4	33.4	8.0	3.5	0.2	0.1	2.2
B+	0.0	0.0	0.0	0.0	0.0	0.0	0.6	0.0	9.7	11.2	25.4	35.6	10.2	3.0	0.2	4.2
B	0.0	0.0	0.0	0.0	0.0	0.0	0.0	3.5	1.4	2.1	11.8	33.6	31.7	5.7	1.5	8.6
B−	0.0	0.0	0.0	0.0	0.0	0.0	0.0	0.0	0.0	1.5	10.8	11.3	51.1	12.5	3.9	8.8
CCC	0.0	0.0	0.0	0.0	0.0	0.0	0.0	0.0	0.0	0.0	2.7	15.0	32.8	28.8	11.8	8.9
Corporate – hard landing (%)																
AA	52.7	36.7	4.6	5.3	0.6	0.0	0.0	0.0	0.0	0.0	0.0	0.0	0.0	0.0	0.0	0.0
AA−	14.1	33.4	29.0	8.7	8.6	6.2	0.0	0.1	0.0	0.0	0.0	0.0	0.0	0.0	0.0	0.0
A+	7.4	15.3	26.8	32.6	14.4	3.4	0.0	0.0	0.0	0.0	0.0	0.0	0.0	0.0	0.0	0.0
A	4.0	34.6	11.2	12.1	20.5	7.3	3.6	1.6	4.9	0.1	0.0	0.0	0.0	0.0	0.0	0.0
A−	5.5	0.0	5.2	12.1	19.0	30.0	21.3	3.3	1.5	0.4	1.5	0.0	0.0	0.0	0.0	0.0
BBB+	0.0	1.6	0.0	4.6	11.0	25.3	40.3	15.7	2.8	0.0	0.4	0.0	0.0	0.0	0.0	0.0
BBB	0.0	0.0	0.0	1.2	4.0	11.0	20.3	33.8	13.5	14.1	0.5	2.0	0.2	0.0	0.0	0.0
BBB−	0.0	0.0	0.0	0.5	3.8	4.7	20.9	26.0	17.5	13.2	9.7	4.0	0.8	0.0	0.0	1.4
BB+	0.0	0.0	0.0	0.0	1.4	2.0	2.6	18.9	41.5	12.5	11.4	5.2	2.5	0.1	0.0	4.7
BB	0.0	0.0	0.0	0.0	0.0	0.2	1.9	6.8	21.2	36.1	20.8	5.7	7.6	0.4	0.0	4.9
BB−	0.0	0.0	0.0	0.0	0.0	0.0	0.4	3.3	10.2	23.6	38.8	5.7	7.6	0.7	0.2	9.4
B+	0.0	0.0	0.0	0.0	0.0	0.0	0.0	0.0	8.1	7.9	18.3	38.7	7.6	5.9	0.3	13.3
B	0.0	0.0	0.0	0.0	0.0	0.0	0.0	0.0	5.2	3.9	11.7	17.6	35.0	4.9	2.2	19.5
B−	0.0	0.0	0.0	0.0	0.0	0.0	0.0	0.0	0.0	3.6	5.6	12.7	15.2	17.2	5.3	40.4
CCC	0.0	0.0	0.0	0.0	0.0	0.0	0.0	0.0	0.0	0.0	0.0	14.4	0.0	19.3	27.1	39.2
Corporate – soft landing (%)																
AA	61.6	17.7	8.3	6.3	3.4	0.6	1.5	0.4	0.3	0.0	0.0	0.0	0.0	0.0	0.0	0.0
AA−	26.8	26.7	18.5	13.5	4.6	4.9	3.8	0.2	0.6	0.2	0.0	0.0	0.0	0.0	0.0	0.1
A+	10.9	19.0	25.8	19.7	10.8	7.5	4.7	0.5	0.7	0.2	0.1	0.0	0.0	0.0	0.0	0.0
A	6.0	10.3	19.7	21.8	16.6	12.1	7.4	4.3	1.8	0.1	0.0	0.0	0.0	0.0	0.0	0.0
A−	2.0	4.4	10.6	18.9	21.7	19.7	13.4	6.2	2.1	0.4	0.3	0.0	0.0	0.0	0.0	0.2
BBB+	1.0	1.6	4.2	9.8	17.4	25.9	21.8	11.2	4.7	1.4	0.5	0.2	0.0	0.0	0.0	0.3
BBB	0.4	0.5	1.2	3.6	6.9	18.1	29.4	21.5	13.5	3.3	1.0	0.2	0.0	0.0	0.0	0.4

(continued)

Table 4.33 (continued)

	AA	AA-	A+	A	A-	BBB+	BBB	BBB-	BB+	BB	BB-	B+	B	B-	CCC	Default
BBB-	0.0	0.2	0.4	0.7	1.9	7.4	21.9	30.7	24.7	7.8	2.9	0.6	0.2	0.1	0.0	0.5
BB+	0.0	0.0	0.1	0.2	0.5	2.0	6.8	18.8	39.3	21.0	7.7	2.0	0.6	0.1	0.1	0.9
BB	0.0	0.0	0.0	0.0	0.2	0.6	2.2	6.7	24.6	34.6	21.2	6.4	1.5	0.3	0.0	1.6
BB-	0.0	0.0	0.0	0.0	0.1	0.2	0.6	2.0	10.3	26.0	34.8	17.3	5.0	0.5	0.1	3.2
B+	0.0	0.0	0.0	0.0	0.0	0.1	0.3	0.9	4.5	11.2	28.0	32.5	14.0	2.7	0.1	5.7
B	0.0	0.0	0.0	0.0	0.0	0.0	0.0	1.0	2.5	5.5	14.5	28.8	30.1	6.9	1.8	8.9
B-	0.0	0.0	0.0	0.0	0.0	0.0	0.4	0.4	2.2	3.3	7.9	19.7	36.6	13.5	3.4	12.6
CCC	0.0	0.0	0.0	0.0	0.0	0.0	0.0	0.0	0.0	1.3	5.6	16.9	31.8	18.2	15.3	10.9

Table 4.34 SME corporate transition matrices

	BBB	BBB–	BB+	BB	BB–	B+	B	B–	CCC	Default
SME corporate – recovery (%)										
BBB	33.9	53.4	9.9	2.5	0.0	0.0	0.0	0.3	0.0	0.0
BBB–	14.0	55.3	19.2	8.1	3.1	0.1	0.3	0.0	0.0	0.0
BB+	0.3	14.4	50.4	22.9	6.8	3.6	0.4	0.0	0.0	1.2
BB	0.1	2.1	31.7	47.9	13.3	2.1	2.0	0.3	0.4	0.0
BB–	0.0	0.1	2.6	38.2	43.2	8.2	4.7	0.4	0.3	2.0
B+	0.0	0.0	0.4	7.4	32.2	46.2	6.4	3.4	0.7	3.2
B	0.0	0.0	1.1	4.7	12.0	35.4	31.4	8.9	2.2	4.3
B–	0.0	0.0	0.0	1.9	2.3	21.3	33.5	17.6	8.8	14.7
CCC	0.0	0.0	0.0	0.0	1.2	7.6	12.1	31.8	14.5	32.8
SME corporate – overheat (%)										
BBB	27.1	58.3	7.3	7.3	0.0	0.0	0.0	0.0	0.0	0.0
BBB–	11.4	50.2	26.9	5.9	4.4	0.5	0.2	0.0	0.0	0.4
BB+	0.3	14.7	44.0	24.2	5.9	4.8	0.1	0.2	0.4	5.2
BB	0.0	1.5	23.3	45.1	18.6	7.2	1.8	0.1	0.2	2.1
BB–	0.0	0.4	3.4	37.0	43.1	8.8	3.6	0.4	1.0	2.3
B+	0.0	0.0	3.1	6.3	23.9	47.5	11.4	3.4	1.1	3.3
B	0.0	0.0	0.5	1.2	8.5	36.9	34.3	8.7	2.3	7.6
B–	0.0	0.0	0.0	0.6	4.9	9.5	48.5	16.6	11.9	8.1
CCC	0.0	0.0	0.0	0.0	0.7	13.1	19.4	34.1	12.4	20.4
SME corporate – hard landing (%)										
BBB	24.4	58.4	11.1	5.4	0.0	0.0	0.0	0.7	0.0	0.0
BBB–	13.9	49.8	19.5	8.8	6.3	1.0	0.2	0.0	0.0	0.6
BB+	0.3	15.3	52.6	12.7	9.1	4.4	0.9	0.2	0.0	4.5
BB	0.1	1.9	19.2	45.1	21.1	4.1	3.7	0.4	0.3	4.2
BB–	0.0	0.5	4.7	20.2	48.8	6.1	7.6	1.4	1.2	9.5
B+	0.0	0.0	2.5	4.3	16.6	50.0	8.3	6.5	1.7	10.1
B	0.0	0.0	1.9	2.2	8.6	19.8	38.7	7.7	3.4	17.6
B–	0.0	0.0	0.0	1.4	2.4	10.1	13.7	21.7	15.2	35.5
CCC	0.0	0.0	0.0	0.0	0.0	8.2	0.0	14.9	18.6	58.3
SME corporate – soft landing (%)										
BBB	41.5	43.5	13.0	1.5	0.0	0.0	0.0	0.5	0.0	0.0
BBB–	13.3	54.0	25.5	4.8	1.7	0.3	0.1	0.0	0.1	0.2
BB+	0.7	15.7	51.3	21.9	6.3	2.3	0.7	0.2	0.1	0.9
BB	0.1	1.9	22.8	44.0	21.9	5.1	2.3	0.3	0.2	1.4
BB–	0.0	0.3	4.7	22.3	44.1	18.7	5.0	0.9	0.7	3.3
B+	0.0	0.0	1.4	6.3	25.9	42.7	15.5	3.1	0.8	4.4
B	0.1	0.0	0.9	3.1	10.5	31.7	32.6	10.5	2.8	7.9
B–	0.0	0.3	0.3	1.3	3.7	17.1	35.9	18.5	10.7	12.0
CCC	0.0	0.0	0.0	0.0	1.4	15.2	19.3	22.1	16.6	25.5
BB	0.0	1.5	23.3	45.1	18.6	7.2	1.8	0.1	0.2	2.1
BB–	0.0	0.4	3.4	37.0	43.1	8.8	3.6	0.4	1.0	2.3
B+	0.0	0.0	3.1	6.3	23.9	47.5	11.4	3.4	1.1	3.3

(continued)

Table 4.34 (continued)

	BBB	BBB-	BB+	BB	BB-	B+	B	B-	CCC	Default
B	0.0	0.0	0.5	1.2	8.5	36.9	34.3	8.7	2.3	7.6
B-	0.0	0.0	0.0	0.6	4.9	9.5	48.5	16.6	11.9	8.1
CCC	0.0	0.0	0.0	0.0	0.7	13.1	19.4	34.1	12.4	20.4
SME corporate – hard landing (%)										
BBB	24.4	58.4	11.1	5.4	0.0	0.0	0.0	0.7	0.0	0.0
BBB-	13.9	49.8	19.5	8.8	6.3	1.0	0.2	0.0	0.0	0.6
BB+	0.3	15.3	52.6	12.7	9.1	4.4	0.9	0.2	0.0	4.5
BB	0.1	1.9	19.2	45.1	21.1	4.1	3.7	0.4	0.3	4.2
BB-	0.0	0.5	4.7	20.2	48.8	6.1	7.6	1.4	1.2	9.5
B+	0.0	0.0	2.5	4.3	16.6	50.0	8.3	6.5	1.7	10.1
B	0.0	0.0	1.9	2.2	8.6	19.8	38.7	7.7	3.4	17.6
B-	0.0	0.0	0.0	1.4	2.4	10.1	13.7	21.7	15.2	35.5
CCC	0.0	0.0	0.0	0.0	0.0	8.2	0.0	14.9	18.6	58.3
SME corporate – soft landing (%)										
BBB	41.5	43.5	13.0	1.5	0.0	0.0	0.0	0.5	0.0	0.0
BBB-	13.3	54.0	25.5	4.8	1.7	0.3	0.1	0.0	0.1	0.2
BB+	0.7	15.7	51.3	21.9	6.3	2.3	0.7	0.2	0.1	0.9
BB	0.1	1.9	22.8	44.0	21.9	5.1	2.3	0.3	0.2	1.4
BB-	0.0	0.3	4.7	22.3	44.1	18.7	5.0	0.9	0.7	3.3
B+	0.0	0.0	1.4	6.3	25.9	42.7	15.5	3.1	0.8	4.4
B	0.1	0.0	0.9	3.1	10.5	31.7	32.6	10.5	2.8	7.9
B-	0.0	0.3	0.3	1.3	3.7	17.1	35.9	18.5	10.7	12.0
CCC	0.0	0.0	0.0	0.0	1.4	15.2	19.3	22.1	16.6	25.5

It is possible to select the three most relevant areas for analysis:

- validation of the rating model;
- validation of the rating process; and
- validation of the dedicated IT system.

This chapter selects and describes the main set of analyses and statistical tests to be performed in order to assess, the appropriate aspects of a rating model for each relevant risk component (PD, LGD and EAD):

- the model design;
- the estimation of the risk parameters; and
- the model's performance beyond the evaluation of the impact of company processes and the evaluation of the judgmental revisions of in relation to the performance of the statistical components of the rating models.

Table 4.35 SME retail transition matrices

	BBB	BBB–	BB+	BB	BB–	B+	B	B–	CCC	Default
SME retail recovery (%)										
BBB	33.9	53.4	9.9	2.5	0.0	0.0	0.0	0.3	0.0	0.0
BBB–	14.0	55.3	19.2	8.1	3.1	0.1	0.3	0.0	0.0	0.0
BB+	0.3	14.4	50.4	22.9	6.8	3.6	0.4	0.0	0.0	1.3
BB	0.1	2.1	31.7	47.9	13.3	2.1	2.0	0.3	0.4	0.0
BB–	0.0	0.1	2.6	38.2	43.2	8.2	4.7	0.4	0.3	2.2
B+	0.0	0.0	0.4	7.4	32.1	46.1	6.4	3.4	0.7	3.6
B	0.0	0.0	1.1	4.6	12.0	35.3	31.3	8.8	2.1	4.8
B–	0.0	0.0	0.0	1.9	2.2	20.9	32.9	17.3	8.7	16.1
CCC	0.0	0.0	0.0	0.0	1.1	7.3	11.6	30.4	13.8	35.7
SME retail – overheat (%)										
BBB	27.1	58.3	7.3	7.3	0.0	0.0	0.0	0.0	0.0	0.0
BBB–	11.4	50.2	26.9	5.9	4.4	0.5	0.2	0.0	0.0	0.5
BB+	0.3	14.7	43.8	24.1	5.9	4.8	0.1	0.2	0.4	5.7
BB	0.0	1.5	23.2	45.0	18.6	7.2	1.8	0.1	0.2	2.3
BB–	0.0	0.4	3.4	37.0	43.0	8.8	3.6	0.4	1.0	2.5
B+	0.0	0.0	3.1	6.3	23.8	47.3	11.4	3.4	1.1	3.6
B	0.0	0.0	0.5	1.2	8.4	36.6	34.0	8.7	2.3	8.3
B–	0.0	0.0	0.0	0.6	4.8	9.4	48.0	16.4	11.7	9.0
CCC	0.0	0.0	0.0	0.0	0.6	12.7	18.9	33.1	12.1	22.5
SME retail – hard landing (%)										
BBB	24.4	58.4	11.1	5.4	0.0	0.0	0.0	0.7	0.0	0.0
BBB–	13.9	49.8	19.5	8.8	6.3	1.0	0.2	0.0	0.0	0.6
BB+	0.3	15.3	52.3	12.6	9.0	4.4	0.9	0.2	0.0	5.0
BB	0.1	1.9	19.1	44.9	21.0	4.0	3.7	0.4	0.3	4.6
BB–	0.0	0.5	4.6	20.0	48.3	6.1	7.5	1.3	1.2	10.4
B+	0.0	0.0	2.5	4.3	16.5	49.5	8.2	6.5	1.7	11.0
B	0.0	0.0	1.8	2.2	8.5	19.4	38.0	7.5	3.4	19.2
B–	0.0	0.0	0.0	1.3	2.3	9.7	13.2	20.8	14.6	38.0
CCC	0.0	0.0	0.0	0.0	0.0	7.6	0.0	13.8	17.2	61.4
SME retail – soft landing										
BBB	41.5	43.5	13.0	1.5	0.0	0.0	0.0	0.5	0.0	0.0
BBB–	13.3	54.0	25.5	4.8	1.7	0.3	0.1	0.0	0.1	0.2
BB+	0.7	15.7	51.2	21.9	6.3	2.3	0.7	0.2	0.1	1.0
BB	0.1	1.9	22.7	44.0	21.9	5.1	2.3	0.3	0.2	1.6
BB–	0.0	0.3	4.7	22.2	44.0	18.6	5.0	0.9	0.7	3.6
B+	0.0	0.0	1.4	6.2	25.8	42.5	15.4	3.0	0.8	4.9
B	0.1	0.0	0.9	3.1	10.4	31.4	32.3	10.4	2.8	8.7
B–	0.0	0.3	0.3	1.3	3.6	16.9	35.4	18.2	10.6	13.2
CCC	0.0	0.0	0.0	0.0	1.3	14.7	18.7	21.3	16.0	28.0

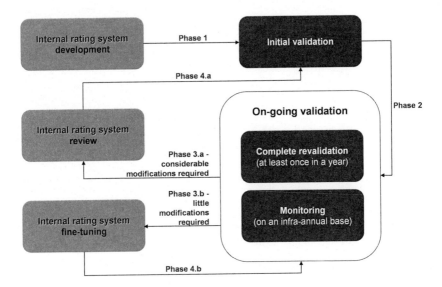

Fig. 4.15   Rating system life-cycle

4.6   Validation of the PD Model

As we can infer from Fig. 4.16 and Fig. 4.17, the validation of a PD model requires the use of both qualitative and quantitative analyses.

The main relevant areas of a PD qualitative validation are:

- the model's design (model type, model architecture, default definition);
- the rating process (attribution of the rating, IT requirements of the rating system); and
- the use test (relevance of the rating information across the credit/reporting processes).

Conversely, a quantitative validation analysis focuses on:

- the model's discriminatory power; that is, the ability of the rating model to discriminate ex ante between defaulting and non-defaulting borrowers (rank ordering and separation tests);
- the stability of the model and representativeness of the development samples over time; and

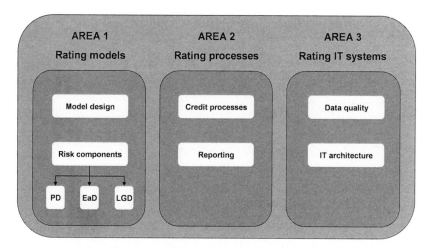

Fig. 4.16   Rating system validation: areas of analysis

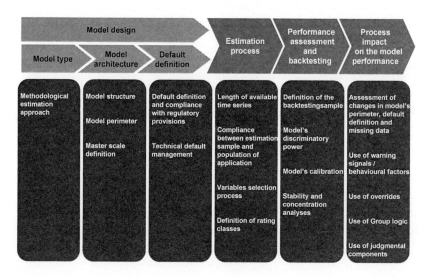

Fig. 4.17   PD model validation: areas of assessment

- the model's adequacy in associating a PD with each rating grade, which gives a quantitative assessment of the likelihood that graded obligors will default (concentration and calibration tests).

The following sections summarize the main analysis to be performed in the PD validation.

4.6.1 PD Model Design Validation

Model design validation is essentially about investigating the methodological approach selected to assess the credit risk profile of obligors assigned to the portfolio under consideration, the rationales supporting the choice, underlying architectural features and the definition of default addressed in the model.

Table 4.18 presents a possible checklist of analyses related to the area of model design validation, grouped by the three dimensions listed in Fig. 4.17: model type, model architecture and default definition.

4.6.2 PD Estimation Process Validation

Table 4.36 illustrates a list of analyses that should be executed during the estimation process validation.

For the dynamic properties of a rating system, refer to: Bangia et al. (2002), Lando and Skodeberg (2002), Bardos (2003) and Basel Committee on Banking Supervision (2005b). For the purposes of estimating risk parameters, banks may elect not to classify so-called "technical defaults" as defaulted – that is, positions that do not reflect a state of financial difficulty on the part of the obligor, such as to generate losses – so long as this is consistent with reference to the various risk parameters (see Bank of Italy 2006) (Table 4.37).

Table 4.36 Model design validation analyses: PD parameter

Dimension	Topic	Main analyses
Model type	Methodological estimation approach	Description of the selected methodological approach
		Assessment of reasons behind the choice: strengths versus weaknesses
		Validation of the comparative analysis carried out during the development stage, to consider possible alternative approaches
		Check the model's adequacy in respect of the portfolio of application
Model architecture	Model structure	Assessment of model's structure: modular versus integrated
		Assessment of number of models: single model versus multiple sub-models
		Rating philosophy point-in-time (PIT) versus through-the-cycle (TTC)
		Definition of relevant input data sources
		Assessment of the adequacy of the model's input variables to predict the borrower's default risk, irrespective of the specific nature of any underlying transaction
		Assessment of the model's functional requisites: updating frequency, validity of rating for operating purposes, computational rules, minimum information requirements, customer/exposure unique rating value
		Assessment of model's main assumptions
	Model perimeter	Definition of relevant variables for model's perimeter scoping
		Definition of relevant segmentation variables for definition of sub-models
		Definitions of exclusions
		Development samples' definition and reconciliation
		Definition and IT acquisition of the model's population (last available date)
		Definition and IT acquisition of a backtesting sample
		Compliance check: IT segmentation rules versus model's development perimeter versus commercial segmentation versus regulatory exposure classes
		Assessment of new clients and management of start-up enterprises
		Assessment of management of group connections

(continued)

Table 4.36 (continued)

Dimension	Topic	Main analyses
	Master scale definition	Definition of adopted master scale
		Assessment of the presence of at least 7 grades for non-defaulted obligors and 1 for defaulted obligors
		Analysis of distribution of rates obligors among various rating classes, in terms of both position and exposure
		Assessment of the absence of excessive concentrations within a single rating grade Assessment of empirical evidence supporting high concentration within a single rating grade
Default definition	Default definition and compliance with regulatory provisions	Regulatory compliance of adopted default definition
		Default assessment for temporal generations
		Duplication check
		Transition status assessment
		Analysis of positions management (exceptions/discriminating events)
		Default contagion (intergroup versus intercompany)
	Technical default management	Assessment of technical default definition
		Validation of selected identification criteria
		Assessment of technical default exclusion from the development sample

Table 4.37 Estimation process validation analyses: PD parameter

Topic	Main analyses
Length of available time series	Verify that PD estimates are not based solely on judgmental considerations, but rely consistently on the long-run default experience and on empirical evidence Verify that PD estimates are based on updated, relevant and representative data of the portfolio under analysis Verify the compliance of the development sample's observation period with regulatory provisions
Compliance between estimation sample and population of application	Assess the presence of a fair number of exposures in the development sample Assess the representativeness over time of the development samples with respect to the bank's most recent portfolio of application (distribution of portfolio and sample by segmentation variables: macro-geographical area, macro-industrial sector, turnover, and so on)
Variables selection process	Definition of explanatory variables' long list(s) Analysis of the economical relevance of long lists' variables with respect to the event of default (coherence of information value's sign) Description of variables' selection process and criteria (univariate versus multivariate analysis, cluster and correlation analyses, regression analysis and so on) Missing values, outliers and exceptions management Assessment of the degree of correlation among selected explanatory variables Assessment of model's output replicability PIT versus TTC adjustment
Definition of rating classes	Definition of internal rating master scale Assignment of obligors to internal rating grades (calibration) Distributive analysis

4.7   PD Performance Assessment and Backtesting

The performance assessment and backtesting consists in analyses such as those listed in Table 4.38.

4.7.1   Process Impact on the PD Model's Performance

Finally, regarding the process impact on the performance of the statistical model, Table 4.39 offers a possible analysis checklist. The quantitative

Table 4.38 Performance assessment and backtesting: PD parameter

Topic	Main analyses
Definition of the backtesting sample	Definition of a backtesting sample univariate analysis on model's short list(s)
	Assessment of short lists' variables distribution
	Analysis of default distribution along the sample Comparison with model's portfolio
Model's discriminatory power	Descriptive statistics (in bonis versus defaults average PD/score and variance)
	Graphical assessment of cumulative accuracy profile (CAP) and receiver operating characteristic (ROC) curves
	Calculation of accuracy ratio (AR) and area under the ROC curve (AUROC) at univariate, multivariate and sub-segment levels Calculation of corrected Gini coefficient (denoted as Gini[a] in the following)
	Calculation of contingency tables: false alarm rate (FAR), hit rate (HR) and misclassification rate (MR)
	Calculation of Kolmogorov–Smirnov distance (KS) Calculation of Pietra index
Calculation of conditional information entropy ratio (CIER)	Calculation of information value
	Calculation of mean difference
	Calculation of divergence statistic
	Calculation of Brier score
	Calculation of other discriminatory power indicators Comparison with model's performance at development stage
Model calibration	Descriptive statistics (in bonis versus default distributions)
	Graphical assessment of realized default rates compliance with estimated PD confidence interval for each rating grade
	Graphical assessment of cumulative default curve
	Chi-square test (Hosmer–Lemeshow, HSLS)
	Binomial test (with and without asset correlation)
	Traffic light test
	Calculation of other calibration measures
	Comparison with model's performances at development stage
Stability and concentration analyses	Analysis of obligors' distribution by rating grades Portfolio's composition by stratification variables
	Calculation of the population stability index (PSI) at univariate, multivariate and sub-segment levels
	Herfindahl–Hirschman index test
	Transition matrices assessment: persistence rate (PR), migration rate within 1 notch (M1C), migration rate within 2 notches (M2C), rating reversal analysis (RR)
	Calculation of other stability/concentration measures
	Comparison with model's performances at development stage

[a]See Brier (1950)

valuation anlysis of PD estimation models are finalized to evaluate, on a ongoing basis:

- the ability of a model to discriminate the in bonis positions from the future defaults (ordering and separation tests);
- its adequacy in representing the correct risk profile of the reference portfolio (calibration); and
- the model's stability and the development samples' representativeness with respect to the current portfolio.

Table 4.39 Process impact on the model's performance: PD parameter

Topic	Main analyses
Assessment of changes in model's perimeter, default definition and missing data	Assessment of changes in model's perimeter during the implementation stage, with respect to the development stage
	Alignment of default definition adopted during model's implementation with that used for development purposes
	Assessment of potential impact of missing data on model's performance
Use of warning signals/ behavioral factors	Assessment of the presence of internal processes that may have a direct influence on the rating score
	Impact on model's performance of irregular positions (so-called "administrative positions")
Use of overrides	Assessment of changes in overrides policy from model's development to implementation phase
	Allowed overrides typologies
	Frequency and size of overrides
	Information gain through overrides
	Impact of overrides' powers on model's performance
Use of group logic	Use of group mapping for rating purposes
	Assessment of changes in group logic from model's development to implementation phase
	Group logic and overrides relationship
	Frequency and size of changes on rating because of group logic
	Impact of group logic on model's performance
Use of judgmental components	Use of judgmental components for rating purposes
	Assessment of changes in judgmental components from model's development to implementation phase
	Judgmental components and overrides relationship
	Impact of judgmental components on model's performance

Next, we offer a brief description of the most common default probability validation tests on portfolio segments characterized by an enough number of defaults.

4.7.2 PD Discriminatory Power Tests

The accuracy ratio (AR) or Gini coefficient is the most common rank ordering power test: it measures the model's ability to order a sample/population according to its level of risk.

The indicator assumes values between 0 and 1: the higher the AR, the greater the model's discriminant power. A model that does not discriminate at all has a null AR, while the perfectly discriminating model is characterized by an AR (in absolute value) equal to 1. The Lorenz curve or cumulative accuracy profile (CAP) is the graphical analysis tool with which to evaluate the efficacy of a model's ordering power.

The x-axis in Figure 4.21 shows the counterparts subject to evaluation rates from more to less risky according to the model's score; the y-axis identifies the cumulative percentage of the insolvencies.

From this, we can obtain the CAP curve corresponding to the analyzed model; this is compared graphically with the curve of the perfect model and of the random model. The curve of the perfect model is obtained by assuming a model capable of assigning the worst possible scores to future insolvents; the random model – represented by the diagonal – corresponds to a model with no discriminant ability that uniformly distributes both in bonis and defaulted customers.

A "real" model falls unavoidably between the two curves: the better its discriminant ability, the closer its CAP curve will be to that of the perfect model.

The receiver operating curve (ROC) is a graphical representation of the "false alarm rate" (FAR) and "hit rate" (HR); this is obtained by letting the separation of solvent and future insolvent customers' cut-off "C" vary from 0 to 1. The false alarm rate identifies the frequency of effectively solvent subjects that have been incorrectly classified as in default; the hit rate identifies the percentage of correct classification of future insolvents (see Fig. 4.18).

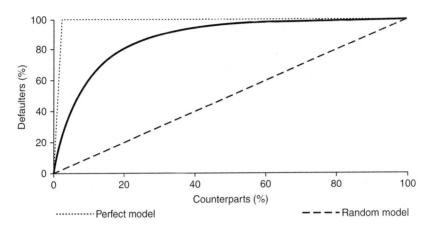

Fig. 4.18 Cumulative accuracy profile: an illustrative example

The information contained in the ROC can be synthesized in the measure denoted as the area under the receiver operating curve (AUROC). The AUROC assumes a value of 0.5, corresponding to a random model with no discriminatory capabilities, and 1 in the event of a perfect model: the higher the value, the better the model.

The AUROC and the AR parameters are linked by the relation: AR = 2 AUROC - 1

The corrected Gini coefficient (Gini*) is defined as: Gini* = AR · (1 − DR) where DR represents the sample default rate.

In Table 4.40, the contingency tables synthesize, within the four possible quadrants illustrated, the information relative to the:

- percentage of counterparties correctly foreseen in bonis by the model (Specificity);
- percentage of bad counterparties incorrectly foreseen in bonis (Type I error);
- percentage of good counterparties incorrectly foreseen in default (Type II error or FAR); and
- percentage of bad counterparties correctly classified (Sensitivity or HR).

Table 4.40 Contingency table: an illustrative example

Forecast status (%)			
Actual status	Good	Bad	
Good	80	20	Type II error (%): 20
Bad	30	70	Type I error (%): 30

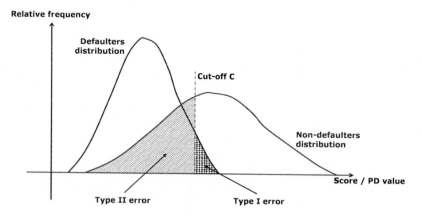

Fig. 4.19 Score distribution of good and bad positions of the sample

As shown in Fig. 4.20, the number of errors of the first and second type depend strongly on the cut-off value (C), settled as a separator of future default (counterparties characterized by a score value equal or less than C) from the futures in bonis (score value greater than the cut-off value).

In general, an error of the first type generates a loss corresponding to the capital and the interest lost due to the insolvency of a counterparty having been incorrectly classified as "healthy" and, hence, approved.

An error of the second type, conversely, produces a more limited loss (at least, in the corporate segment), originating from lost earnings in terms of fees and interest margin due to the incorrect classification of the healthy customer as a future insolvent. Once the cut-off has been defined, the following indicators are determined:

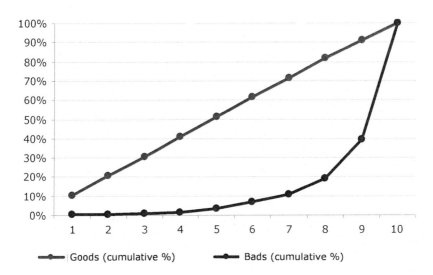

Fig. 4.20 The cumulative distribution of bads and goods per score decile: an illustrative example

- the misclassification rate (MR) – the percentage of counterparties wrongly classified (good as future default; bad as future solvent) over the whole sample positions set; and
- the hit rate (HR) – the percentage of correct classifications of bads over the total of the defaulted positions.

Table 4.41 shows the two rates of correct (HR) and incorrect (MR) classification, coherent with the illustrative contingency table proposed in Table 4.40.

The Kolmogorov–Smirnov distance (KS) evaluates the degree of separation between the solvent and defaulted positions, measuring the maximum vertical distance (in absolute values) between the empirical cumulative distributions of goods and bads. The variation in its values is the [0; 1] interval: the greater the index, the better the model's separation ability.

On the basis of the KS computation, Figure 4.20 illustrates the cumulative distribution of goods and bads in the same sample; Fig. 4.21 compares the trends of the KS test on two different samples: development and validation.

Table 4.41 Hit rate and misclassification rate: an illustrative example

Test	Value (%)
Hit rate	70
Misclassification	25

For further insights into discriminant power tests, see Brier (1950), Bamber (1975), Lee (1999), Engelmann et al. (2003), Sobehart and Keenan (2004) and Basel Committee (2005b).

4.7.3 PD Calibration Tests

The aim of calibration analysis is to evaluate the accuracy of the estimated (and calibrated) PDs with respect to the default rates effectively observed per rating class. Such analysis has particular importance: a rating system that underestimates the probability of insolvency of one or more credit portfolio segments requires careful monitoring (and, in some cases, a deep revision), because the estimation of capital requirements could be not aligned with the risks effectively assumed by the bank. (Fig. 4.23)

Before beginning the calibration test, a series of descriptive analyses (both graphical and tabular) must be conducted to represent and compare by quantiles and rating classes:

- the distributions, joint and separate, of the bads and goods of the estimation and validation samples; and
- the trend and the level of the observed default rate, with respect to the PD forecast by the model.

Tables 4.42 and 4.43, and Figs. 4.21, 4.23 and 4.24 give some examples.

Generally, three types of tests are used to check the adequacy of the model to represent the correct risk profile of the reference portfolio, :

- binomial (with and without asset correlation);
- Hosmer–Lemeshow χ^2 (chi-square); and
- the traffic lights approach.

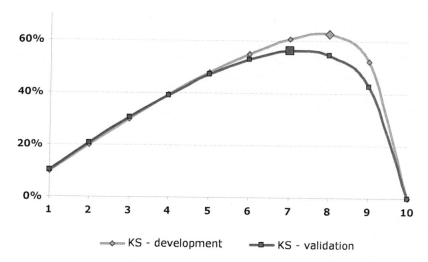

Fig. 4.21 The Kolmogorov–Smirnov statistic per score decile: an illustrative example

Table 4.42 The Kolmogorov–Smirnov statistic per score decile: an illustrative example

Decile	development sample (%)			Validation sample (%)		
	Percentage of bad	Default rate		Percentage of bad		Default rate
1	0.2	4.0	0.06	0.4	7.4	0.20
2	0.4		0.11	0.7		0.33
3	0.5		0.15	1.0		0.47
4	0.9		0.29	2.1		1.00
5	2.0		0.61	3.1		1.47
6	3.1	96.0	0.97	5.0	92.6	2.33
7	4.7		1.44	7.7		3.60
8	8.4		2.58	12.7		5.93
9	18.9		5.82	24.3		11.33
10	61.0		18.81	42.9		20.00
Total	100.0	100.0	3.08	100.0	100.0	4.67

The binomial test is based on a comparison, for every rating class, of the default rate observed values with the estimated PD. It is a "conservative", unidirectional test applied to single classes and – in its original formulation – based on the default independence within the risk classes.

Table 4.43 An illustrative example of risk and distribution per rating class: validation sample

Rating class	Total	Good	Bad	Default rate (%)	PD (%)
1	4819	4816	3	0.06	0.03
2	11,245	11,210	35	0.31	0.12
3	19,277	19,170	107	0.56	0.45
4	28,916	28,612	304	1.05	1.24
5	40,161	39,400	761	1.89	2.01
6	53,012	50,800	2212	4.17	3.87
7	24,096	22,000	2096	8.70	7.49
8	11,245	9500	1745	15.52	15.08
9	4819	3620	1199	24.89	23.22
10	2410	1540	870	36.09	40.17
Total	200,000	190,668	9332	4.67	

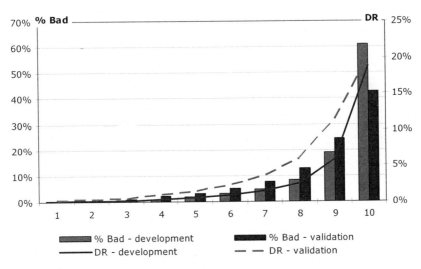

Fig. 4.22 An illustrative example of the percentage distribution of bad and default rates per score decile: development versus validation sample

For a given level of confidence, the null hypothesis (H_0) underlying the test is: "the PD estimated for single rating class is correct"; and the alternative hypothesis (H_1) is: "the PD is underestimated". As outlined in Basel Committee on Banking Supervision (2005b), the default independence hypothesis is not adequately confirmed by the empirical evidence.

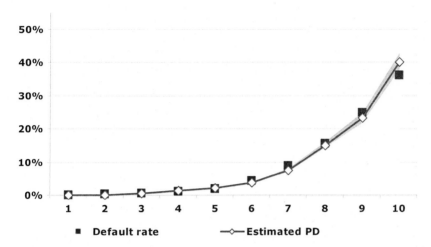

Fig. 4.23   An illustrative example of a comparison between default rate and PD per rating class

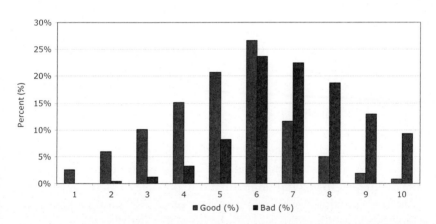

Fig. 4.24   An illustrative example of the percentage distribution of bads and goods per rating class: validation sample binomial test usually includes in its workings the regular asset correlation with respect to different levels of confidence

For this reason, the Hosmer–Lemeshow χ^2 (chi-square) test consists of overriding one of the binomial test limits: the verification of the model's capacity at a single class level separated from the synthetic indication of the whole model calibration. The Hosmer–Lemeshow test applied to the whole portfolio presumes a default independence within and among the rating classes.

Setting a determined level of confidence, the test verifies the alignment between the estimated PDs and the number of observed defaults in the classes: a null hypothesis rejection can imply, therefore, both an under-estimation, and an overestimation of the effective number of defaults. Finally, the traffic lights approach – applied to single rating classes – is a parametric test of a conservative type. Setting a determined level of confidence, it is possible to identify two thresholds – lower (PD^{inf}) and upper (PD^{sup}) for each rating class ($i = 1, \ldots , 10$).

If the default rate observed in the class i (DR_i) is lower than PD^{inf}, the test outcome is "green for go" (overestimation of the effective insolvency rate); if it is "red for stop" (underestimation) a re-calibration action is needed; otherwise the outcome is "yellow" (coherent estimation).

For further insights on calibration tests, see Blochwitz et al. (2003), Tasche et al. (2003) and Basel Committee on Banking Supervision (2005b).

4.7.3.1   PD Stability Tests

Stability analysis checks the alignment over time between the distributions of the development and validation samples, in order to identify possible differences that could originate future possible model instabilities.

Internal stability is evaluated by means of (i) the computation of the population stability index, and (ii) the transition matrix analysis.

The population stability index (PSI), is a synthetic indicator used to measure the representativity of the estimation sample with respect to the current portfolio, and for the stability of a single indicator or of the entire model, respectively, for bands of assumed values or for rating classes.

Once the variable subject to examination (e.g. the rating class), its possible modality (the 10 classes effectively evaluated) and the percentage distribution of the variable (with respect to the rating classes) of the estimation and validation samples have been identified, it is possible to define the PSI as follows:

$$PSI = \sum_{i=1}^{k} \left(P_i - C_i \right) \cdot \log\left(\frac{P_i}{C_i} \right)$$

where k is the number of modalities subject to analysis (in this example, the 10 evaluated classes), $P_i (i = 1, \dots , k)$ denotes the percentage of the validation sample assigned to the class i, while $C_i (i = 1, \dots , k)$, the percentage of the estimation sample.

The indicator defined in this way assumes a value of between zero and $+\infty$: the small values of PSI are expressions of a good level of stability/representativeness of the sample used for the model estimation; high values are a symptom of instability.

Transition matrices allow us to examine the evolution of the portfolio over time, highlighting possible variations in the positions of the different rating classes, both upgrading and downgrading.

The population stability degree is evaluated through the calculation of the permanence rate in the same class (persistence rate, or PR), the migration rates within one or two classes (migration rates M1C or M2C) with respect to the rating assigned initially and at the rating reversal analysis.

Table 4.44 shows figures and percentages of the class changes of opposite signs, inferred by the observation of the rating assigned across a consecutive three-year horizon, confirming the stability over time of the PD model adopted for illustrative purposes.

Table 4.44 An illustrative example of rating reversal analysis over three consecutive years

Type of rating reversal	Number	Percentages	
Reverse	1,491	12.4	
downgrade – upgrade	774	6.5	12.4
upgrade – downgrade	717	6.0	
Stable	10,509	87.6	
upgrade – stable	1,516	12.6	
stable – upgrade	937	7.8	24.3
upgrade – upgrade	463	3.9	
stable – stable	3,499	29.2	29.2
downgrade – stable	1,332	11.1	
stable – downgrade	1,559	13.0	34.1
downgrade – downgrade	1,203	10.0	
Total	12,000	100.0	

5

SME Credit Rating Models: A New Approach

This chapter describes the methodology and the estimation and validation process of a proprietary SME Credit Rating Model (DefaultMetrics™
2.0) developed by Capital Investment S.r.l. based on mid-corporate and
SME commercial bank databases. The accuracy of the model relies on
the integration of accounting information and behavioral information.
The related modeling incorporates the author's 20-year experience in
applied research and in modeling customer–bank relationships. This
model gains leverage on data from the Italian CCR, which is strongly
predictive of default events as explained in this chapter and in Sects. 4.6,
4.7, 4.8, and 4.9.

5.1   Definition of Default

The model estimates the probability of default over the 12 months following the moment a company's creditworthiness is assessed.

The definition of default, whereby a counterparty is defined as solvent
(good) or insolvent (bad), is that established in the Basel II and Basel III
regulations, largely based on bank-specific and CCR data.

© The Author(s) 2017
G. Oricchio et al., *SME Funding*,
DOI 10.1057/978-1-137-58608-7_5

With regard to the provisions set out in the supervisory regulations in force, defaulted exposures pursuant to the regulations are defined as:

1. substandard loans; and/or
2. bad loans; and/or
3. restructured loans; and/or
4. exposures past-due on a continuing basis.

More specifically, the following regulatory definitions apply:

1. Substandard loans: on- and off-balance sheet exposures to borrowers facing temporary objective difficulties which may be expected to be remedied within a reasonable period of time;
2. Bad loans: on- and off-balance sheet exposures to borrowers in a state of insolvency (even if insolvency is not legally ascertained) or in essentially equivalent situations, regardless of any loss forecasts made by the bank;
3. Restructured loans: on- and off-balance sheet exposures for which a bank (or a pool of banks), as a result of the deterioration of the borrower's financial situation, agrees to amendments to the original terms and conditions, giving rise to a loss;
4. Past due on a continuing basis (or abnormal past due, to be distinguished from short-term, natural past due): the company's exposures are past due and/or overdrawn for more than 90 consecutive days and do not normalize in the following months. For the purpose of determining the amount of past due and/or overdrawn exposures, such exposures on some credit lines may be offset with margins available on other existing credit lines granted to the same borrower.

One of the following two values is equal to or greater than the 5 % threshold:

1. Average past due and/or overdrawn amounts out of the entire exposure, measured on a daily basis over the previous 90 days;
2. Past due and/or overdrawn amounts out of the entire exposure measured as of the 180th day (since the loan has become past due and/or overdrawn).

For the purpose of calculating materiality in the numerator:

1. Any amount that is past due by less than 90 days with respect to other exposures must be taken into account;
2. Any default interest claimed from the customer must not be included.

In calculating the denominator, securities must be accounted for on the basis of their book value; other loans must be accounted for on the basis of their cash exposure

The default definition is very clear from a regulatory point of view. All 90-day past dues that generate a loss given default (LGD) greater than zero must be considered as default (bad company). However, in several banking markets not all 90-day past dues generate an LGD greater than zero.

A clear separation must be drawn between 90-day past dues that do not generate a LGD greater than zero (or past dues associated with a 100 % cure rate) and 90-day past-dues that generate an LGD greater than zero (past dues associated with a 100 % danger rate). With regard to Basel regulations, the former (false past dues) are not to be considered as default whereas the latter (true past dues) must be considered as default (Fig. 5.1).

It is simple to demonstrate that if false past dues (with a 100 % cure rate) are also taken into account in capital requirements, the excepted loss does not change, while the unexpected loss (or capital requirement) decreases dramatically; this is due to Basel algebra.

The process of collecting and examining past due data requires great attention and scrutiny in the cleaning and validation of the data. It is necessary not only to identify the past due event, but also to determine whether this event has subsequently generated an economic loss (LGD>0) or has not generated an economic loss (LGD = 0).

Only past due events which, subsequent to their capture, have generated an economic loss should be considered true defaults and designated as bad. If this approach is not followed, especially in EU fringe countries, there will be a phenomenon of inflated false bads, which dilutes both the predictive capacity of rating models and also the savings on capital requirements.

In balanced development samples, only true 90-day past due exposures were considered as "bad" enterprises. These were 90-day past dues associated with an LGD greater than zero; that is, those which subse-

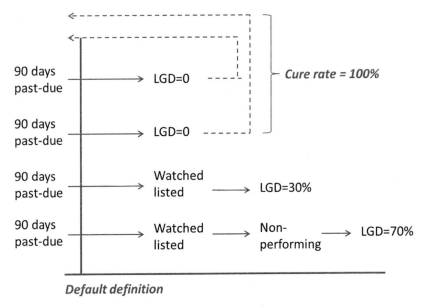

Default definition

Fig. 5.1 90-day past dues with 100 % cure rate are different from 90-day past dues with 100 % danger rate

quently deteriorated, falling into a substandard, bad or restructured loan classification.

5.2   Data Description

5.2.1   Data Exclusions

Default characteristics must be similar for the firms and industries treated in the model. The data does not include financial institutions – that is, banks, insurance companies and investment companies – in order to improve the accuracy ratio. This exclusion is due to the fact their balance sheets present higher leverage compared with private firms; also, their regulation and capital requirements set them widely apart from middle-market companies. Other companies excluded from the data are:

1. Holding companies with no operating activity: In estimating the credit risk of such businesses, the lending activity of which is asset-based, accounting information is not as relevant as the value of their assets.
2. Real estate developers and investment companies: Since the activity of such companies centers on asset-based rather than cash flow-based lending, less information on credit risk is found in the annual their profit and loss accounts.
3. Public and not-for profit institutions: The financial results of public institutions cannot be compared with those of private institutions. Likewise, the financial ratios of not-for-profit and for-profit institutions are very different.
4. Companies whose net sales are below €2,500,000 are not included due to the lesser value of their accounting information, along with the greater value of information from the CCR with regard to estimating credit risk.
5. Companies in the first two years of existence: Given the high volatility of financial data for these companies, such data cannot be used to evaluate their creditworthiness.

5.2.2   Descriptive Statics of the Data

The model is designed to estimate the default risk of companies with a production value ranging from €2.5 million to €100 million.

5.2.2.1   Overview of the Data

The model has been developed and validated using an extensive data set of Italian companies' balance sheet and CCR information.

Figure 5.2 presents the distribution of Italian firms and defaults used in validation and calibration: about 147,000 units of information for the period 2008–2012 were sourced; a unit of information means either a balance sheet or a firm's CCR status (Source: Capital Investment Research).

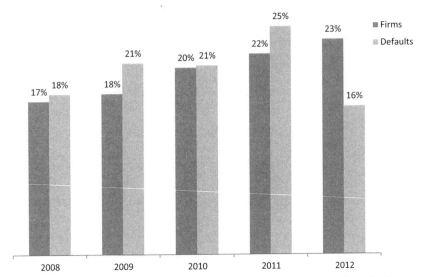

Fig. 5.2   Date distribution of Italian units of information and default data

5.2.2.2   Robustness of the Data

The data set used in the construction and validation of the model is extremely broad and representative of the real circumstances in which Italian SMEs operate, in terms of their sector of activity (Fig. 5.3) as well as their geographical location (see Fig. 5.4). The number of defaults examined in the analysis is equally representative of real conditions.

5.2.3   Cleaning the Data

Data cleaning was a key process in the development of the model, and is necessary to better define input variables and improve the accuracy ratio. Great attention was paid to:

- the correct identification of what is and what is not a proper regulatory default (see Sect. 2.3 for the definition of default);
- the correct reading CCR data;

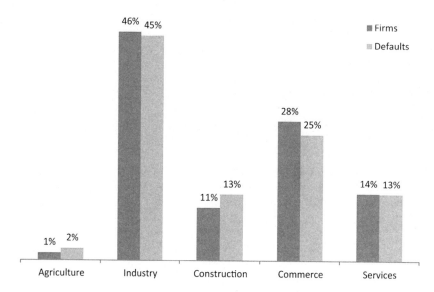

Fig. 5.3 Distribution of Italian defaults and firms by industry

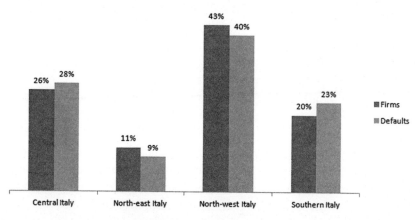

Fig. 5.4 Distribution of Italian defaults and firms by geographical area

- the correct identification of a hausbank relationship as opposed to a multi-banking relationship; and
- verifying the degree of consistency between balance sheet information and CCR information.

5.3   Model Architecture

The model estimates the PD over the 12 months following the moment a company's creditworthiness was assessed. It has a modular structure composed of three sub-modules:

(a) Hausbank Behavioral Module (or Leading Bank Behavioral Module) based on SME-bank data from the CCR;
(b) Multiple Banks Behavioral Module (or Non-Leading Banks Behavioral Module) based on the SME-aggregate non-leading banks data from the CCR;
(c) Financial Module based on financial statements data, with an approach similar to best international practice).

All sub-modules process three scores in a separate and parallel manner: these scores are calibrated and validated for the purpose of estimating the counterparty's PD. Through calibration, each score is turned into a PD which, on a scale from 0.03 % (lowest risk) to 20 % (maximum risk), reflects the probability that, during the 12 months following the analysis, the borrower will become insolvent, according to the adopted definition of default. These modular PDs are subsequently combined, on a weighted average basis, into a single PD.

As noted previously with regard to the behavioral modules, it is considered preferable to develop two distinct credit performance models based on the different behaviors observed in the banking system; this relates to banks that have a predominant relationship with a firm and banks that have a marginal position with the same firm. A banks that has a predominant relationship with a firm tends to provide greater support to that firm, given the bank's greater share in terms of loans granted and disbursed. Also, the bank can cover the credit lines that may be canceled by other banks with a more marginal position with the firm. A bank that has a marginal position with a usually carries out these transactions with a view to acquiring new customers; however, if the credit situation deteriorates they are more prone to classify the position (i.e. to classify the firm as being in a state of default according to the regulatory definition) and are less likely to reach negotiated settlements.

It follows that two distinct categories of banks, each reflecting substantially different commercial behavior, can be distinguished in the multiple banking relations usually held by domestic firms behavior: the leading bank(s) and the non-leading banks. For the purposes of modeling, a leading bank is that defined as the bank considered to be leading by the company's managers. In the absence of this indication, the single bank whose exposure to the firm in terms of the amount drawn down on a revocable facility/amount drawn down on revocable facilities with the banking system exceeds 40 % on the date the PD is calculated (i.e. the most recent CCR data). If two banks exceed this threshold, the leading bank is defined as the bank that has the highest ratio of the amount drawn down on revocable facility/amount drawn down on revocable facilities with the banking system.

5.3.1 Model Development

The model has been developed on the basis of the structured process shown in Fig. 5.5.

Step 1	Step 2	Step 3	Step 4	Step 5
Definitions, data collection and sampling	Univariate analysis	Multivariate analysis	Selection of the final model	Calibration and integration
- **Definition of default** - **Request for data** - **Data collection** - **Data Control** - **Distribution analysis** - **Construction of samples**	- Longlist - Expert opinion - Statistical testing - Factors transformation - Shortlist - Expert opinion	- Correlation and cluster analysis - Statistical regression - Check coverage of relevant categories - Identification of candidate modules - Expert opinion	- Modules testing - Expert opinion - Selection of best module by category	- AP estimate - Calibration - Modules integration - Breakdown analysis by class - Model testing - Expert opinion

Fig. 5.5 Development of each of the three modules

The various activities carried out in each step of module development are described in this book within the relevant chapters, which also describe their practical implementation.

According to published analysis, logistic regression is one of the best methods for estimating the function that associates the probability of a dichotomous attribute (in this case, bad = 1, good = 0) with a set of explanatory variables (financial, performance-based or qualitative).

The model has been developed on the basis of international best practices, which consider logistic regression as the best methodology for estimating the probability of default. Logistic regression is a special form of regression analysis where the dependent variable Y is dichotomous and has a binomial distribution, and the estimated Y, as it varies between 0 and 1, assumes the meaning of probability:

$$P\{Y = 1|x\} = \pi(x) \text{ i.e.,}$$

$$Y = \begin{cases} 1, & \text{with probability } \pi(x) \\ x, & \text{with probability } 1 - \pi(x) \end{cases}$$

The logistic regression function appears as:

$$\text{logit}(\pi(x)) = \beta_0 + \sum_{i=1}^{n} \beta_i \cdot x_i = \mathbf{X} \cdot \beta$$

where logit $(\pi(x))$ denotes the natural logarithm of the ratio between the probability of success (i.e. the probability that the analyzed position becomes insolvent in the 12 months following the assessment) and the probability of failure (i.e. solvent), given the vector $\mathbf{x}$ of n predictor variables (e.g. performance data on the concerned position):

$$\text{logit}(\pi(x)) = \ln\left[\frac{\pi(x)}{1 - \pi(x)}\right]$$

Since $\pi(x)$ denotes the probability that Y has a value of 1 depending on the explanatory variables x, the probability of Y can be expressed as a logistic function:

$$\pi(x) = \frac{e^{X \cdot \beta}}{1 + e^{X \cdot \beta}}$$

The logit chosen to describe the function that links the probability of Y to the combination of the predictor variables is based on the finding that the probability gradually approaches the limits 0 and 1, describing an S-shaped figure (called a "sigmoid"). While this is not the only function by which it is possible to model the probability of a given event, the logit is preferred over others because it represents a transformation of the ratio between two complementary probabilities (a quantity known as "odd"); that is, the number of successes for each failure of the event in question.

5.3.2 Development Samples

The baseline datasets for the development of the model consist of 21,770 firms in the SME segment, observed for five years up to December 31, 2007, and representative of the Italian economy both from a geographical and a sectoral perspective (see Fig. 5.6).

Each of the three modules has its own development sample.

The balanced development sample for the Financial Module consists of over 2200 enterprises; over 1100 were good enterprises and the remainder comprised bad enterprises (see Figs. 5.7, 5.8 and 5.9).

The balanced development sample for the Non-Leading Banks Behavioral Module consists of over 3000 enterprises; 1500 were good enterprises and the remainder comprised bad enterprises (see Figs. 5.10, 5.11 and 5.12).

The balanced development sample for the Leading Bank Behavioral Module consists of over 2100 enterprises; around 1000 were good enterprises and around 1000 were bad enterprises (see Figs. 5.13, 5.14 and 5.15).

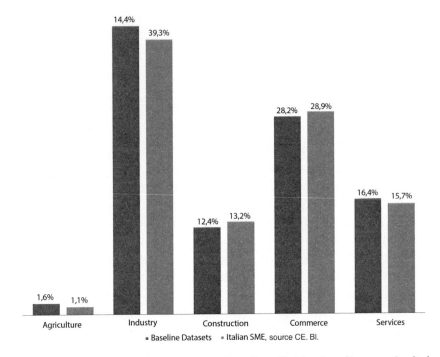

Fig. 5.6 Baseline datasets versus SME Italian distribution (Source: Capital investment research)

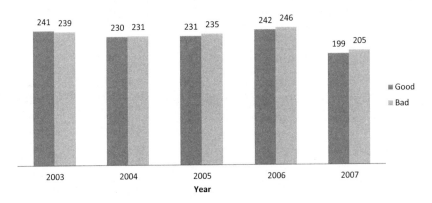

Fig. 5.7 Financial module development sample: good/bad time distribution

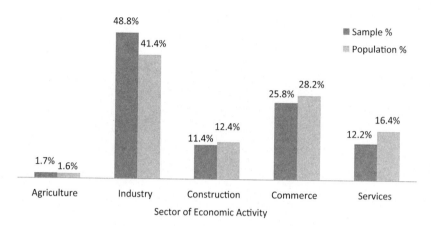

Fig. 5.8   Financial module development sample: industry distribution

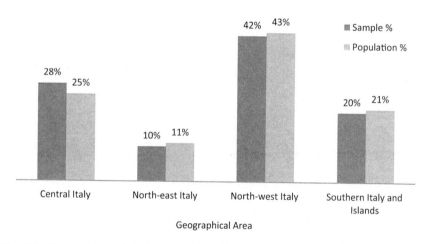

Fig. 5.9   Financial module development sample: industry distribution

The development samples for both the financial module and the behavioral modules were each built separately, in three steps:

Step 1 – Analysis of the reference portfolio;

Step 2 – Identification of the sample of bad firms and verification of their representativeness with respect to the economic activity and the geographical areas of all the identified insolvent positions;

Step 3 – Construction of the sample of good firms by adopting a random sampling methodology without replacement and stratified with

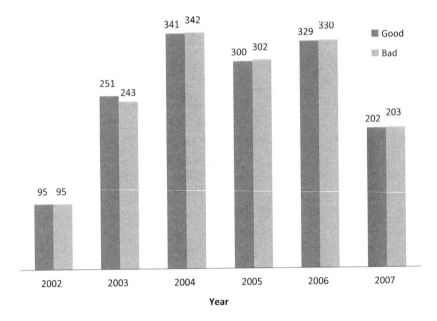

Fig. 5.10 Non-leading banks behavioral module development sample: good/bad time distribution

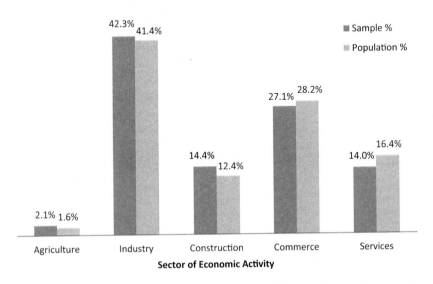

Fig. 5.11 Non-leading banks behavioral module development sample: industry distribution

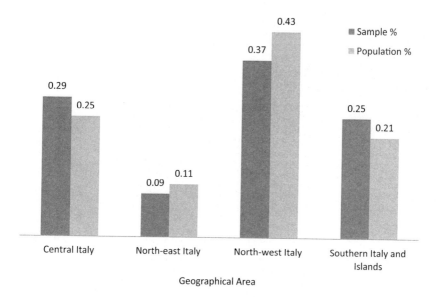

Fig. 5.12 Non-leading banks behavioral module development sample: geographical distribution

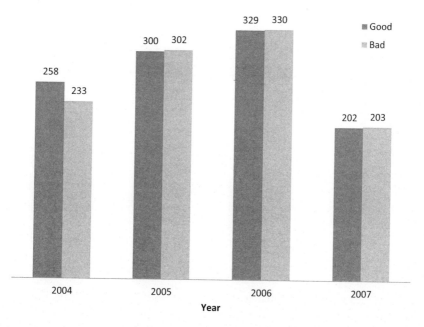

Fig. 5.13 Leading bank behavioral module development sample: good/bad time distribution

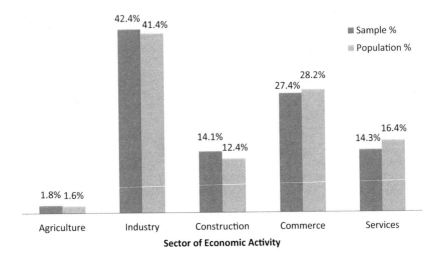

Fig. 5.14 Leading bank behavioral module development sample: industry distribution

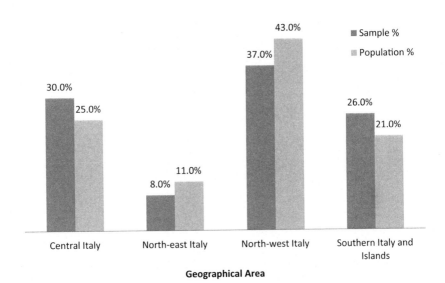

Fig. 5.15 Leading bank behavioral module development sample: geographical distribution

respect to the representativeness variables and the year of default, with constant sampling probability (simple sampling) across subgroups.
The sample thus obtained was tested to verify:

1. the completeness of the information;
2. compliance with the evidence identified in the population at December 31, 2007 (non-compliance with any of these conditions would have resulted in a new extraction of the sample).

The estimation samples of the Financial, Leading Bank and Non-leading Bank modules' financial, internal performance and external performance modules were tested for representativeness using the Population Stability Index (PSI).

Financial and CCR information was attributed to the positions within the SME estimation samples according to the criteria shown in Fig. 5.16.

If d indicates the time of default of a generic bad position, the data observation period for the (bad) position in question and the corresponding good position ranges from:

- d-12 to d-15 for the behavioral indicators – so that, for example, it is possible to build quarterly averages;
- d-19 to d-43 for the financial variables – in order to simulate the actual availability of the financial statements when applying the model.

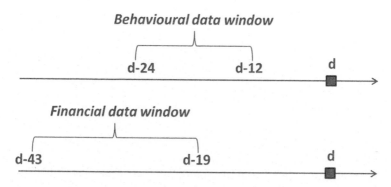

Fig. 5.16 Behavioral data window versus financial data window

5.3.3   Univariate Analysis, Multivariate Analysis and Model Weights

This section describes the methodology used to identify the long list, the selection of the short list, the multivariate analysis for the definition of each sub-module and the final integrated model.

The first analysis, conducted separately on each factor in the long list, is aimed at identifying U-shaped relationships (that must also be confirmed by the financial analysis) between the range of values taken by the indicator and the default rate.

The analysis was carried out by breaking down the range of values of each variable into sub-intervals (more precisely, quantiles) with respect to which the observed default rate was calculated.

The median value of each sub-interval and the corresponding default rate were identified, respectively, on the X and Y axes of a Cartesian plane to obtain a graphic representation of the relationship of each indicator with the default rate.

Given the U-shaped pattern, and having fixed the point $(x0;\ y0)$, where the sign of the first derivative of the underlying implicit function changes (ideally, the minimum point of a parabola facing upward), the best preliminary transformation (piecewise linear or quadratic) (defined as U) that could ensure vicinity to the point $(x0;\ y0)$ and simultaneously minimize the mean square deviation between the interpolating curve and the observed values was identified.

At the end of the preliminary analysis, all factors in the long list were *monotonic* (increasing or decreasing, in terms of their financial meaning) with respect to default, leading to a more accurate assessment of their predictive ability.

The subsequent analysis conducted on the factors in the long list (preliminarily transformed by the U operator, where appropriate) was intended to identify, for each of them, the range of values $[xl;\ xu]$ where:

- a significant portion of observations (at least 80 %) would fall; and, at the same time,
- the monotonic relationship with the default event proved to be particularly evident.

Once the extremes of this range, called the "upper" and "lower" bounds, respectively, and denoted as $x\,u$ and $x\,1$, were identified, the discriminating power of each factor within the $[xl;\ xu]$ interval was enhanced (through a logistic (deterministic) transformation, L_d), while it was flattened outside the interval where the relationship with the default event was found to be less obvious.

In analytical terms, by defining the percentage of observations falling on the left-hand side of the interval as l (lower), the percentage falling on the right as $1 - u$ (u = upper) and the generic value included in the identified interval as $x[xl;\ xu]$, the transformation of x is defined as:

$$L_d(x) = \frac{1}{1 + e^{-p \cdot (x-f)}}$$

where

$$= \frac{\text{logit}(u) - \text{logit}(l)}{x_u - x_l} = \frac{\ln\left(\dfrac{u}{1-u}\right) - \ln\left(\dfrac{1}{1-l}\right)}{x_u - x_l}$$

is the average slope of the curve in the interval $[xl;\ xu]$ and

$$f = \frac{x_u + x_l}{2}$$

is its point of inflection, while for the values falling outside the interval $[xl;\ xu]$, the following relations apply:

$$L_d(x) = \begin{cases} L(x_l), & \text{if } x < x_l \\ L(x_u), & \text{if } x < x_u \end{cases}$$

At the end of the transformation determined by the L_d operator, an analysis was carried out to assess the discriminatory power of the individual indicators, based on an evaluation of their accuracy ratio and the consistency of the ratios with respect to the economic meaning attributed to them, as well as the likelihood that the directors' discretion in the preparation of the financial statements might be precursory to any type of window-dressing practices.

As previously noted with regard to the Behavioral Modules, the development of two distinct credit performance models for predicting the PD was considered preferable: one based on a firm's bank account data with the leading bank and the other on the firm's aggregate data with non-leading banks.

The standardization and transformation of the CCR variables used for the Leading Bank Behavioral Module and Non-leading Banks Behavioral Module were thoroughly analyzed. The related long list consists of approximately 180 behavioral indicators, derived from the various types of exposure included in the Italian CCR, which were reprocessed to obtain absolute values, differences, ratios and min–max deviations.

On the basis of the indicators' ability to sort default events and economic meaning, a short list for each sub-module was defined.

With regard to the credit performance module, we have extracted the short list from the long list for both bank module types:

1. Leading Bank Behavioral Module (hausbank commercial relationship): 32 variables with high univariate accuracy ratios;
2. Non-leading Bank Behavioral Module (multiple bank commercial relationship): 22 variables with high univariate accuracy ratios.

Below are some examples these analyses:

The relationship between the average quarterly amount drawn down/ revocable lines and credit commitments offers an evaluation of the extent to which an SME has used its overdraft facilities during the previous 12 months, in relation to the number of overdraft facilities it has obtained from all lenders, without differentiating self-liquidating credit lines. It is one of the indicators typically used to reveal the adequacy/sustainability of an SME's credit lines. The analysis yields an accuracy ratio of 47.1 % (see Fig. 5.17).

The relationship between the average quarterly amount drawn down on revocable facilities/revocable lines granted shows the quarterly average of an SME's usage of revocable overdraft facilities obtained from all lenders over the previous 12 months, and is the key indicator of the economic strength of the corporate treasury. The analysis yields an accuracy ratio of 63.2 % (Fig. 5.18).

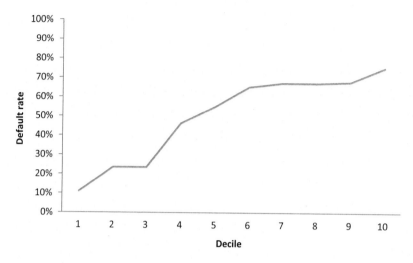

Fig. 5.17 Average quarterly amount drawn down/revocable lines and credit commitments

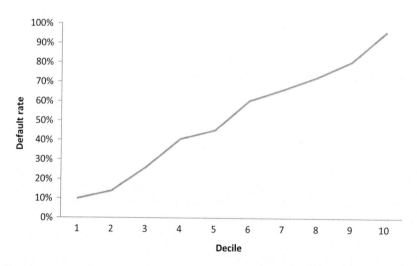

Fig. 5.18 Average quarterly amount drawn down on revocable facilities/ revocable lines granted

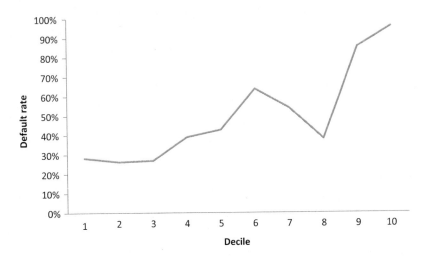

Fig. 5.19 Overdrawn exposure/revocable facilities and credit commitments

The overdrawn exposures on revocable facilities and credit commitments indicator shows a positive value where credit limits have been breached and is a point-in-time indicator of stress, or the absence thereof, affecting the SME's credit lines with the banking system. The analysis yields an accuracy ratio of 46.1 % (see Fig. 5.19).

The indicator of the maximum quarterly overdrawn exposures on revocable facilities/revocable facilities granted is intended to capture the maximum levels of overdrawn exposure on revocable facilities in relation to the total facilities granted during the previous 12 months, and allows an evaluation of the adequacy of the facilities themselves in relation to the cyclic nature and seasonality of the business. The analysis yields an accuracy ratio of 66.0 %. (Fig. 5.20)

The next step was a correlation analysis between the short-listed variables, a multivariate analysis and the selection of the sub-module considered as optimal.

The three modules show the following accuracy ratios in development samples on a stand-alone basis (in sample, excluding missing values). It will be seen later that the accuracy ratio of the overall model is much higher than the average accuracy ratio of each stand-alone module. The accuracy ratios of the three modules are:

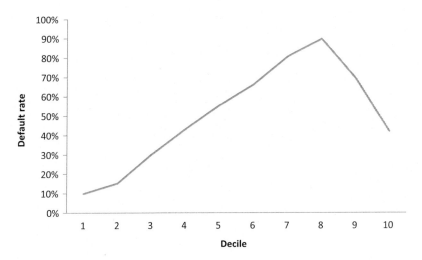

Fig. 5.20 Maximum quarterly overdrawn on revocable facilities/revocable lines granted

1. Accuracy ratio of Leading Bank Behavior Module = 69.7 %;
2. Accuracy ratio of aggregate Non-leading Banks Behavior Module = 69.9 %;
3. Accuracy ratio of Financial Module = 61.9 %.

5.3.4   Central Tendency

Estimates of long-run aggregate probabilities of default (or central default tendency) are an important issue, as they form an anchor point for the model. The default probabilities are calibrated in a 12-month horizon and an expert team supports the estimation of the anchor point year by year. In 2013–2014, the anchor point was 2.08 %.

5.4   Validation of the Model

The validation of the model was carried out on very large out-of-sample and out-of-time (2009–2012) datasets. Each module was validated individually and the Combined Model was validated as a whole. A summary

Table 5.1 Out-of time and out-of-sample validation datasets

Sample	Performing positions at the beginning of period	Of which in default within the next 12 months	Default rate (%)	Accuracy ratio multi-year range (%)
Leading Bank Behavioral Module	64,221	929	1.45	57–60
Non-leading Banks Behavioral Module	77,327	1054	1.36	60–68
Financial Module	60,151	429	0.71	58–70
Combined Model (on single/intersection)	41,954	293	0.70	78–85

of out-of-sample and out-of-time datasets and accuracy ratios is reported in Table 5.1.

The Combined Model, which maximizes the overall accuracy ratio and ensures a good balance between the three modules, has the following weights:

1. Leading Bank Behavioral Module: 30 %;
2. Non-leading Bank Behavioral Module: 35 %;
3. Financial Module: 35 %.

The selection was made by reducing the following methodological aspects to common factors:

1. The results of simulations to determine the optimum accuracy ratio according to changes in the various weightings of the three modules;
2. The opinion of the group of experts called upon to carry out their qualitative evaluation of the balancing of the various modeling elements;
3. The desire to keep each module distinct and separate from the others in order to be able to work on each module individually in evaluating credit risk. With this approach, we preserved the richness of information obtained from reading the PDs derived from hausbank relationships separately from PDs derived from multi-engagement

relationships. In the same way, we preserved the richness of information obtained from contrasting PDs based on balance sheet data with PDs derived from CCR data. In doing so, however, we gave up the ability to optimize a collective accuracy ratio, which could have been obtained had the scores of each module been harmonized into a single score, and subjected to validation and calibration.

In order to verify the robustness of the model's accuracy ratio estimate, calculated on out-of-time and out-of-sample datasets, we proceeded to apply the Mann-Whitney test to establish the confidence interval.

The model's aggregate accuracy ratio is 81.4 %

The Combined Model accuracy ratio on the overall out-of-time and out-of-sample datasets is 81.4 % with a Mann-Whitney test confidence interval of 78.2 % (lower bound) and 84.6 % (upper bound).

The restricted interval of the accuracy ratio supports its validity.

5.5   Leveraging Behavioral Data and Enhancing Model Accuracy

SME credit rating models based on balance sheet information as well as behavioral information held in CCRs regarding bank–client relationships are proved to be highly predictive

While the accuracy ratios of each of these two approaches (financial and behavioral), if taken individually, falls between 66 % and 70 %, in the new approach the model's overall accuracy ratio reaches 80–84 %.

This result can be explained by the different role played in forecasting a state of insolvency by information from financial statements, as opposed to information based on credit performance.

With respect to SMEs, for which audited financial statements are not required, financial statement data:

(a) is by its very nature available on a delayed basis;
(b) is potentially subject to creative accounting practices;
(c) is provided on an annual basis.

In essence, financial statements are useful to estimate the probability of default over a period of 24–36-months following publication. However, they show little flexibility in capturing a situation of strained liquidity or overstretched credit lines vis-à-vis the banking system on an ongoing basis. This fact is especially relevant under the Basel regulations since default – before reaching pathological conditions such as those envisaged in banks' classifications in watch-listed or in non-performing loans, or those resulting in the cessation of business – is defined as credit lines overdrawn for an extended period of time (i.e. past-due).

Conversely, the information available in CCRs:

(a) is not subject to corporate practices of creative accounting;
(b) is available within a week;
(c) is updated on a monthly basis;
(d) has a stronger correlation with the past due definition of default;
(e) provides a reliable picture of an SME's liquidity situation.

In modeling CCR behavioral variables, it is important to take into consideration the different relationships between SMEs and banks according the two principal schemes: the hausbank (or leading bank) relationship and multiple bank relationships (aggregate non-leading banks).

This methodological choice resulted from the different behaviors observed in the banking system between banks that have a predominant relationship with a firm, compared with banks that have a marginal position with the same firm.

By combining the predictive ability of the financial statement approach with the predictive ability of the behavioral approach (in terms of a hausbank or multiple banks position), it is possible to achieve a synergistic effect in the overall accuracy ratio. The accuracy ratio improvement is in the region of 14 percentage points.

The higher accuracy ratio of the model under the new approach allows for the optimization of the predictions in EU systems, which are predominantly bank-centric, as evidenced by the IMF's Financial Stability Reports.

The new methodology leverages CCR data, follows a flexible approach and differentiates between the hausbank (leading bank) model and the multiple-bank (non-leading banks) model when evaluating the relationship between the bank and the SME. This mathematical flexibility is useful in applying the methodology in EU countries other than Italy.

5.6   Two SME Credit Risk Assessment Cases

In order to better explain the added value of CCR data compared with typical balance sheet data, two examples using real company data are offered.

5.6.1 Company A

Company A operates in the manufacturing sector with annual revenue of €8,320,000. On December 31, 2012, the company presented the following healthy balance sheet:

Net debt/EBITDA	4.8
Interest costs/EBIT	46 %
EBITDA/sales	4.3 %
Debt/equity	2.5

An evaluation of credit risk using a model based on balance sheet data gives an estimated 12-month expected default frequency of 0.35 %.

An examination of CCR data yields additional information, some positive and some negative; in particular:

1. Company A does not have a leading bank relationship, but works with four different credit institutions.
2. The ratio of credit reserve to credit used across all lenders contracted over the last three months went to 7.4 % from 12.9 %.
3. The safety margin associated with the use of revocable lines of credit contracted over the last three months went to −10.4 % from 200 %; also, the company breached its credit limits twice during the last two months. The company's treasury is consequently under pressure and is compelled to undertake the rapid regeneration of liquidity (i.e. by disposal of non-core assets, etc.).

An evaluation of credit risk using a model based on CCR data gives an estimated 12-month expected default frequency of 5.35 %, which is clearly in the elevated risk zone.

Based on a combined reading of balance sheet information and information on commercial relationships with the banks, the estimated credit risk is of the order of 3.1 %; that is, in the high-yield sector.

5.6.2 Company B

Company B operates in the food producing sector with annual revenue of €11,675,000. On December 31, 2012, the company presented the following relatively healthy balance sheet:

Net debt/EBITDA	6.3
Interest costs/EBIT	51 %
EBITDA/sales	7.8 %
Debt/equity	0.6

An evaluation of credit risk using a model based on balance sheet data gives an estimated 12-month expected default frequency of 0.61 %

An examination of CCR data yields additional positive information; in particular:

1. Company B has a leading bank relationship (in which 50 % of the drawn credit lines are concentrated) and also works with two other credit institutions.
2. The ratio of credit reserve to credit used across all lenders has remained constant during the last three months, at around the 160 % mark.
3. The safety margin associated with the use of revocable lines of credit has increased during the last three months, to 240 % from 200 %, with no credit limit breaches. The company's treasury position is consequently very good and an expansion of business activities may be envisaged.

An evaluation of credit risk using a model based on CCR data gives an estimated 12-month expected default frequency of 0.22 %, which is clearly in the low-risk zone.

Based on a combined reading of balance sheet information and information on commercial relationships with the banks, the estimated credit risk is of the order of 0.4 %; that is, at investment grade level.

The following are the main points of the new proposed methodology:

1. The capacity to transform CCR behavioral data from the commercial bank-SME relationship into a PD, in line with the regulatory definition of default (i.e., past-due with a 100 % danger rate);
2. The capacity to differentiate between commercial bank–SME relationships of a hausbank type and commercial bank-SME relationships of a multiple engagement type, thus producing different behavioral PDs (the algebra incorporates two different types of commercial behavior);
3. The capacity to exploit fully the synergies between financial models and behavioral models, resulting in the notably improved predictive capability of (an out-of-sample and out-of-time jump in accuracy ratio to 81 % from 68 %);
4. A modular and flexible approach which allows the new methodology to be extended in the 14 EU banking markets that offer CCRs (in all EU countries, SME funding is excessively bank-centered, according to the IMF's Financial Stability Reports) and potentially also in the 41 countries outside the EU that have a CCR system;
5. The "open architecture" by which the model can be further empowered through developing and inserting new behavioral modules based on SME energy consumption, on SME phone and data utilization, on SME web indexing and reputation, and so on. According to the writers, an upward or a downward "jump" in the IT or energy consumption is always linked to a "not-normal" situation that can be used in an "early warning" credit rating system in terms of accuracy ratio improvements.

5.7 SME Credit Risk: An Empirical Analysis

This section discusses the dynamics of the credit risk on a sample of 10,000 Italian SMEs studied in 2010–2014 (Source: Capital Investment Research on commercial bank databases). The analysis is based on the application of the model described in this chapter.

The crisis has had a significant effect in terms of bankruptcies, cessation of trading of companies and a rise in unemployment. The progressive reduction of bank credit led to a phenomenon of "polarization" and selection of SMEs: the best SMEs on one side, with high turnover abroad, mainly self-sufficient in economic and financial terms and on the others; on the other side were the SMEs experiencing financial difficulties. The top group of SMEs has a good internal rating grade and their loans present a low absorption of regulatory capital: therefore, the banking system has offered credit in abundance and low prices. The second group of SMEs progressively lost the support of the banking system.

In this perspective, the European Central Bank Long-Term Refinancing Operations (LTROs) and Targeted Long-Term Refinancing Operations (TLTROs) did not improve the health of SMEs. More precisely, banks mainly used LTROs to buy government bonds and profit from the spread between the cost of funding and the yield on government bonds. The final effect was that a very low level of funding reached the so-called "real economy". Banks used TLTROs according loans to SMEs with the best internal credit rating (lower bank capital absorption) and not used to fund SMEs with a lower internal credit rating (higher bank capital absorption): this bank selection contributed to the phenomenon of "bias/polarization" described above.

The reason for this behavior lies in the fact that LTRO-TLTRO operations solve a problem of bank liquidity and not a problem of bank capital. Under Basel Regulations, the allocation of credit is based on the allocation of capital: there is an abundance of credit only if there is abundance of bank capital; there is a reduction of credit if there is bank capital shortage.

In sum, the "bottleneck" that hampers the restarting of bank lending to SMEs is the shortage of bank capital and not a shortage of bank liquidity. The European Central Bank is taking two directions: increasing bank liquidity, in order to avoid any bank failure; and, at the same time, increasing bank capital requirements, thus discouraging lending to marginal firms.

Figures 5.21, 5.22, 5.23 and 5.24 illustrate the distribution of the probability of default of the Italian small and medium-sized enterprises in the years 2011–2014 (Source: Capital Investment Research on the BNL-BNP Paribas database).

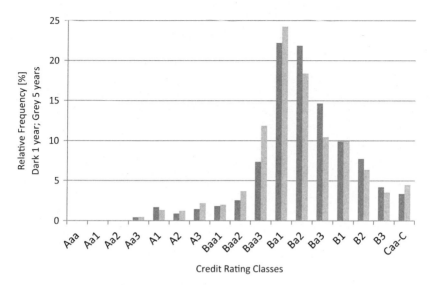

Fig. 5.21   Credit rating distribution 1–5 years, 2011

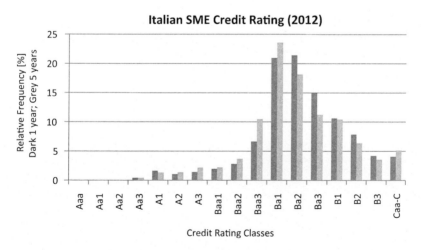

Fig. 5.22   Credit rating distribution 1–5 years, 2012

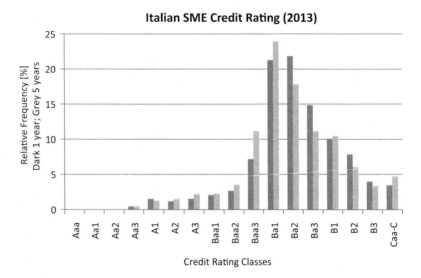

Fig. 5.23 Credit rating distribution 1–5 years, 2013

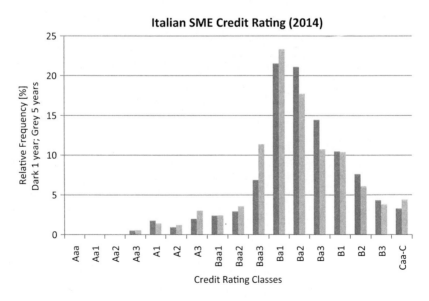

Fig. 5.24 Credit rating distribution 1–5 years, 2014

As you can see from the above figures, the percentage of Investment Grade companies remains very low, apart from the class Baa3. The larger classes are consistently Ba1, Ba2 and Ba3. It is also interesting to note that, in all the years examined, the 5-year probability of default tends to improve compared with the 12 month probability of default for classes Baa2, Baa3 and Ba1, while the 5-year probability of default tends to deteriorate compared with that at 12 months for classes Ba2 and Ba3. This gap can be read as a result of the "polarization" described above.

6

Restarting the Credit Engine in Europe

6.1   Introduction

Small and medium-sized enterprises (SMEs) are a major concern for European policy-makers, as the fixed costs required to access the financial markets may be too high for SMEs. Consequentially, their financing relies mainly on bank credit. However, as the unit size of loans to SMEs is usually smaller than average, while screening costs are fixed, banks tend to minimize the cost of collecting and processing information on SMEs (e.g. using scores instead of ratings) (IIF-B&C 2013). On their part, SMEs are less transparent; their financial statements are less informative and are often unaudited. In some countries, this is also for tax purposes. This translates into greater informational asymmetries and higher transaction costs for potential investors. These are discrepancies that could be mitigated by long-term customer relationships. In presence of imperfect information and adverse selection, banks tend to act as demonstrated by Stiglitz-Weiss (1981), allowing credit rationing to SMEs. As a consequence of becoming more risk averse (as was the case after the financial crisis), banks tend to increase credit rationing to SMEs. Firms faced by credit constraints are more likely to exit the market, lower their

© The Author(s) 2017
G. Oricchio et al., *SME Funding*,
DOI 10.1057/978-1-137-58608-7_6

employment, spend less on technology, invest less in new capital and in marketing, and, on the whole, are less likely to enter export or import markets.[1] Long-term investment is also an important policy issue. There are major challenges to higher allocations to such assets. Infrastructure investments frequently involve very high up-front costs. The risks associated with them are often specific to the project. Examining these project-specific risks requires dedicated resources that can take years to build, and which many smaller institutional investors (such as many pension funds and insurers, in particular) lack. Furthermore, the scarcity of high-quality data on infrastructure makes it difficult to assess the risk in these investments and to understand correlations with other assets. Technological and environmental risks may be very difficult to quantify. In addition, regulatory barriers in some countries prevent institutional investors from investing in these assets (Kaminker-Steward-Upton 2012; OECD 2013).

These challenges may have recently increased. Banks are now less willing to issue the kind of long-term loans required for the build phase of larger projects (AFME-Oliver Wyman 2013). The bank business model has become increasingly dominated by non-lending activities. Coupled with increasing fiscal constraints on government spending, this is causing a growing mismatch between the amount and time horizon of available capital and the demand for long-term finance. New banking regulation also negatively affects the supply of long-term financing by banks and by institutional investors such as pension funds and insurance companies.

Several public and private-led initiatives have been taken to revive credit to SMEs and infrastructure in Europe since the peak of the crisis. Many actors (described in Sect. 6.2) have taken initiatives (reviewed in Sect. 6.3) to re-issue credit to enterprises and with regard to long-term finance in general. This chapter will review these initiatives, focusing on their different scopes, and identify their pros and cons. Subsequently, based on the preceding critical review, we will examine what different players could (but also should not) do to revitalize credit, exposing innovative proposals. We will not, however, consider initiatives and proposals related to

---

[1] See the literature quoted in Holton et al. (2013) and Wehinger (2014).

taxation, accounting standards or financial prudential regulation, or proposals that are just suggestions or recommendations to the private sector.

6.2   The Actors

6.2.1   Promotional Institutions

Government intervention in credit can be direct (providing funds through debt, equity, or hybrid instruments) or indirect (improving the availability of credit information, providing explicit guarantees, or facilitating methodologies for financial statement analysis). These products and services may be provided through different channels and by different institutions.

Public policy mandate defines what can be considered as promotional institutions (PIs). This mandate can vary in scope from general missions (such as banking groups that target SMEs, or firms located in certain regions as part of their general activities) to general-interest missions (these comprise financial institutions targeting certain areas or sectors with a social value but are not necessarily profitable). Promotional institutions may play an important role during financial crises, as their propensity to risk is more stable. In PIs, the government is the implicit guarantor of funds (Robano 2014)

The oldest, and probably largest, government promotional institution to support SMEs is the German KfW Group. The KfW Group, founded in 1948, is active in different financing fields (e.g. promotion of SMEs, housing, municipal infrastructure, environmental protection, international project and export finance, developing countries), but the focus is on the support of German SMEs through the business sector KfW *Mittelstandsbank*. The subsidiary KfW-IPEX Bank provides project and export finance (Denzer-Speck & Lob 2013).

Spanish public support for SMEs is developed mostly through two public institutions: the *Instituto de Credito Oficial* (ICO), a state-owned bank; and the *Empresa Nacional de Inovation* (ENSIA), a public company attached to the Ministry of Industry, Energy and Tourism.

In Italy, the biggest role is played by the joint-stock company under public control: *Cassa Depositi e Prestiti*.

Furthermore, governments may offset possible financial market failures either by providing export financing directly, or by insuring against certain risks through a PI commonly known as an export credit agency (ECA). In addition, an ECA can offset market failures through auxiliary actions such as gathering and sharing information on risks, and by providing relevant assistance to exporters. An example of an entirely state-owned ECA is UK Export Finance.

As for the role played by PIs in the infrastructure industry, Canadian and Australian infrastructure financing models are widely recognized as using the best practices in government support to infrastructure investments. Through Infrastructure Canada and Infrastructure Australia, the respective federal governments have significantly bolstered infrastructure spending. Infrastructure Canada has set up the Infrastructure Stimulus Fund, the Building Capital Fund and the Green Infrastructure Fund (Bassanini and Reviglio 2014).

Since the global financial crisis of 2008/2009, PIs have become increasingly important in financial markets, addressing short-term financing gaps and mitigating cyclical fluctuations in lending activities of private banks. Following the sharp reduction in business lending activities, new functions have been attributed to PIs; also, a broader set of areas and players has been targeted, posing new challenges to PIs.

In December 2012, the French government created the *Banque Public d'Investissement* (BPIfrance), which has been operative since February 2013 in a similar role to that of KfW. BPIfrance incorporated the major public institutions involved in financing and supporting French SMEs (including the *Caisse des Dépôts et Consignations*, the *Fonde Strategique d'Invstissement*). Portugal has set up its PI (Istitução Financeira de Desenvolvimento) in 2014.

6.2.2 Central Banks

When interest rates reach very low levels, as is currently the case, traditional monetary policy becomes limited. For this reason, central banks must look to non-standard measures in order to further ease monetary conditions. Either these policies can affect the overall monetary stance in the economy (a general easing), or they can be more targeted toward sectors that are most acutely affected. Alternatively, they can perform a combination of both.

Collateral requirements to access central bank lending facilities can be changed in order to favor lending to particular sectors. Options include reducing the minimum rating requirements and the restrictions imposed on certain types of assets (for instance, on SME loans or Asset Backed Securities: ABSs), or on pools of assets. If a central bank makes the conditions on usage of a certain asset (for instance, loans to SMEs) more favorable, it encourages bank lending to this sector. Changes to the collateral framework can clearly be effective in easing financing constraints to banks and access to finance to sectors of the economy, such as SMEs. However, changes in relation to pools of assets can be complex and could increase risks for the Eurosystem.

Central banks around the world have also implemented purchase programs or non-recourse repurchase (repo) programs for ABSs and other credit related securities. By purchasing ABSs in secondary markets, central banks could improve investor confidence through a portfolio balance effect, increased liquidity, or simply through signaling support for this asset class. This could have the effect of narrowing spreads and fostering activity in the primary issuance market. The Federal Reserve System (Fed) (USA) undertook such asset purchases to reduce long-term interest rates and improve financial conditions. For example, the Fed bought mortgage-backed securities in order to attempt to increase the availability of credit for house purchase. Another version of this type of policy involves non-recourse loans (repo agreements) given to investors through eligible counterparties using ABSs as collateral with a haircut, similar to the Fed's Term Asset-Backed Securities Loan Facility (TALF). This means that borrowers could leave the underlying security with the Fed, rather than repay the loan, should the value of the security fall below the amount of money owed. This arrangement leaves the investor with potential upside gains, while removing the chance of extreme losses.

6.2.3 European Institutions

The European Investment Bank (EIB) provides finance and expertise to promote investment activity that will increase growth and employment in the EU, with a special focus on SMEs, resource efficiency, infrastructure, innovation and skills. The European Investment Fund (EIF), which is part of the EIB Group, focuses on venture capital, guarantees and micro-finance. In 2012, the EIB capital was increased by €10 billion, which allowed for an extra €60 billion in lending between 2013 and 2015. This measure was expected to unlock €180 billion in additional investments. The EIB supports SME financing primarily through financial institutions that on-lend to SMEs and other counterparties, either directly or through guarantees.

The European Investment Fund (EIF) manages the Program for Competitiveness of Enterprises and SMEs (COSME) of the European Commission. In the period 2014–2020, COSME will boost support for SMEs through a loan facility, as well as equity facility and finance for research and development.

As an example of the cooperation between the EIB and promotional institutions, in September 2013 the EIB and BPIfrance signed an agreement according to which the EIB group has made available a €200 million guarantee under the EIF Risk Sharing Instrument, co-financed by the European Commission, to support loans to innovative firms.

6.2.4 Public-Private Partnership

Public support is often essential to overcome market failures. However, government support should be designed to ensure and avoid excessive transfer of risk from the private to the public sector. As a general principle, all additional parties involved (SMEs, banks, guarantee schemes) should retain a sufficient share of the risk and responsibility to ensure proper functioning of the system. In addition, where market failure is a coordination failure, or where the solution is potentially profitable, the public may act as a catalyst for private initiatives.

Governments are increasingly turning to public-private partnerships (PPPs) for investments in public infrastructures. The largest share of such investment to date has been in transport.

There are two main types of PPP: remunerated by tolls levied by the private partner or remunerated by the availability of payments from the contracting agency.[2] Both types of PPP create liabilities for the taxpayer that need to be contained by transparent public accounting rules and budget procedures that identify them as on-balance sheet commitments. Tolled facilities tend to require larger equity investment, at higher costs. Availability payment-based PPP projects represent a lower risk for investors and attract bank loans with accompanying insurance and hedging instruments. Many availability payment-based projects involve only "pinpoint equity"; that is, a very small equity holding, sometimes less than 1 % of project finance.

Regulated utility-based models for investment attract a larger range of investors. They are a more familiar class of assets, with returns determined in relation to investment by a regulatory formula. An independent regulator is required in this model to arbitrate between the interests of investors, government and the users of the infrastructure. The regulator sets quality standards and user charges; these are subject to periodic review, which provides a useful degree of flexibility in the context of long-term concessions (OECD 2013).

However, there are few "investment grade" projects in the pipeline; these are projects that are not only bankable, but also adapted to more prudent categories of investor. The complexity of the construction and financing of major projects, especially in sectors with high regulatory or macroeconomic risk, requires agreement with various entities working together.

6.2.5 Initiatives by Aim

This section reviews the main initiatives (mainly public, but also private-led) in place or recently announced to restart credit both at the EU and at the national levels. Regarding the latter, the focus is on the largest countries (France, Germany, Italy, Spain, the United Kingdom), but also addresses relevant initiatives in other countries (Austria, Ireland, Latvia, Portugal, Romania, The Netherlands).[3]

---

[2] An availability payment is a payment for performance made irrespective of demand.

[3] See Infelise (2014), for a review of policies in the four major EU countries. Best practices are reviewed in IIF-B&C (2013). For an extensive review of policies to support credit to SMEs in

It is important to consider a number of issues when assessing policies in this area. For instance, does the introduction of policy support lending; that is, lending that would not have occurred in the absence of the policy? The policy must not distort the credit allocation mechanism by diverting funds to borrowers who do not have viable investment propositions. Similarly, policies must have structures in place to ensure that the lending decisions made are free of political or bureaucratic influence that would lead to sub-optimal credit allocation. Finally, there must be transparent and rigorous ex-post analysis of policy to ensure the effective use of taxpayers' money (Holton et al. 2013).

6.2.6   Reducing the Cost of Bank Funding

The leading intermediaries in most European countries are banks. In the years leading up to the crisis, European banks had relatively high loan-to-deposit ratios in international comparison and they relied heavily on credit from other sectors to fund their lending – namely, the rest of the world and insurance, mainly achieved through the securitization market and maturity transformation (i.e. borrowing short and lending long). As confidence vanished during the sub-prime crisis, the interbank market and the securitization markets dried-up, increasing the cost of bank funding (EC 2013a,b). With the sovereign debt crisis and the risk of re-denomination, bank funding pressures have increased again, particularly for banks heavily invested in certain sovereigns. Private-sector borrowing costs have started to diverge substantially according to geographic location.

6.2.6.1   National Initiatives

Funding for Lending (FLS) was a joint flagship program from the Bank of England and HM Treasury. The scheme was initiated in August 2012 and renewed until January 2015, and was aimed at boosting the lending

Ireland, see Holton et al. (2013). Major initiatives at the EU level are reviewed in Giovannini and Moran (2013).

of commercial banks to households and SMEs. The idea was to allow banks to borrow at a preferential rate from the Bank of England (collateral swap) on the condition that they increased their net lending positions to non-financial corporations. In practice, FLS allowed banks to borrow UK Treasury bills (which could be used to back cheap borrowing on financial markets) at the off-market rate of 0.25 %. Banks were allowed to borrow up to 5 % of their actual lending exposure and, subsequently, up to the total amount of new lending to SMEs. If this preferential borrowing did not lead to an increase in the bank's net lending, the rate at which Treasury Bills needed to be repaid was raised to 1.5 % (Churm et al. 2012; Infelise 2014).

In the UK, there is also a National Loan Guarantee Scheme, launched by HM Treasury in March 2012, with the objective of lowering interest rates on loans by providing national guarantees on banks' unsecured borrowing (Infelise 2014).

While these funding programs can be very effective in alleviating credit constraints, particularly when banks have liquidity problems, the effectiveness of such programs can be difficult to assess and communicate. It is arduous to estimate what the likely evolution of credit conditions would have been in the absence of the scheme (the "counterfactual"). Targeted programs may prove complex in their set-up.

6.2.6.2   Europe-Wide Initiatives

The European Central Bank

Untargeted central bank refinancing operations (fixed or flexible rates) aim to alleviate bank funding pressure, as central banks are capable of supplying essentially unlimited liquidity to banks against eligible collateral, in a manner similar to that of the ECB with its fixed rate full allotment policy. Central banks can also increase the maturity of their operations to reduce bank uncertainty, as the ECB did with its Longer-Term Refinancing Operations of up to one year (introduced in the second half of 2009) and three years (introduced at the end of 2011).

Central banks can change the collateral requirements for their operations to alleviate bank funding stress and reduce financing obstacles. The ECB has made a number of such adjustments; for example, by reducing the rating threshold for certain ABSs and by allowing national central banks (NCBs) to accept additional "credit claims" (i.e. bank loans) as collateral. In July 2013, it reduced the rating requirements and haircuts on certain ABSs in the collateral framework to ease financing conditions further.

In June 2014, the ECB launched Targeted Long-Term Refinancing Operations (TLTROs), which aimed to lower the funding cost of credit to non-financial private enterprises. The initial allowance of up to 7 % of outstanding loans to the non-financial private sector (excluding mortgages) can be increased in the next two years up to three times the net lending in excess of a specified benchmark. The interest rate will be fixed at the rate of the main refinancing operations prevailing at the time of take up plus a spread of 10 basis points. If net lending is below the benchmark, the borrowings will have been repaid in September 2016.

In June 2014, the ECB announced a plan aimed at Outright Purchase of covered bonds (which started in October 2014) and of simple and transparent ABSs.

Prime Collateralized Securities (PCS)

Before the crisis, European banks had a large and increasing funding gap; that is, the difference between deposits and loans. Between 2000 and 2007 in the Euro area, the bank funding gap rose from €830 billion to €1,540 billion; that is, 18 % of deposits in 2007. ABS issuance – including Residential Mortgage Backed Securities (RMBSs), Commercial Mortgage Backed Securities (CMBSs) and Collateralised Debt Obligations (CDOs) – filled about 77 % of the increase in the funding gap over the same period.

Due to different structural peculiarities (i.e. diversified providers of collateral management services and no quasi-monopolistic recourse to a tri-party system owned by systemic important financial institutions, minor recourse to sub-prime assets used as collateral, large adoption of international standard legal contracts), the collateralized funding market in Europe has proven to be more resilient and not a source of systemic risk. The downgrade ratio and the default rate of European ABSs during the sub-prime crisis were significantly lower than that of US ABSs, with the exception of CMBSs.

During the crisis, the European securitization market also closed down and new ABSs were mainly retained in bank balance sheets to be used as eligible collateral at the European Central Bank or the Bank of England.

After the crisis, the relevant financial regulation was adjusted:

1. Credit Rating Agency (CRA) conflict of interest has been addressed by oversight (EU Directive, Dodd-Frank Act);
2. Incentive misalignment has been addressed by the introduction of an obligation for sponsors of ABSs to retain at least 5 % of the credit risk of the assets underlying the securities ("skin in the game");
3. Transparency is being addressed by the Global Joint-Initiative of issuers associations and by the loan-by-loan initiative lead by central banks (see Sect. 2.4).
4. Interconnectedness has been addressed by Basel 3 (particularly by the revision of counterparty risk).

Banks will need this product to refinance away from central bank funding and potentially to manage capital. In order to facilitate economic growth, a reconnection between capital markets and financial institution asset portfolios is essential. Other secured and unsecured bank debt products are insufficient; neither are they the answer in all cases. The need to restart the securitization market has been posited since 2009.[4]

---

4 Given the pivotal role of securitization as an alternative and flexible funding channel, failure to restart securitization would come at the cost of prolonging funding pressures on banks and a diminution of credit. (IMF 2009)Securitization helped cause a crisis that killed it. A proper reincarnation should help the recovery. (FT 15 September 2010)

To revitalize the securitization market in Europe, three things are necessary:

1. Restoration of investors' confidence;
2. Regeneration of market liquidity overcoming the coordination failure that was freezing the market: "No investors without liquidity, no liquidity without investors";
3. The tightening of spreads to make issuance economically viable.

The PCS is a new, standardized, high-quality and highly transparent investment class. It is based on a market convention between representatives of issuers, investors and arrangers that provides standards on quality, transparency and structure. The EIB Group, European Central Bank and Bank of England participated as "observers" in the PCS initiative. As the issuer can credibly certify the quality of the asset it is selling and as private information is less relevant because the loans are less opaque or more standardized, spreads are expected to be lower. The market is organized and relies on a light structure (the PCS Secretariat), which will also be engaged to improve, over time, the conditions and organizational market features of a liquid secondary market.

The PCS initiative was publicly announced in June 2012 and formally launched in November of the same year with the announcement of the appointment of the PCS Board, chaired by the former head of Market Operations at the European Central Bank, Francesco Papadia. The first PCS labeled issuance followed a few weeks later (http://pcsmarket.org/).

The PCS includes four categories of assets: residential mortgages, auto loans, SME loans and consumer credit. PCS eligible SME loans are loans or leases advanced by an originator to an obligor that is a small or medium-sized enterprise for general business purposes, where the originator has full recourse to the obligor. As factoring type of instruments are not yet sufficiently standardized across countries, they were not included in the PCS eligibility criteria.

In addition to the general eligibility criteria, which are applicable to all asset classes, each PCS Eligible Issuance, where the underlying assets are European SME Loans, must comply with additional criteria that were

defined in close consultation with the European Investment Bank Group
(EIB and European Investment Fund):

1. The number of Obligor Groups is not less than 500;
2. The aggregate outstanding principal balance of the Underlying Assets
   due from any single Obligor Group does not exceed 0.75 per cent of
   the asset pool;
3. The originator of the Underlying Assets has provided a representation
   and warranty that the Underlying Assets in the asset pool are not of a
   lower credit quality (including tenor) than comparable assets retained
   by the originator (including previous securitizations) and (ii) None of
   the Underlying Assets are loans in arrears, non-performing loans or
   restructured loans;
4. Each Obligor Group has made at least one scheduled payment under
   each relevant Underlying Asset Agreement or (ii) there has been a
   lending relationship between the originator and each Obligor Group
   for at least 12 months; and
5. The number of Underlying Assets in the asset pool, which have no
   scheduled principal payments due in the next 5 years, is not greater
   than 25 per cent of the asset pool.

The securitization of SME loans indirectly creates a secondary market
combined with funding for the originator. Investors buy a tranche (or
several tranches) of the notes and, often, they intend to hold the notes
until maturity, while the junior tranche is retained in full or in part by
the originator.

The securities backed by SME loans (SMELBS) are traditionally a small
fraction of the securitization market, which is dominated by RMBSs – less
than 15 % of the European securitization volume over recent years. SME
loans are, in principle, less homogenous than residential mortgages (with
regard to size, legal forms, collateral, etc.). Most SME securitization has
traditionally originated from a few countries, such as Spain, Germany,
Italy (especially leasing), Benelux, Portugal and the United Kingdom.

The EIF typically provides guarantees on junior and mezzanine triple
A tranches, but can also act as guarantor for senior tranches of SMELBSs
for funding-driven transactions (Kraemer-Eis et al. 2010).

The only PCS labelled SMELBS (€600 million) so far has been originated by GEFA (*Gesellschaft für Absatzfinanzierung mbH*), the leasing German subsidiary of *Societe Generale*.

6.2.7 Sharing Risk and Lowering Interest Rates

6.2.7.1 Direct Lending

Government can provide funding to the SMEs either by means of the direct provision of funds through a state bank, or through the provision of funds that are leveraged by private sector investors. Both forms of intervention are common across developed countries. Government provision of SME financing can act as a counter-cyclical substitute for bank financing in times of financial distress. Furthermore, government involvement allows policy-makers the opportunity to set strategic objectives and to target segments of the economy that are the most likely to be disproportionately affected by a tightening of bank lending. This can include sectorial targeting; for example, for the purposes of infrastructure, or to high-potential sectors of the economy with which banks are unfamiliar or where tangible collateral is less readily available.

The most pertinent risk associated with direct government funding for SMEs relates to the misallocation of capital, deriving from either political interference or the lack of a profit motive to incentivize those making capital allocation decisions. Numerous academic studies have shown that higher state involvement in the banking sector is associated with weaker financial development, higher default rates, lower interest rates for firms in areas with stronger political patronage and a higher probability of incidence of a banking crisis (Holton et al. 2013).

With the risks highlighted above, it is often judged preferable to follow the public-private model, where private firms, who then take full control of credit allocation decisions on a commercial basis, leverage government funds.

For example, in the KfW Entrepreneur Loan program, applications are submitted to KfW by a commercial bank, which can be freely chosen by the applicant. KfW finances up to 100 % of the total investment.

KfW does not require any specific collateral, which, in turn, has to be negotiated by commercial banks. KfW Entrepreneur Loan targets established enterprises (those with an annual turnover of up to €500 million with more than three years in business), providing them with loans at favorable interest rates of up to €25 million for medium- and long-term investment projects. Loans can be used for a broad set of activities, such as the acquisition of land, properties and buildings; construction costs; acquisition of machinery; external services or patents.

KfW Entrepreneur Loan – Subordinated Capital aims at improving the capital structure of SMEs older than three years by providing loans up to €4 million in a two-tranche formula: a debt capital tranche of 50 % and a subordinated debt tranche of 50 %. Loan applications need to be submitted by a commercial bank. KfW can finance up to 100 % of the total investment. The debt capital tranche has to be secured by posting collateral, while the subordinated tranche does not; the latter will not represent a liability for the commercial bank.

The KfW ERP Innovation Programs I and II support firms in meeting their long-term financing needs for investments in market-oriented research, research and development for new products, process and services (Program I) and for the introduction of new products in the market (Program II). Program I provides loans of up to €5 million to firms that are at least two years old and that have a turnover of less than €500 million; Program II provides loans of up to €1 million at favourable interest rates to SMEs that are at least two years old. The procedure and the package is the same as in the Entrepreneur Loan – Subordinated Capital, although the two tranches may vary between 50 % and 60 %.

6.2.7.2   Guarantee Schemes

In many countries, credit guarantee schemes (CGSs) represent a key policy tool that supports credit to SMEs and to infrastructure projects. Well-structured CGSs spread some of the risk and thereby enable banks to extend loans to firms that would find it difficult to access credit otherwise. Relative to GDP, the highest volume of guarantees is currently provided in Italy (2.3 %), followed by Portugal (1.8 %), Hungary (1.4 %) and Romania (1.3 %) (EIB 2014).

The actual costs of a well-designed CGS may be lower than the social costs (loss of output, rise in SME bankruptcy, increased unemployment) of not proving this kind of support. Some loans supported by guarantees displace loans that banks would have provided even without guarantee. However, CGSs free up capital (the risk weight of the guaranteed portion is zero) and thus enhance banks' total lending capacity (Infelise 2014).

Depending on the ownership structure and role of shareholders in the management of the schemes, CGSs can be classified into three main typologies: public guarantee schemes, public-private guarantee schemes, and private schemes.

6.2.7.3   Public Guarantee Schemes

Public guarantee schemes are generally managed by government-related agencies, but guarantee services may also be provided in a de-centralized manner, through the financial system, with little intervention on how the guarantee scheme is run. In other cases, the public guarantee services are delivered through legal entities started on public initiatives and with majority participation of public entities. The government can play a direct role in the guarantee schemes by providing financial support, participating in their management, or, indirectly, by granting counter-guarantees whereby the government takes over the risk from the guarantor up to a predefined share of the guarantee.

Public CGSs are preferable to direct government lending schemes as, given that funds continue to be channeled through the banking system, appropriate credit quality assessments on prospective borrowers are more likely to be carried out. To achieve this, the risk coverage offered by the government on defaulted loans must be sufficiently low that banks have the necessary "skin in the game" to be incentivised to assess credit risk appropriately. A further possible advantage of CGSs lies in the re-direction of credit allocation. Banks are likely to favor borrowers with tangible collateral and this could arguably lead to misallocation away from intangible-intensive sectors such as information technology, business services and other production involving research and development. By shifting the incentives of banks to lending to such sectors, a CGS can increase a bank's experience and expertise in lending to these sectors and, therefore, have a potentially positive long-run effect. However, the additional of public guaranteed SME lending may be difficult to identify. It is possible that such a scheme will exist merely to allow banks to reduce their exposure to default risk on loans that would have been made without the scheme, while charging borrowers an unnecessary premium.

The design of CGSs is crucial for their effectiveness and sustainability. Targeted enterprises, coverage ratio, credit risk management and fee structure should ensure additionality. A major challenge for the additionality of CGSs comes from selection mechanisms. As financial conditions of guaranteed credits are generally more favorable than ordinary loan contracts, the scheme may attract borrowers with solid creditworthiness that may able to obtain funds without the support of a guarantee. At the other extreme, loan guarantees may attract firms that seek finance for highly risky projects (adverse selection). In an attempt to maximize additionality, some schemes (e.g. the UK Enterprise Finance Guarantee and the Irish SME Credit Guarantee Scheme) restrict eligibility to those firms that have been denied credit on the loan markets. In some cases, additionality is sought by narrowly defining the target of the program, which may be a sector or specific categories of firms for which severe market failures were identified (OECD 2012).

According to the IIF (2013), Portugal's guarantee schemes are highly effective in providing credit to SMEs. The Portuguese schemes focus on export or investment credit, providing mutual government guarantees for bank loans. The high uptake is related to the advantageous credit terms for SMEs, including extended repayment and grace periods; reduced costs of borrowing for SMEs; easy access to the guarantee lines, directly through the banks; and a high level of SME awareness. Conversely, upfront fees and long lending terms were the main barriers to uptake in the Netherlands.

Public guarantees are also used to support credit to infrastructure projects. The UK Guarantee Scheme for Infrastructure Projects, launched by HM Treasury in July 2012, assigns the UK sovereign rating to infrastructure project guaranteed debt instruments (Giovannini and Moran 2013).

6.2.7.4   Mixed Schemes

Privately funded schemes and public-private schemes are characterized by the direct participation of the private sector, SME organizations and banks in the funding and management of the schemes. An interesting model of a private or mixed scheme is that of mutual guarantee schemes (MGSs). MGSs are private societies created by borrowers to improve their access to finance. Governments may provide financial support to MGSs, mainly in the form of counter-guarantees. These enhance the guaranteed credit volume that can be made available to SMEs, as well as the credibility and reputation of the scheme.

   MGSs are characterized by strong ties with the local communities and territorial system and, often, members operate in a specific sector or value chain. This provides a specific information advantage to the schemes: they evaluate their members, assess their creditworthiness, express recommendations to lending institutions and are involved in the recovery of losses should the borrower default. Therefore, MGSs act as signaling device for large banks, which have greater difficulty accessing information on SMEs. However, MGSs may also provide incentives for moral hazard behaviors, as the collateral is external to the firm. However, the peer review process may act as a powerful mechanism for controlling risk and limiting opportunistic behavior. Members have strong incentives to monitor their peers closely, which may prevent borrowers from excessively risky behavior and increase the probability of the repayment of the loan. Local and central governments may participate in the capital of MGSs or top up the guarantee: in these cases, incentives for moral hazard behaviors are higher. A multi-layered guarantee structure exists in Italy (*Confidi*) and Spain (*Sociedades de Garantia Reciproca*). The Italian system is very fragmented; however, a concentration process is ongoing, particularly in the north-east (Mistrulli and Vacca 2011).

   Evidence shows that GCSs have been effective in mobilizing a large amount of credit and in easing access to finance for a large number of enterprises (ADB-OECD 2013; Öztürk et al. 2014). Most countries have expanded credit guarantees to SMEs to induce banks to re-open their credit facilities, thereby reducing the additional risk that banks need to take on their balance sheet when granting new loans. The amount of funds was increased substantially and eligibility constraints were eased, a higher percentage of each loan was guaranteed, and applications were processed more rapidly (ECB 2014). In most cases, government guarantees provided to SMEs increased dramatically during the crisis. In some countries (e.g. France), as crisis measures were phased out and new programs introduced to foster growth and job creation, some guarantee instruments were tailored to specific categories of SMEs, such as start-ups or innovative firms. In other cases, guarantee schemes were introduced to support equity investments, addressing, among other things, the need for de-leveraging firms and supporting them in key transitions, such as expansion or ownership transmission.

MGSs have also been successful in providing support for lending to SMEs; however, their credit quality has deteriorated rapidly: in Italy, for example, the default rate for enterprises with mutual guarantees has been twice the default rate of other enterprises (Mistrulli and Vacca 2011). Nonetheless, the higher recovery rate for mutual guaranteed loans has maintained the Loss Given Default (LGD) at a lower level than that for non-guaranteed loans, keeping interest rates on guaranteed loans lower than those on non-guaranteed ones (in Italy, between 20 and 30 basis points).

The counter-cyclical expansion of MGSs has brought about an important change in scale and exposure to risk. This change is taking place with the ongoing transformation induced by Basel III. This has increased the need to upgrade the organizational efficiency and skill level of these schemes. The response to these challenges has been a change in scale with mergers and consolidation. This can help reduce the relative cost of service, as well as broaden the offer of guarantee instruments. At the same time, a trade-off may emerge between efficient scale and proximity to borrowers, which has been, so far, the competitive advantage of MGSs. This trade-off may be addressed by setting up a chain scheme that includes a local layer close to the firms, a regional or inter-sector layer that provides mainly counter-guarantees and a national and/or European counter-guarantee fund.

6.2.7.5   Europe-Wide Initiatives

The European Commission and the EIB work together on blended risk-sharing instruments, leveraging the EU budget with the EIB lending capacity to finance further special activities in EU priority areas. In November 2012, the Commission and the EIB launched the Project Bond initiative to support capital markets in financing long-term infrastructure investments (EC-EIB 2013).

6.2.7.6   Credit Insurance

Three European institutions dominate the private credit insurance landscape: Euler Hermes, Coface and Atradius. The firms provide insurance on accounts receivable, allowing SMEs to manage risk associated with the financial default of their customers, both in the domestic market and abroad. Each has a detailed proprietary risk analysis by country, activity sector and company. Barriers to higher uptake are low awareness and the relatively high cost of insurance. Regulatory risk weighting for prudential capital requirements of these private guarantees is significantly less favorable than for public guarantees (IIF 2013).

6.2.7.7   Favouring Non-bank Financing

European non-financial companies finance their investment largely through bank loans. During the crisis, many banks started to de-risk their business in order to adjust to pressure in their funding through de-leveraging their balance sheets (by increasing equity capital and/or disposing of assets), as well as changes in funding structure. This process has been reinforced by changes in regulation (higher capital requirements, introduction of liquidity requirements) and may last for several years, with the consequence that credit may become less available and more costly. Therefore, since the onset of the crisis, non-financial companies have relied more on market-based funding, including different financial instruments (such as equity, debt securities, inter-company loans and trade credit). However, although EU corporate bond markets have developed in recent years, non-financial corporate bonds still account for only 15 % of non-financial corporate debt, compared with almost 50 % in the USA. Unless corporate – and, especially, SMEs – have access to alternative sources of finance, any decline in bank lending is likely to have an adverse impact on corporates' ability to finance investment (EC 2013a, b).

Insurance companies and pension and mutual funds are the biggest institutional investors in Europe. The investment strategies of insurers and pension funds are driven primarily by the characteristics of their liabilities in bonds, which provide stable and long-dated cash flows. However, for several reasons (increasing competition among insurers, agency problems for pension funds, performance evaluation, recency bias) institutional investors are increasingly affected by short-termism (OECD 2011). The largest share of their activities is invested in corporate bonds.

As banks are less able to meet the long-term funding needs of borrowers, there is an opportunity for insurers and pension funds, because they tend to have long-dated liabilities that match the part of the credit market from which banks are retreating. Infrastructure investments are attractive to institutional investors as they can assist with liability-driven investments and provide duration hedging. Infrastructure projects are long-term investments that could match the long duration of pensions and insurance liabilities.

Institutional investors have traditionally invested in infrastructure through listed companies and fixed income instruments. Although growing rapidly, institutional investment in infrastructure is still limited (OECD 2013). To encourage institutional investors to invest in infrastructure projects, it is necessary that they are standardized and collected in dedicated portfolios (Bassanini and Reviglio 2014).

Long-term investors (principals) often invest via "agents" such as fund managers. Agents usually have better information and different objectives than their principals. The net result may be that agents misprice securities and extract rents. Large investors and authorities could address these problems requiring agents to adopt a long-term investment approach based on long-term dividend flows, rather than on short-term price movements (EC 2013a, b).

6.2.7.8   Equity Finance

Equity can be a better financing instrument for long-term, high-risk investments, as well as for investments with significant information asymmetries and moral hazard. However, since the crisis, macroeconomic uncertainty and the low interest rates may have affected companies' demand and risk appetite for long-term equity capital.

Current tax laws in most countries favour debt over equity. A welcome exception is Italy's recent Allowance for Corporate Equity (ACE), which aims to enhance the capital structure of Italian companies by giving firms incentives to build up additional equity by allowing 3 % of new equity to be deducted from income taxes.

Equity listings of SMEs remain limited. Initiatives aimed at developing trading platforms to raise equity capital for SMEs have been developed in each major country. Access to these markets is typically designed for enterprises that are small and medium-sized, rather than for micro firms, as the structure and the size of these operations still requires a structural minimum assets size. This feature allowed relatively faster growth of these platforms in countries such as the UK and Germany, where capital markets have been traditionally more developed and where the share of medium-sized firms is higher compared with other countries. In order to improve the visibility and the attractiveness of a public listing, the operators of these markets are offering a broad range of complementary services aimed at supporting firms that could access these markets, but that lack the necessary expertise to exploit this possibility (Infelise 2014)

One successful case is Alternext Paris, founded in 2005, which lists almost 190 SMEs. After the successful launch in more flush times, access was eased in 2009 by adapting and streamlining the regulatory framework and rules (IIF 2013). The UK AIM (Alternative Investment Market) is also considered to have been successful due to a network of advisers that is experienced in supporting companies from the time they first consider a flotation, through helping them raise capital and through a knowledgeable investor base (Giovannini-Moran 2014). Non-EU successful examples are the Stock Exchanges of Tel Aviv and Toronto, as they enjoy a highly localized, sector specific and interconnected ecosystem.

6.2.7.9   Capital Markets

Capital markets represent an important alternative source of funding, but they are accessible mainly for large corporates domiciled in larger countries with more developed corporate bond markets. SMEs that face the more severe consequences of the credit crunch cannot afford the costs of bond issuance.

Alternative investment markets designed for the issuance of SME bonds are relatively more recent and less developed compared with analogous platforms targeting SME stocks. Exploiting less stringent regulation, those markets aim at overcoming the major barriers in terms of costs and transparency requirements that usually prevent SMEs accessing external finance through bond issuance.

SME high-yield bond issuance has attained considerable importance in Germany. Four of the eight German exchanges have started trading "*Mittelstand bonds*". In Stuttgart, the BondM platform gives mid-cap SMEs the opportunity to issue bonds that can be sold direct to retail investors without an investment bank underwriting the issue. Covenant and documentation provisions and costs are also kept to a minimum (EC 2013a, b).

Italy launched a bond market in 2013. It allows non-listed SMEs to issue mini-bonds, which enjoy tax relief on interest costs and issuance expenses. Mini-bonds issues may benefit from a guarantee provided by the export credit and insurance public company *Servizi Assicurativi del Commercio Estero* (*SACE*) up to 70 % of the principal to the extent the mini-bond is issued to finance an internationalization project.

Created in 2000, Euronext is the first pan-European exchange, spanning Belgium, France, the Netherlands, Portugal and the UK. In May 2013, Euronext launched EnterNext (https://www.enternext.biz/en), designed to develop and promote its stock markets specifically for SMEs. Drawing on its pan-European presence, EnterNext brings together all Euronext Group initiatives for companies with market capitalization under €1 billion, including companies listed on Alternext (the French equity market for SMEs). EnterNext has dedicated teams and offices across Europe in Belgium, Portugal and the Netherlands, as well as in several regions of France. EnterNext covers around 750 SMEs listed on Euronext markets in these countries.

However, the majority of specific SME markets or segments are struggling to attract companies: the smaller the company, the more disproportionate is the cost to the benefits of being listed. The main barriers to accessing these markets and segments are (ESMA SMSG 2012):

- High cost of capital due to limited investor interest;
- Lack of appropriate research coverage – SME research is generally not in itself a profitable activity;
- Low liquidity; SMEs' trading volumes tend to be limited;
- Higher transparency requirements impact on SMEs governance structure;

6.2.7.10   Funding Escalator

There are other different sources of funding that firms can access at different stages of maturity (seed financing, business angels, venture capital, private equity, and so on). These forms may combine to form a "funding escalator", providing debt and equity as firms grow and their funding needs evolve. These schemes are more targeted than guarantee schemes and are restricted to specific groups of firms (ECB 2014).

As a way to reinvigorate private funding sources, several countries are using tax incentives designed to attract new investment funds. The French scheme allows French citizens to invest up to €12,000 per year in pooled managed funds, which then invest in SMEs. The Irish Employment and Investment Incentive Scheme allows individual investors to make direct investments in SMEs and obtain income tax relief on capital up to €150,000 per year.

Sometimes, public intervention aims to support young entrepreneurs in setting up their own business. In the UK, Start-up Loans support entrepreneurs aged 18–30 by providing them with loans even if they lack real collateral or a proven track record. Loans are supplied on evaluation of a viable business plan; the program, which started in May 2012, backed more than 12,000 businesses with an average loan size of £5700.

Applicants need to pay back the loans within five years at a 6 % fixed interest rate.

In Germany, through the ERP Start-up Loan (StartGeld and Universell), KfW helps business founders, self-employed professionals and SMEs (with an annual turnover of up to €50 million) with less than three years in business by providing loans of up to €100,000 at a favorable fixed interest rate. Loans need to be used to finance the expansion of young enterprises, for the succession of an enterprise, or for the takeover of an enterprise. Applications are submitted to KfW by a commercial bank, of which the applicant has free choice. KfW finances up to 100 % of the total investment. KfW does not make any specific requirement on collateral, which, in turn, has to be negotiated by commercial banks. The StartGeld scheme (for small enterprises with annual turnover of up to €10,000) is supported by a guarantee of the European Investment Fund (EIF), which implements the Competitiveness and Innovation Framework Programme (CIP). The commercial bank bears 20 % of the credit risk in the StartGeld scheme, and none in the Universell scheme.

The Netherlands is pursuing private-public partnerships with the goal of securing more seed funding. For example, to provide funding banks and the state are pooling resources through Qredits, a microcredit institution, while the EC and EIB Group are providing first-loss credit insurance.

6.3   Non-bank Financing: Credit Funds, Peer-to-Peer Lending and Crowd Funding

6.3.1   Shadow Banking Definition

Shadow banking transforms opaque, risky, long-term assets (collateral) into money-like, short-term liabilities. Regulated banks make short-term deposits, redeemable at any time, to create medium-/long-term credit. Convertibility is granted because deposit and cashing activities have become "worry free" thanks to deposit insurance. Deposit insurance makes the value of bank deposits "information insensitive". In other words, similarly to currency, diligence to the transaction is not strictly required.

Likewise, shadow banking uses securitized finance (such as covered bonds) and securitization techniques (asset pooling, tranching techniques and credit enhancements) to create information insensitive debt to be "converted" into credit in financial markets (such as repo markets). As with demand deposits in the traditional bank sector, senior tranches of securitizations used as collateral to obtain credit in the collateralized funding markets were perceived until the crisis as "information insensitive". The presence of "information insensitive" debt led financial operators to underestimate the counterparty risk. This is not an issue per se, provided the collateral used in the transactions is transparently of high quality. Secured markets in themselves are in fact, ceteris paribus, a less risky funding source compared with unsecured lending (i.e. inter-bank borrowing).

Securitization is a form of credit risk transfer (CRT), similar to syndicated loans and credit derivatives. Securitization includes Asset Backed Securities (ABSs), Mortgage-Backed Securities (MBSs, of which RMBSs are the Residential MBSs), Collateralized Loan Obligations (CLO), and Collateralized Debt Obligations (CDO). The three main benefits to issuers are: (1) an additional funding channel; (2) portfolio risk-management; (3) arbitrating regulatory capital requirements.

Typically, the originating bank sells loans to a Special Purpose Vehicle (SPV), which then sells the securities to the investors. The SPV is sponsored by the bank itself, although often, before the crisis, the SPV was not consolidated from a regulatory perspective in the bank's balance sheets. SPVs contributed substantially to the creation of credit, in many cases for the purposes of regulatory arbitrage, rather than for channelling credit to the real economy. From that perspective, vehicles investing in long-term assets and issuing short-term asset-backed commercial papers (ABCPs) played a crucial role. Starting from August 2007, the ABCP market closed abruptly to non-bank investors and shrank in terms of size.

The securities could then be sold in the repo market. A repo agreement, also known as a repo, is an agreement in which the seller is to buy back the securities at a later date. The party that originally buys the securities actually acts as a lender; the original seller is, indeed, acting as a borrower, using the security as collateral for a secured cash loan at a fixed interest rate. This practice is known as hypothecation.

Re-hypothecation occurs when a lender re-uses assets pledged as collateral by borrowers as collateral for its own borrowing. Re-hypothecation contributed to the increase in the amount of debt exposures. The IMF calculated that, at the inception of the crisis, US banks were receiving over US$4 trillion worth of funding by re-hypothecation, much of it sourced from the UK. In 2009, the IMF estimated that the funds available to US banks due to re-hypothecation declined by more than half.

These shadow banking activities are implicitly enhanced by official guarantees, either directly (because they are guaranteed by a government agency, as in the US) or indirectly (because they are off-balance sheet liabilities of regulated financial institutions). Among the latter, partnership between direct lending funds and banks increased since the peak of the crisis. In general, banks underwrite debt using their credit expertise and their close relationships with companies and distribute to insurers looking to diversify their investments. In this way, banks limit the impact of these loans on their capital requirements and the lending funds enjoy the indirect official credit guarantee. French asset manager Amundi, for example, has partnered with UniCredit to offer financial support to the German mid-market. Likewise, in the UK, Barclays announced its partnership with private debt lender BlueBay Asset Management (a unit of Royal Bank of Canada) to provide a uni-tranche debt facility for mid-market private equity deals.[5] Generali has signed a joint deal to finance Germany's *Mittelstand* with Dusseldorf-based bank IKB and Gothaer, a local insurance group.

In addition, a wide range of credit intermediation activities have appeared on the scene which do not require official credit enhancement, such as security lending activities of insurance companies, pension funds and certain asset managers (Pozsar et al. 2012). Corporations remain the major users of securitization, through both the securitization market and ABCP programs. Large and medium-sized corporations frequently use

---

[5] A uni-tranche debt facility is a single tranche term facility, provided principally by credit funds. More narrowly, it is a term facility which, from a borrower's perspective, contains only one class of lender and under which a common interest rate is charged.

ACBP programs to raise cash from the sale of trade receivables and leases in a cost efficient manner (AFME 2013). Non-bank institutions may compete with traditional banks as far as they are able to get information advantages alternative to relationship banking – a result mainly achieved through specialization in the assessment of specific credit risks, related to either the company stage or its main activities. Non-bank lending can take off regardless of traditional banks only if it can benefit from a direct official enhancement.

6.3.2 Shadow Banking and the Crisis

The financial crisis that began in 2008 was triggered by the losses on US sub-prime RMBSs; that is, losses on securities backed by mortgages to households with low credit merit (low-income earners, temporary workers, etc.), following the burst of the real estate bubble in the USA. However, it is still a matter of debate whether the mortgage lender side or the security issuer side is to blame.

The lender side is associated with the so-called "Originate-to-Distribute" (OtD) model: the underwriters (originators) of the sub-prime mortgages (mainly US non-banks) used to fund themselves selling (distributing) the mortgages, often mis-rated by CRAs, to other financial institutions that would then securitize the loans. This model is supposed to have misaligned incentives, weakening the monitoring exercise of lenders and loosening lending standards.

The issuer side is associated with securitization techniques allowing the slicing and subsequent pooling of credit risks and their distribution to a myriad of investors, freeing capital and lowering the cost of funding. These securities could then be re-used in even more complicated derivatives (such as synthetic securities, re-securitization and CDOs). This process was finalized to produce new assets that could be used in the repo market to generate liquidity and allow financial institutions to meet the increasing demand for credit. While simplified information (in the form of ratings) allowed an enlargement in the plateau of potential buyers of these securities at the same time, the entire securitization process was, in fact, a machine to reduce transparency. As a consequence, supervisors and central bankers, no less than market participants, were progressively affected by an information gap as to the extent and allocation of risks.

Certainly, the panic generating the crisis led to the shadow banking sector in the USA. US shadow banking grew in parallel to the development of low-income households' policies. Bill Clinton was the initiator of these policies, which were then continued by President Bush. These policies were promoted by the enhanced role of the government-sponsored enterprises (GSEs), Fannie Mae and Freddie Mac; highly leveraged banks which invested in mortgages and developed the securitization of sub-prime mortgages.[6]

Securitization played a crucial role both in the availability of "information insensitive" collateral and in the leverage effect, as collateral may be re-packaged and its credit quality enhanced, increasing overall credit supply.[7]

Low-quality collateral (often sub-prime mortgages), which was perceived as information insensitive debt, *suddenly* became "information sensitive" debt, as a consequence of deterioration of the underlying credit following the burst of the real estate bubble. However, financial operators did not judge it necessary, or were often not properly equipped, to assess the risk embedded in those assets (rating was often one of prevailing factors for decision-making). As a consequence, uncertainty on the true value of the ABSs underlying collateral and other derivatives fluctuated widely, while diversification brought no significant risk reduction.

CRAs played a special role between the lender and the originator sides. Securities have to be rated in order to be sold to a large set of investors; furthermore, regulation requires banks and other investors to invest only in (highly) rated assets. The ratings proved to be inaccurate, at least. In fact, some 90 % of triple-A rated securities that were supposed to have a minimum life expectancy of seven years were downgraded over a very

---

[6] On GSE, see Acharya et al. (2011a) and Acharya et al. (2011), who define them as the "world's largest and most leveraged hedge funds". Since 1992, GSEs were supervised by the Office of Federal Housing Enterprise Oversight (OFHEO), lodged in the Department of Housing and Urban Development (HUD). GSEs started lowering their underwriting standards since the mid-1990s.

[7] It may be noted that the abrupt cessation of the securitization market to convert a broad range of collateral into credit in the market was substantially mitigated by the central banks' collateral frameworks (broad eligibility criteria and stable haircuts) and accommodating liquidity management policies. These were the most important policies and tools for systemic crisis management.

short time span after July 2007. Four factors are usually mentioned to explain why (Mullard 2012):

1. Conflict of interest, arising from the "issuer pay" model that had pre-vailed since the 1970s[8] and from the possibility of providing advisory services both to the structuring of securities and to their rating;
2. The CRAs' oligopoly position[9] set barriers to entry (economies of scale, advantage of experience, brand name reputation);
3. Flaws in the mathematical models designed to estimate default prob-abilities – in particular, in catching innovations (such as adjustable rate mortgages) and system breaks (the latter being common to other mathematical models used in finance);
4. The legal framework, which exempts CRAs from legal accountability, as ratings are usually assimilated to "investment opinions".

One point is missing in this usual list: combined with the oligopolistic position of CRAs, the huge size and concentration of investment bank-ing since the 1990s[10] created an oligopoly-monopsony market prone to seller (in this case, CRA) cooperation (Spriggs and Sigurdson 1985). This seller cooperation was implicitly provided by the common adoption of backward-looking methodologies (which are likely to produce similar outcomes across different models) and aversion to innovation (on the latter, see Mullard 2012).

Therefore, CRAs tend to maintain their market share (and thus their short-term profits) at the expense of accuracy (and long-term reputa-tion), being complacent with issuers. Securities were therefore overrated. Inflated triple-A ratings increased the demand for securities by institu-tional investors, including pension funds. The rapid downgrading of a

---

[8] This was not the case at the beginning provided CRSs were rating corporate bonds and therefore issuers tended to be small. In this case, losing an issuer to a competitor is not an issue. Things changed with securitization (see fn 9).

[9] For example, Moody's and Standard & Poor's were responsible for 94 % of ratings in the US market (see fn 10).

[10] Twelve underwriters account for 80 % of the deals in the USA (Mullard 2012). In this situation, losing a single issuer is a major concern.

large number of securities in July 2007 contributed to undermining market confidence.

The collateralized funding market in Europe has proved more resilient and not to be a source of systemic risk. The downgrade ratio and the default rate of European ABSs during the sub-prime crisis were significantly lower than that of US ABSs, with the exception of CMBSs. The main difference between the US and the European shadow banking is that the US shadow system relied more on government implicit guarantees provided by the GSEs, while the European banking sector relied more on the indirect guarantee provided by the traditional banking sector. Also for this reason, there were relevant different structural peculiarities in European shadow banking: diversified providers of collateral management services avoided the quasi-monopolistic recourse to a tri-party system owned by systemic important financial institutions, subprime assets were used as collateral less frequently and there was a larger adoption of international standard legal contracts.

6.3.3   Regulation of the Shadow Banking System

Shadow banking remains largely unregulated and the CRAs market remains structurally the same; that is, an oligopoly-monopsony market.

Furthermore, Europe is registering a recent and growing interest for direct financing to SMEs by non-bank institutions (Lugaresi 2015). European non-financial companies finance their investment largely through bank loans. During the crisis, many banks started to de-risk their business in order to adjust to pressures in their funding by de-leveraging their balance sheets (by increasing equity capital and/or disposing of assets), as well as applying changes to funding structure. This process was reinforced by changes in regulation (higher capital requirements, introduction of liquidity requirements) and may last for several years, with the consequence that credit may become less available and more costly.

Therefore, concurrently, increasingly regulated traditional banks complain that they have to face the unfair competition of unregulated shadow banking; the systemic risk of shadow banking has only been reduced, while shadow banking is now also expected to play its role in providing non-bank credit to SMEs. How may fair competition be restored, system risk further reduced and, at the same time, non-bank credit favored? Let us revert to the analogy between the traditional bank system and shadow banking to discuss the regulation of shadow banking. From this perspective, understanding the rationale that led to the current regulatory framework for banks and related implications is crucial:

- Increase in bank capital requirements has the effect of reducing the relative size of the regulated banking sector and, therefore, increases the room for shadow banking.
- In the past, a bank charter became a title to future monopoly profits. Shadow banking reduces bank charter value. In attempts to maintain profitability, banks enter new activities, very often in riskier activities (including shadow banking).
- Financial innovation is largely driven by regulation and taxes.
- A logical consequence of the above considerations is that:
- The introduction of any new regulatory initiative should be duly calibrated in order to account for its potential unintended consequences (for instance, mis-calibrated regulatory arbitrage initiatives that would foster and de-stabilize the shadow system, rather than limit and stabilize it). As already stressed, shadow banking is the natural/unintended by-product of regulatory requirements introduced in the banking sector.
- Existing differences in the regulatory and supervisory environment across countries should be given due consideration as they are exacerbating the unlevel playing field.

Keeping that in mind, we suggest the following paths for intervention:

1. Strengthen supervision and market discipline for all financial players:

    - An adequate transparency framework should allow market discipline to work effectively and supervisors to perform powerfully in their role/duty. Lack of transparency in markets can lead to abusive behavior and facilitate violations of competition rules. Lack of transparency makes it difficult, for authorities and risk managers, to monitor where risks are concentrated.

- Transparency is crucial to allow market discipline to function properly. For instance, the percentage of asset segregation on total assets of a bank could be properly disclosed. This would imply several benefits. First, it would limit outright the volume of securitization. Second, it would allow market discipline to work effectively (the higher or lower percentage of segregated assets on total assets will significantly change the risk profile of a bank with significant implications for its cost of funding). Third, it would maintain a balance between ABS note-holders and senior bond-holders in the context of bail-in (the excessive recourse to ABS issuance would undermine the position of senior bond-holders, since the latter would become structurally subordinated, with the risk making it increasingly difficult from the bank perspective to tap into the senior investment base).

2. Provide an adequate framework to better manage risks in the collateralized funding markets:

- Standard contracts should be extended as far as possible among financial players, both in and outside Europe.
- Strengthen market infrastructures: activities in Central Clearing Counterparties (CCPs) may help to increase transparency, efficiency and manage counterparty risk. However, it is important that the authority properly monitors the risk control measures adopted by the CCPs in order to avoid a situation where their unexpected generalized changes have unintended disruptive consequences.

3. Introduce measures to internalize negative externalizations arising from shadow banking. A well-designed financial transaction tax (as introduced in Italy) may serve this purpose.
4. Reform the CRAs market. Prudential supervisory authorities and competition authorities should make an in-depth investigation of the CRAs market. The breakdown of large investment banks and of CRAs may be necessary.

6.3.3.1   Direct Lending

There is a recent and growing interest for direct financing to SMEs by non-bank institutions; for example, by the setting up of specialized debt funds. However, the leaner structures of funds and their management limit their ability to obtain the level of grass-roots information efficiently.

In Germany, there is a large private placement market, known as *Schuldschein* (€10 billion issuance in 2012). *Schuldschein* are bilateral, unregistered and unlisted loan instruments sold directly to investors. In contrast to bonds, *Schuldschein* loans are not securities and are traded over-the-counter. The large German commercial banks and *Landesbanken* typically act as arrangers and intermediaries for *Schuldschein* loans. There is a limited secondary *Schuldschein* market, but it is less liquid than the bond equivalent. There is no specific *Schuldschein* regulation; however, their issuance is regulated under German banking regulations. There are several benefits of *Schuldschein* loans over bonds: short documentation, unrated issuance, confidentiality, flexibility of terms and conditions, and restricted distribution to institutions only (*Schuldschein* cannot be sold to retail investors directly).

France has been an innovator in direct lending: since August 2013, insurance firms have been allowed to invest up to 5 % of their liabilities in loans to unlisted companies (only listed bonds were allowed previously), either directly or through special funds (so called loan-to-real-economy funds or *Funds de Prêts à l'Economie*).

Partnerships between direct lending funds and banks have increased since the peack of the crisis. In general, banks underwrite debt using their credit expertise and their close relationships with companies, and distribute to insurers or asset managers looking to diversify their investments. In this way, banks limit the impact of these loans on their capital requirements and retain their clients while de-leveraging. The lending funds indirectly enjoy the official credit guarantee that banks enjoy directly. French asset manager Amundi, for example, has partnered with UniCredit to offer financial support to the German mid-market. Likewise, in the UK Barclays announced its partnership with private debt lender BlueBay Asset Management (a unit of Royal Bank of Canada) to provide a uni-tranche debt facility for mid-market private equity deals. Generali has signed a joint deal to finance Germany's *Mittelstand* with Dusseldorf-based bank IKB and Gothaer, a local insurance group.

In UK, the Business Finance Partnership (BFP) is a program run by the UK Treasury aimed at stimulating funding through non-bank loans. The program was started in autumn 2012 and will invest £1.2 billion in different tranches. BFP stimulates private fund managers to invest in SMEs and medium-sized companies by co-funding up to 50 % of the loans' value. The Treasury manages the BFP and chooses which applicant funds to support, and fund managers operate independently according to their investment strategies (Infelise 2014).

6.3.3.2 Crowdfunding

Crowdfunding is the practice of funding a project or venture by raising monetary contributions from a large number of people, typically via the Internet. There are three types of crowdfunding (ESMA 2014): (1) reward-based crowdfunding, where the return to investment consists of a copy of the finished product; (2) security-based crowdfunding, where the return consists of securities or unlisted shares in a company, usually in its early stage; (3) loan-based crowdfunding, where the Internet platform collects the credit requirements and matches them with pools of investors willing to accept the credit terms.

Reward-based crowdfunding is popular mostly for creative endeavors such as films, music, games, free software development and scientific research (Standard and Poor's 2014). Examples of loan-based crowdfunding platforms in the USA are Lending Club and Prosper.

There are different types of risks associated with crowdfunding: fraud, liquidity and legal platform failure. In Europe, most countries do not have any specific regulation of crowdfunding; rather, they leave it to be dealt with under the existing relevant regulatory framework. In the case of pure investment crowdfunding (security-based), absence of specific regulation leaves it under the limits as stated in the Prospectus Directive: a Europe-wide requirement of a prospectus for issues larger than €5 million, and no obligation at all for issues under €100,000 (ESMA 2014).

Some EU member states have decided to take regulatory action on crowdfunding (among which are Italy, the UK, France and Spain). In July

2013, Italy become the first country in Europe to implement complete regulation on security-based crowdfunding, which applies only to innovative start-ups, and establishes a national registry and disclosure obligations for both issuers and portals. Other EU Member States have, instead, issued guidelines (Germany, Belgium and the Netherlands). Germany has not produced any specific regulation of crowdfunding, and yet is one of the European countries where equity crowdfunding has been more active.

In March 2014, the European Commission has published a Communication entitled "Unleashing the Potential of Crowdfunding in the European Union". While the Commission does not intend to come up with legislative measures in the near future, it will carry out a study and will set up the European Crowdfunding Stakeholder Forum.

6.3.3.3   Peer-to-Peer Lending

A particular form of crowdfunding is peer-to-peer lending (P2P), whereby individuals lend to each other and small business via a website. P2P has been growing in the USA,[11] Germany and the UK.[12] By avoiding complex structures and the procedures of normal banks, and thus some overhead costs, as well as regulatory burden, a P2P lender can offer credit at relatively low rates and offer relatively higher returns to their investors, to whom the loans are sold in slices. Many of these lending websites are now becoming more active in lending to SMEs (Wehinger 2012).

Of the £1.2 billion funding of the UK government's Business Finance Partnership, roughly £85 million has gone to seven "alternative funding" providers. The inclusion of these platforms in the scheme is a signal of the growth potential and growing acceptability of P2P among UK policy-makers. This process has been accelerated further by the inclusion of P2P lenders under the regulation of the Financial Conduct Authority from April 2014.

---

[11] The most prevalent market participants are Lending Club and Prosper.

[12] The main platforms in the UK are Funding Circle and Zopa, with the former focusing on SMEs and the latter on consumer lending. An overview of all P2P market participants in the UK can be found at http://www.p2pmoney.co.uk/companies.htm

Survey evidence in the UK suggests that 60 % of SMEs that used Funding Circle had tried previously to obtain bank financing, and 32 % would not have received funds from any other source. Such numbers suggest that, when assessing P2P against the "additionality" principle, there appears to be scope for improving credit access for SMEs. However, as the matter currently stands, retail investors considering P2P are not protected by legislation on issues such as anti-money laundering or fraud; neither are they guaranteed a transparent disclosure of the platforms' credit checking processes. Furthermore, P2P platforms generally do to not have any "skin in the game" in the loans transacted on their websites.

6.3.4 Summary

These initiatives provide some useful lessons. First, non-bank institutions may compete with traditional banks as far as they are able to get information advantages alternative to relationship banking. This may be achieved mainly through specialization in the assessment of specific credit risks, related either to the company stage, or to its main activities. Second, non-bank lending can take off independently of traditional banks only if it can benefit from a direct official enhancement or a well-functioning securitization market, which allows the transfer of risks.

7

Alternative Funding Options: E-platforms

With every passing week, a brand new electronic platform pops up in another location across the different market segments offering financial services to clients. In fact, a definitive and reliably updated list of these *arrivistes* no longer exists because it hardly seems feasible. Nevertheless, we can still list the commonalities and points of interest amongst these new players and examine the causes and effects, as well as risks and rewards.

7.1   Why E-platforms?

The beauty of launching an electronic platform (or E-platform) is the low costs, with barely any entry barrier to speak of; technology costs are thus increasingly reduced and the software market offers ready-to-use platform functionality. In turn, E-platforms leverage the connecting power of the Internet to provide a highly effective alternative to traditional models in financial mediation, a function historically performed by commercial and investment banks. Needless to say, this is not news in other industries such as travel services, retail products or services, where players such as Airbnb, Uber, Expedia, Amazon and Thumbtack have re-defined entire industry segments by challenging the competitive status quo.

© The Author(s) 2017
G. Oricchio et al., *SME Funding*,
DOI 10.1057/978-1-137-58608-7_7

In many of these cases, challengers have confronted existing market regulations and struggled with incumbent players. This challenge has occurred in different fashions across individual geographical markets. The emerging competitive scenario in such a situation is that of a leaner distribution chain, a more direct user/supplier relation that often crowds out the middleman. Regardless of the industry, the leading development pattern has been to define a scalable service model in a large enough geography (typically, the US market), then roll it out internationally in a "global-to-local" sequence. Internet technology has facilitated this pattern, including the offer of multi-lingual and multi-currency user experiences. Such an approach has allowed a series of unexpected positive results in terms of the speed of international development and client ownership. These two factors appear to prevail on revenues or profit as key drivers of today's E-platforms equity valuations – leadership has its privileges.

The outcome in these cases generally results in a pro-innovation landscape in less regulated businesses, with more regulated markets – such as, for instance, taxi services, or the distribution of pharmaceutical

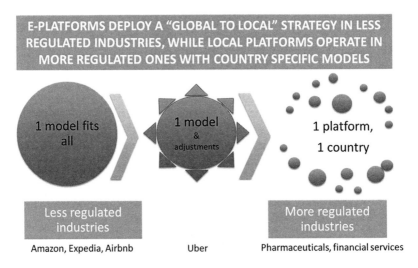

Fig. 7.1   E-platform business model

products – witnessing higher tensions. Think of how Uber somehow mitigated its momentum in Europe as it (thus far) abstained from the full deployment of its model following the UberPop disputes with local authorities and incumbents (see Fig. 7.1).

7.2 Upstream (of Capital)-Side Driven Opportunities

Upstream opportunities are emerging in today's current economic scenario as a consequence of low returns on debt securities that provoke investors to seek new territories. This is somewhat typical and goes with interest rate cycles: in market phases with low inflation and interest rates, investors are inclined to take more risks and explore new markets and new types of investments. In today's markets, one emerging asset class is that of consumer or SME debt. These instruments have traditionally witnessed premium pricing by banks and therefore attract those investors interested in seizing the excess return premium: E-platforms appear to be the most efficient mean to access that type of risk.

In particular, peer-to-peer (P2P) E-platforms such as Lending Club (USA), Lufax (China), Funding Circle and Market Invoice (UK) or Work Invoice (Italy) offer access to a well-organized myriad of potential borrowers. Besides important access features, these P2P E-platforms provide the additional function of spreading the investor's money over multiple borrowers, hence mitigating risk via a portfolio effect. This scenario attracts new investors to the game, such as specialized funds or high net-worth individuals (HNWIs).

7.3 Downstream Opportunities

Downstream opportunities for E-platform development appear to be structural, as they are connected both to the new technology and to the new regulation situation. In particular, the new technology available in web-based customer experiences, risk management tools and payment services allows new players to compete with highly focused offers to con-

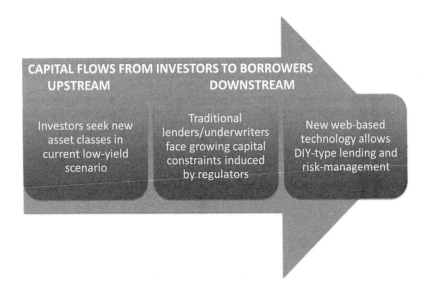

Fig. 7.2   Upstream and downstream

sumers and SMEs. Such offers range from invoice discounting, consumer lending, mini-bonds, and so on.

On the regulatory side, new capital adequacy requirements are also imposing a more selective credit approach to commercial banks and, similarly, a lighter proprietary trading approach to financial markets to investment banks, causing an overall reduction of the banking sector's ability to respond to the needs of borrowers and fundraisers. This scenario is perhaps the main instigator of all shadow banking (or better, alternative finance) E-platform initiatives (see Fig. 7.2).

7.4   The Need for Liquidity

The success of financial markets – electronic or not – is a reflection of their ability to attract liquidity. Liquidity then attracts more investors, traders, issuers, followed by more liquidity. The quality of the product itself is a necessary condition in a market's strategy for success, but it is not sufficient. Choosing the right timing and analyzing competition create the conditions necessary for establishing a new E-platform and turning it into a success. The key point, however, comes when the new platform is able to build up volume momentum and reach that tipping point when market participants start leaving other platforms, or simply decide to start committing liquidity to the new marketplace. They do this because it is where price formation is perceived as most efficient, where it is more likely to enter in a certain investment or, in the event, trade out of that investment and cash in with minimum transaction costs.

Let us look at this as if we were bankers – say, *arriviste* E-platform bankers in search of nightlife after a hard day on the terminals; we will look at platforms as if they are dance halls.

There are basic rules for choosing which dance hall to go to: more dancers and longer queues to enter the hall are signs of success that attract further dancers. Therefore, the basic consumer benefit of a disco appears to be that there are many (interesting) people. A large number of dancers make a successful dance hall or disco. Likewise, for successful E-platforms, a crowd appears to be a defining condition in the financial services world. Platforms not only need to define their marketing strategy and be well-launched on the web, they also need to have many users. Just like dance halls, in fact, successful E-platforms are a small portion of the growing market, according to a "leader takes it all" principle that seem to apply to individual segments.

The international E-platform scene is further enriched by a variety of several different operators. Currently, E-platforms focus on individual geographical markets and there are hardly any multi-national players. However, many new formats are defining trends; for example, the P2P lending platforms, as well as the platforms dealing with securities, are attracting different types of investor. They also often focus on specific types of needs, such as short-term or longer-term financing. There is a regulatory pattern that tends to aggregate alternative finance operators into two major families that attract two different regulatory environments: lending-based and investment-based.

Lending-based crowdfunding operators are (or will be) ruled by lending/payment regulations and supervised by the relevant authorities in that area.

Investment-based crowdfunding operators are (or will be) ruled by securities regulations and supervised accordingly.

In the EU, the economic effects of this two-rule system apply to E-platform operators and could reflect the different regulatory perimeters: generally country specific for the lending business, and more EU-wide for investment services, thanks to the implementation of the Markets in Financial Instruments Directive 2004/39/EC (MiFID) as an umbrella regulation. Securities firms appear to have an easier life when setting up a multi-country EU business.

This regulatory framework appears to affect the ability to develop larger operators that can achieve the economies of scale proper to the whole EU market as opposed to that of a single country. The following sections describe several aspects relevant to qualifying as existing or emerging market segments, such as types of investor, fundraisers, types of platform and types of financial instruments.

7.5   From One-to-One Lending to Aggregators

E-platforms attract investors and fundraisers of different types seeking new financial market experiences. As far as E-platforms are concerned, investors seem to value the ability to provide improved access, higher transaction speed or lower costs. Borrowers – or, more generally, fundraisers – value the opportunity to contact multiple potential lenders/investors so as to achieve improved conditions in terms of both pricing and speed. The idea is that a greater number of players can come together in those virtual marketplaces by streamlining processes and simplifying the product offering.

The consequent concentration of liquidity and information creates the conditions for delivering competitive overall results and a superior experience is clearly relevant to the development of P2P lending E-platforms, especially if compared with the service level of commercial lending. This assumption has, in fact, driven the development of E-services and originated from the ambition to deliver a more competitive arena for the benefit of borrowers.

The starting point for this sea change came in the early 2000s with the development of aggregator web services. These allowed borrowers to access multiple banks via a single website, to compare conditions and even to send a credit application on standardized products such as mortgages or personal loans. The "end of the line" of the traditional aggregator is, nevertheless, still a bank that performs services, simply adding a commercial intermediary (the aggregator) as a customer interface. The aggregator merely acts as a broker.

Clearly, the presence of the aggregator results in twofold bad news for the banks: (a) more competition in pricing, and, hence, a lower interest margin; and (b) lower fees, including the rebate typically due from the bank to the aggregator. However, there is some good news for banks. An active bank, large or small, can use the aggregator to reach new clients and to integrate the customer experience with its own strengths, such as physical proximity, face-to-face service and bundle pricing. The customer acquisition function performed by aggregators is often leveraged by smaller and local banks that gladly pay a fee to outsource the task of broadening their market; in this case, banks could face the risk of operating in geographical markets where their credit database is of little help in assessing risks.

Overall, it appears that aggregators have instituted a transparency process that has provided benefits to the market and to the customer. In particular, aggregators have enhanced the visibility of credit products that are comparable: in order to be comparable, products need to be simpler and therefore more understandable for clients. More aggregators, fewer footnotes. Many successful aggregators such as PersonalLoans.com (USA), LoanWala (India), PrestitiOnline (Italy) and AFG (Australia) are still active. (Fig. 7.3)

7.6   From Aggregators to E-platforms

Aggregators have pursued an improvement in access to product, transparency and overall competitiveness. Most importantly, aggregators acted as ice-breakers vis-a-vis an online customer experience: clients looking for a personal loan, families looking for a mortgage loan, small business owners

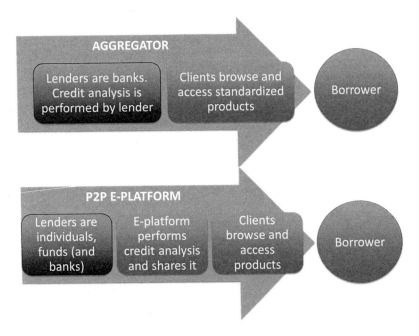

Fig. 7.3 P2P E-platforms

looking for a loan – all regularly browse aggregators to check products and compare rates. In many cases, these clients even complete their transaction online; yet, aggregators provide a mere connection function and add little value, since they act as middlemen. The analysis engine as well as the pot of lending capital stays upstream with the lending bank affiliated to the aggregator.

By comparison, in E-platforms such as Lending Club or Funding Circle, the borrower experience resembles that of an aggregator website: a credit application, background checks, and so on. However, the end of the cycle is different, since the lender is replaced by an type of auction system in which several anonymous lenders compete to fund multiple credit requests. Allowing new potential borrowers to the market, E-platforms add further strength to competition by starting to level the playing field through offering detailed credit information on potential borrowers. Actually, given their huge volume of clients and transactions, E-platforms can develop very accurate default prediction analysis by leveraging their data sets.

Therefore, E-platforms bring in potentially more liquidity as a result of the opportunity for new and non-regulated players to join regulated entities such as banks and funds in the lending market. The platform itself is, indeed, the regulated piece of the chain as it typically performs the function of a payment hub, thus settling all micro-transactions on behalf of both borrowers and lenders. Technically, this is achieved by carving out the pure lending function (highly capital intensive) from the money management function (attracting minimal capital requirements) that is performed by a payment institution – that is, the platform. Payment institutions are regulated according to standards that differ from country to country, but it is generally true that E-platforms performing P2P lending services have much lower capital requirements than banks. At the same time, they provide a possibly superior customer experience.

Besides the effects in capital requirements, the development of P2P lending E-platforms brings a further major strategic innovation that is deserves comment. The so-called credit-engine – that is, the borrowers credit file, the credit analysis scoring and rating models, and the ability to calibrate the credit models by backtesting their predictions on empirical data – now has a potential best owner in the E-platform. It is, in fact, reasonable to expect that the appeal of a credit scoring/rating agency stands on the breadth of its data source and ability to calibrate its predictions. The leading P2P lending E-platforms' growing market share suggests that they are, or will soon be, in the best position to produce and share most accurate credit analysis. This skill will probably represent their key strategic advantage and sustainable growth factor.

All in all, aggregators have succeeded in offering access to products and better choice to borrowers. The impact of the P2P platform is clearly about access: the beauty of direct relations for both borrowers and lenders, and the opportunities granted by a wider choice.

Nevertheless one additional achievement of significance is perhaps less visible. It is also about the shift of the credit "brain", the market intelligence part of the lending engine that is moving away from being an exclusive advantage of banks. As P2P platforms grow, there is, in fact, a greater reason for them to leverage their customer flows: to develop more accurate lender insight, thus becoming the best owner of consumer credit performance prediction models. High lending volumes could therefore lead to better accuracy and to improved business leadership. This represents a shift towards an emphasis on "quality" thresholds as a way to look at possible developments in the financial services business.

7.7   A Brief Thought on Responsible Borrowing (and Lending)

Financial products resemble prescription drugs: over-the-counter availability of lending products does not necessarily represent the best solution for the consumer: that is, price is not everything, simply because personal loans or mortgages are neither commodities nor consumer products. A loan lasts months or often years and can heavily disrupt a family's financial soundness and lifestyle. Recent events have further highlighted the risks of abundance of easy credit and ill-informed borrowing and, aside from the issue of fair pricing and the level information field, E-platforms, aggregators and hard-selling commercial banks do not appear to consider the relevance of this important responsibility. The very fact that a borrower takes on a lasting obligation with the loan (a durable liability) represents a substantial difference from non-durable or even durable consumer products. Moreover, variable rate loans are often "sold" with little regard to the potential side effects on monthly payments of future interest rates hikes.

In other words, whereas information on credit analysis can be practically shared, there is, in fact, no substantial level playing field as far as awareness and decision-making are concerned. In a regulated environment such as commercial banking, local authorities can implement borrower protection standards but, in the new world of P2P lending E-platforms, there are only self-imposed standards implemented by individual operators to address the issue of prudent borrowing: there is no clear framework. In reality, consumers need more than a wide choice, fair pricing and complete information; they frequently may be confused by the abundance of these three items and behave unwisely.

For example, they may end up entering a potentially dangerous cycle of over-borrowing and over-spending. This is because unsophisticated consumers may set their living and spending standards on the size of credit lines available at certain point in time, rather than according to a realistic assessment of their future ability to redeem debt. Consumers need honest and independent professional advice. It is therefore important to consider appropriate advisory services to ensure a substantial – and not merely formal – awareness by less sophisticated clients such as families and small businesses.

Regulators drafting the model for consumer oriented financial E-platform should cope with this need.

7.8 Lending-based and Investment-based E-platforms

The ambitions and benefits of E-platforms operating in the area of financial services appear to be common to different types of players. The key characteristics that segment this market seem to refer to:

1. The distribution model with two solutions appearing to cover the alternative finance market: lending-based versus investment-based E-platforms;
2. Investor base: E-platforms targeting all types of investors, including retail versus those with access restricted to qualified investors only;
3. Fundraisers: private individuals, SMEs of different sizes or start-up companies;
4. Type of financial instruments: loans, invoices financing, commercial paper, bonds, stocks.

Let us look at different distribution models: lending-based versus investment-based. Differences include operations, technology and regulation. The operating model of P2P lending E-platforms is the most innovative and, perhaps, complex. It applies to a large number of borrowers (typically, consumers or small businesses); hence, it involves a large number of transactions on the borrower side. The platform manages the individual borrower's positions as well as performs ex ante credit analysis and credit monitoring. Managing a borrower's position includes activities such as "know-your-client" (KYC) procedures that are often driven by regulation guidelines in the areas of anti-money laundering and anti-terrorism. There is an intense administrative workload connected to the opening of individual memberships.

E-platforms compete in handling this issue of customer care with the highest degree of automation and smoothness of operation, possibly along a paperless process. The credit assessment procedure is often integrated within the client onboarding experience. The E-platform undertakes payments, if authorized to conduct this activity, or an affiliated financial institution can handle them. The smaller the client, the greater the number of administrative activities and the consequent need of greater investments in ad hoc technology to support a P2P lending E-platform's user experience and process controls. (See Fig. 7.4)

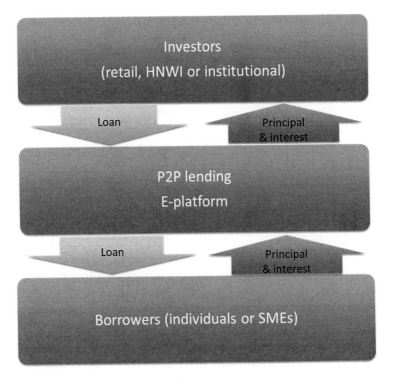

Fig. 7.4 Investors and borrowers flow

The upstream side of the process – that is, the lender side – involves the opportunities for lenders to access and possibly satisfy an individual borrower credit request. The leading models also offer lenders the opportunity to lend money to a basket of borrowers, thus fragmenting the invested sum. In these cases, the platform performs a complex activity that shields the names of the individual borrowers, highlighting different static portfolio solutions that consist of groups of loans with different degrees of credit risk.

The lender is therefore presented with the opportunity to invest in a basket of loans, each to an anonymous borrower. Baskets are defined on the basis of the combined risk effect deriving from the quality and degree of dispersion of the individual borrowers. E-platforms also offer tailor-made solutions that include the opportunity for the investor to blend different units of credit risk by calibrating the risk-weighted portions of their investments. Investors are attracted both by the possibility of fragmenting risk and the fact that the pricing of each risk-bearing micro-investment is consistently rewarding the risk.

This risk assessing and pricing activity – generally an intimate part of commercial banks' internal procedure – is made available to each investor in an extraordinary act of innovative transparency. The concept relies on an intensive technological process that achieves the spreading of relevant investment decision support data, while preserving the privacy of individual borrowers' names and credit status. At the same time, the investors are provided with up-to-date potential loss (PL) ratios and corresponding interest rates associated with clusters of specific borrowers. The decision-making chain tends to be based on three phases: Phase (1) rates to PL ratios; Phase (2) PL ratios are associated with clusters of borrowers; these clusters become the de facto lending target; (3) clusters are associated by the E-platform with the individual borrower. Phases (1) and (2) are visible to the investors; Phase (3) is generally hidden to protect a borrower's privacy.

All in all, a key success factor of the leading P2P lending E-platform consists of the ability to streamline extremely cumbersome processes, thus offering a direct procedure that is easy to use. P2P lending targeting consumers and small businesses relies on a scoring-based quantitative risk model that integrates financial, commercial and past credit performance information. Developing, maintaining and calibrating these models in an effective manner requires large volumes of lending transactions, a large borrower universe and a sufficiently long time series of data. In this respect, those E-platforms that have succeeded in aggregating customer data in such width and depth do compete with large commercial banks in terms of credit analytics. This wealth of information is offered for the small lender's decision-making process by the unique open model provided by P2P lending E-platforms. Another significant element is brought by the reliance of P2P lending E-platforms on a fully automated credit analysis and on a risk dispersion mechanism; these functions satisfy most investors' requirements and facilitate investment in loans to anonymous borrowers. The greater the statistical universe, (potentially) the more accurate the prediction risk model offered by the platform. Investors do not need much more than that in terms of analytical support on which to base their decision, so P2P lending platforms' no-name standard for borrowers does not limit their reach to local markets where lenders require knowledge about their borrowers.

For example, Lending Club, the US P2P lending E-platform, has quickly developed nationally with a highly automated decision support system. Lending Club highlights eight steps in its service model:

1. An investor/borrower direct relationship made possible by a fully digital experience;
2. The selection of a potential borrower is performed through a KYC and credit process directly managed by the E-platform;
3. A standardized pricing process based on the assignment of a specific credit grade to each potential borrower from a seven-tier scale ranging from A to G. The consequent pricing of each borrower's loans is a direct consequence of the credit grade: one grade corresponds to one specific interest rate. This is a transparent system which is extremely easy to use and track, and that reassures all lenders as to a fair opportunity;
4. The fragmentation of risk is realized by assigning standardized securities (notes) to the borrowers. This allows investors to build a portfolio with micro units, each represented by a US$25 note, creating a Lego bricks-type model. This also allows extreme efficiency and, at the same

time, allows each investor to design and execute their investments, mixing all possible combinations of notes.

5. A monthly flow of loan interest payments acts as the heartbeat of the credit system;

6. A clear and timely procedure tackles borrowers' missing payments on a specific loan, raises a red flag and instigates possible actions against delinquent borrowers;

7. A simple math model to compute an investor total return after credit charges and fees;

8. The ability to monitor the overall E-platform credit performance, highlighting the measure of net returns in the different credit grades. This is a typical competitive advantage of large players that can improve the accuracy of their prediction models thanks to a broader statistical universe. Investors can evaluate updated default risk predictions connected to each credit grade before entering into transactions. This service allows investors the opportunity to build and adjust their lending portfolio adopting an extremely professional risk assessment process.

9. The result is a function of Lending Club's investments in technology and operations, funded by approximately US$200 million raised by the company in the first four years of its life. Retail oriented P2P lending E-platforms such as Lending Club appear to be requiring great doses of capital to fund their development. In particular, the large amount of micro transactions that are instigated by each consumer loan traded on the Lending Club imposes a solid technology platform and calls for relevant software investments. This creates the current condition of relatively high entry barriers in consumer oriented P2P lending ventures, as a consequence of the investments needed in the technology, marketing, operations and compliance areas.

In practice, today's P2P lenders face large technology investment requirements in order to cope with their volume intensive activity. In addition, they operate in a regulatory environment similar to that of banks that imposes country-specific set-ups. Consequently, the development of a multi-national strategy appears to be happening more slowly than in other industries, or even within the FinTech space, if compared with solutions that are impacted by less country-specific regulations. Moreover, such strategy is constrained within country-specific roll-outs and therefore benefits from relatively fewer economies of scale, if compared with those available to E-platform players active in less regulated industries.

Investment-based E-platforms, on the other hand, apply FinTech innovations to the securities business, rather than to banking (or the lending business) as in P2P lending E-platforms. In this field of business, investors underwrite a security such as a bond or a stock directly issued by the fundraiser. The security is generally negotiable and can therefore be listed in a public exchange for a possible secondary market resale. When an E-platform operates in the area of securities or investments services, it typically comes across a well-defined regulatory framework. Clearly, authorities understand the evolution process that technology and market players have instigated in this area of business. It is therefore reasonable to expect specific regulatory actions with regard to E-platforms. Such actions will be aimed at updating the current regulation to make space for the innovative presence of E-platforms. In the EU, investment services aimed at both qualified and retail investors fall under MiFID.

7.8.1 A Special Focus on Investment-based E-platforms and Their Future in the European Union

The very fact that securities-based (also referred to as investment-based) E-platforms operate in a well-defined regulatory space in Europe would seem provide the following conditions:

* A solid development pattern within the already defined rules;
* A broader single market: the whole EU under a common umbrella set of rules.

The European Securities and Markets Authority (ESMA) is focusing on what it is defining as "investment-based crowdfunding", as distinct from other kinds of crowdfunding such as donations or loans. In an opinion paper published in December 2014, ESMA highlighted its awareness that crowdfunding's recent developments had imposed clarifications and, possibly, the introduction of new specific requirements by Member States. ESMA assessed typical investment-based crowdfunding models in order to promote regulatory convergence at EU level.

SMEs capital markets attract specific risks as a consequence of the fact that securities issuers are smaller, information is limited and investments lack the degree of liquidity that could grant the investor's ability to trade out of an unwanted investment. ESMA is also focusing on the platforms' model as a source of risk; this refers to possible conflicts of interest, the effects of an E-platform's failure and the quality of due diligence (if any) performed by the E-platform on the securities offered.

It is also clear, both to ESMA and the European Commission, that there is an opportunity cost in not facilitating the development of crowdfunding, given its potential to improve access to finance for the real economy and, at the same time, widen the investment opportunities available to investors. The innovations introduced by the alternative finance sectors appear to carry a long-lasting and positive effect, and to instigate momentum in the financial services community. Incumbents such as commercial and investment banks will need to innovate in order to keep up with the new level of competition, transparency and consequent customer awareness. In this respect, the European Commission has produced a Green Paper on a possible Capital Markets Union (CMU) that appears to have become an official manifesto of modern interaction between European retirement institutions, investors and the real economy.

The Commission has set six goals to be achieved by the CMU in order to:

1. Create a single market for capital by removing barriers to cross-border investments;
2. Improve access to financing for all businesses around Europe;
3. Diversify the funding of the economy and reduce the cost of raising capital for SMEs;
4. Maximize the benefits of capital markets, so they can support economic growth and job creation;
5. Help SMEs raise finance more easily;
6. Help the EU to attract investments from all over the world and become more competitive.

Since the Treaty of Rome in 1957, it has been noted that the free movement of capital is one of the fundamental freedoms of the EU and should be at the heart of a single market. The Green Paper defines the practical effects that the CMU implementation should bring to the real economy as the six goals are achieved: they involve, in practice, the fact that an SME can raise financing as easily as a large company and that obtaining credit through the capital markets is increasingly straightforward even across different Member States. Ideally, all investors should be joining banks in a set of market-specific benefits and capital requirements, thus competing fairly. For example, a Spanish SME should end up presenting its investment projects to multiple potential investors in different Member States and, eventually, receive financing from investors based in Germany and Italy. At the same time, for example, an investor based in France should be able to diversify its portfolio of bonds issued by pharmaceutical companies investing in SMEs from Holland, Portugal or Greece.

7.9   The UK's Focus on FinTech

Among Member States, the UK seems to be particularly persuaded that the new CMU scenario will offer a significant and brand new business space to those players adopting the FinTech recipe with an EU-wide scope of business. The CMU could, indeed, work as an alternative territory offered to those UK-based operators that experience the Eurozone's banking regulations as a barrier to achieving a smooth financial mediation channel to the real economy. Despite being out of the Eurozone, the UK is in a strong position to carry on its leadership in the financial services sector. It is, in fact, a key ambition of the CMU to provide a single market that will encourage FinTech operators to invest in technology and involve collateral technologies such as CRM, big data analytics and mobile payments.

An analysis published by the Bank of England in February 2015 highlighted that the CMU can support growth and stability by bringing together savers and borrowers and, consequently, improving the system's allocation efficiency. The study also highlighted that the involvement of the private sector in "risk sharing could lead to lower volatility of incomes and consumption, thereby supporting economic stability". The concepts of risk sharing, diversification and transparency are among those that make E-platforms a highly effective means with which to connect multiple investors to multiple borrowers, regardless of their size or risk appetite. In general, FinTech values the ability of the Internet to connect demand and supply in a "many-to-many" paradigm.

The British Financial Conduct Authority (FCA) is particularly involved in a mission to promote the conditions that would establish the UK as the premier location for starting, growing and maintaining innovative financial technology businesses. In March 2015, the FCA published its vision regarding the role of the UK government in providing leadership and catalysis, that of academics and businesses in developing and delivering business models, and that of regulators in ensuring that existing and new risks are identified and managed effectively.

In particular, the FCA has issued a list of seven recommendations that appear to be underlying the strategic importance of this effort with regard to the financial services industry, jobs creation and UK leadership. The highlights of the seven recommendations are:

1. A clear vision from Government, combined with a stable policy environment, will encourage the private sector to invest in FinTech. However, what is also needed is coordination across Government, regulators, business and academia and we therefore propose that the Government establishes a 'FinTech Advisory Group' with representation from the Government, regulators, trade associations, academia and business.
2. Challenge competitions can be an effective way of catalyzing the application of new technologies to new areas where the market alone may be insufficient as catalyst. This leads to our second recommendation: the Government should create a program of grand challenges on FinTech for academia, business and the third sector to answer. This would enhance the exchange of ideas and knowledge and provide inspiration to the FinTech community by challenging creative start-ups and incumbents to find innovative solutions to global problems.

3. Research Councils and Innovate UK should support research in all areas of FinTech, including big data, analytics, and the social and economic impacts of FinTech. The UK should build academic and technology leadership in the FinTech sector. The Alan Turing Institute should be well positioned to take on a major role, working closely with universities and industry. A key enabler for this research will be access to world-class financial data sets. A FinTech Advisory Board working with Research Councils and Innovate UK would have a role in helping to inform the research agenda.

4. Horizon scanning will be essential to anticipate, monitor and assist in the management of emerging risks and threats in FinTech. There is an important leadership role for a FinTech Advisory Group working closely with regulators and the Bank of England.

5. FinTech modules should be included in relevant degree courses to expose students to the FinTech industry and in turn to expose the FinTech industry to an educated and work-ready body of students.

6. Government should consider developing action plans to harness opportunities to develop regional hubs for FinTech outside London and the South East.

7. Government must be an expert strategic commissioner of FinTech. It should encourage all entrants to market, from start-ups to established players. The Government is an important purchaser of technology and has an opportunity to encourage innovation by expert commissioning of products and services.

7.10 Investors

Reaching investors and attracting their money with an easy-to-use E-platform is one thing, doing so with a sustainable service model is the challenge. The Internet and FinTech have often been synonymous with "access for everyone". Providing access to products and raw information need not be not an excluding factor, some players might tend to consider investors as a whole, the new Internet-enabled arena as one single big market to be pursued.

However, differences in risk awareness and price discovery tend to segment investors in two broad categories: qualified investors and retail investors. In broad terms, qualified investors are those who are organized and experienced in assessing and managing risks, are prepared to identify the negotiated terms, and are big enough to allocate their portfolio in a diversified manner.

Retail investors are not among qualified investors; a different activist attitude seems to identify two different stances towards the developing alternative finance: that of those assuming a leadership role versus that of less active players that assume a follower's role. A three-tier segmentation of the market appears to represent today's investors' arena with regard to the different E-platforms. This takes into account business attitudes rather than only considering parameters imposed by regulation.

This segmentation is perhaps the basis of a possible growth path for those platforms that leverage the wealth of analysis and risk-taking skills embedded in certain experienced investors.

E-platforms have learned to value lead investors as a precious component of their model. Their activity enriches the platform by providing steady liquidity and professional selectivity of the primary market's pipeline of deals (see Table 7.1).

Lead investors are also a significant element in the pricing process. In order to broaden the investor base, investment-based E-platforms tend to treat potentially "lead investors" as premium clients. The strategy of some investment-based E-platforms is to focus on a small target group of investors that would act in a similar fashion as "specialist dealers" in government bonds primary markets. A loyal "lead" investor is an important element to the growth strategy of an investment-based E-platform. It facilitates demand and supply convergence into closed deals that signal the key attraction of the platform. More deals call for more investors and more issuers (see Fig. 7.5).

The very fact that transactions are endorsed by the lead underwriting of a professional and respected investor signals the quality in the evaluation process and enriches the set of information provided by the platform to "follower" investors. "Hard" information such as financial statements, independent ratings and opinion, business plans, KYC filters is complemented by the simple but enriching fact that one or more specific

Table 7.1 E-platforms key features

Market function	Leaders	Followers/backers	Marginal
Investor description	Specialized fund managers, some insurance companies, (some) qualified HNWIs, (some) family offices, banks	Family offices, qualified HNWIs, small banks, insurance companies, pension funds	Non-qualified HNWIs, retail investors
Investor profile	Have the ability to understand or assess the risks involved in investing in SMEs, and the will and resources to perform in-depth analysis of individual issuers; Play an active role in both the structuring and the pricing of capital markets transactions as lead investors; Have the financial resources to build a well-diversified portfolio of SME securities.	Have the ability to understand or assess the risks involved in investing in SMEs; Lack the will or the resources to perform an in-depth analysis of individual issuers, hence they rely on independent risk ratings and market driven price discovery; Have the financial resources to build a well-diversified portfolio of SME securities.	Lack the ability to understand or assess the risks connected to investing in SMEs; Often lack the financial resources needed to build a well-diversified portfolio of SME securities.
Suitable investment targets	All kinds of security accorded as consistent with specific investment policies, including equities, senior bonds, high yield bonds, equity-linked bonds, commercial paper; Direct lending instruments such as loans, including services offered by P2P lending E-platforms	Direct investments in securities such as equities, senior bonds and commercial paper; "Portfolio type" investments such as specialized investment funds; Direct lending instruments such as loans, including services offered by P2P lending E-platforms	"Portfolio type" investments such as specialized investment funds or P2P-diversified lending – direct investing in individual securities is not suitable for these investors

Fig. 7.5 The growth cycle

professionals have evaluated the security, priced it at a visible level and underwritten it for a certain visible amount. To a potential investor, all this becomes relevant pre-trade "soft" information that the E-platform is more than willing to provide to its customer as a distinctive key feature. For an emerging E-platform, this is a possible way to start the positive cycle of liquidity, by building up volumes and calling for more liquidity.

The leader/follower situation tends to apply to many forms of investment-based crowdfunding E-platforms and seems to address a chronic issue deriving from the necessary level of trust needed by investors in their decision-making path. E-platforms compete in providing more and more information and analysis on possible targets; however, investments SMEs and start-up companies require a higher level of insight and understanding. This is often due to general concerns regarding transparency and integrity, but is also related to the fact that SMEs and start-up companies' business models often tend to be unique and, hence, incomparable.

7.10.1 Fundraisers

E-platforms target the following kind of fundraisers:

- Consumers interested in borrowing money at lower rates, as well as those with poor credit ratings or a bad credit history –banks would not consider these eligible clients.
- Small businesses, including small merchants. In this case, borrowers can rely on a developing market of E-platforms providing ad hoc credit-scoring engines, specific loan structures and invoice financing.
- Start-up companies are the quintessential type fundraiser that relies on equity-crowdfunding platforms. This segment is perhaps the least regulated and platforms tend to specialize in each of the typical start-up companies' growth stages. The more advanced the development stage requiring equity financing, the bigger the size of investments tickets, the more structured and possibly regulated the function of the platform.
- SMEs can raise equity funding via specialized pre-Initial Public Offering platforms. Debt products range from self-liquidating short-term solutions – such as invoice financing to securitized financial products such as commercial paper, mini-bonds, or even convertible bonds. The majority of E-platforms typically specialize by product. Product focus is, indeed, the key to a successful acceleration. However, given that, the value of an active investor franchise, marketing and technology, and competition might push players to offer more products on the same platforms. In this perspective, E-platforms insisting on the same client base of the same geographical market will be very likely to consider sharing certain functions, or even merging in order to further the achievement of critical mass. This will be particularly likely in smaller geographical markets.

7.10.2 Financial Instruments

In addition to the standard lending products offered by P2P E-platforms, the FinTech market has allowed a strong development of other funding solutions. For example, in invoice financing, start-up equity fundraising or mini-bonds, the community of possible investors has been attracted by risk/return profiles that were once either a restricted hunting ground for banks or simply did not exist.

FinTech growth was triggered due to new crowds of investors, enabled by the web-based offering. More importantly, they have perceived a relative value opportunity in accessing new asset classes with new funding solutions. Access has enabled the opportunity.

7.11 Why E-Platforms?

Considering the emerging SME-driven flow of investments, long-term investors such as insurance companies and retirement funds will play a key role in enabling the structural growth of the real economy. As highlighted by the EU CMU scenario, this will become a continental priority. In this context, investment-based E-platforms seem to address the challenges that investing in SMEs has witnessed so far. In particular, the possible breakthroughs introduced by these models are:

- The opportunity for investors to meet SME fundraisers in a cost-effective context that is transparent and prudent. E-platforms appear to be in a better position to deliver this benefit than traditional investment banks, which lack the focus and organization to serve this market segment efficiently.
- The syndicate model experienced with venture capital equity investments and highlighted by the example of AngelList can be extended to SME bonds and equity fundraising.
- The fact that E-platforms are independent players, typically acting as brokers, mitigates possible conflicts of interest.

8

The Epic Case Study

In order to provide a practical example of a multi-asset investment-based crowdfunding E-platform, this chapter describes the Italian based E-platform Epic (SIM) S.p.A. Epic is an investment company authorized and regulated by Consob and Bank of Italy that started its activity in Italy in 2014. It operates an investment based E-platform managed and founded by a team of professionals from the fields of financial markets, investment banking, and strategic consulting.

Epic is Italy's first FinTech platform where Italian SMEs can present their development projects to a selected audience of institutional investors (investment funds, family offices, banks, insurance companies, investment companies, pension funds) and private investors classified as qualified under MiFID.

Investors, in turn, have the opportunity to evaluate investment opportunities proposed by SMEs in a transparent, prompt, efficient, economic and "social" way, due to the standard information format used on the platform, obtained not only from companies, but also from independent institutions (e.g. credit rating agencies and research/analyst firms) and from other investors interested in the deal. Investments may take the form of bonds, shares, convertible bonds or commercial papers (see Fig. 8.1).

© The Author(s) 2017   **237**
G. Oricchio et al., *SME Funding*,
DOI 10.1057/978-1-137-58608-7_8

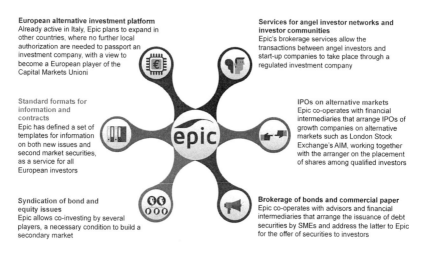

Fig. 8.1 Epic positioning (Source: Epic presentation.)

It was pointed out that E-platforms can operate in many different segments, identified by type of distribution model (lending or investment-based), type of investor (retail or qualified investors only), types of fundraiser (individual consumers, small businesses, or SMEs) and, finally, types of financial instrument (loans, bonds, equities). Epic's positioning in this four dimensional map is as:

• an investment-based E-platform;
• qualified investors only; retail investors that are considered unsuitable for the complexity and lack transparency with regard to investing in SMEs are excluded;
• targeting European SMEs (starting with Italian and subsequently Spanish and Portuguese);
• dealing in securities such as bonds, equity-linked bonds, commercial papers and equities.

In a two-dimensional diagram highlighting the positioning of different investment-based E-platforms with respect to the type of investor (consumers versus professional/qualified) and the type of issuer (start-up companies versus established SMEs), Epic seems to position itself in a

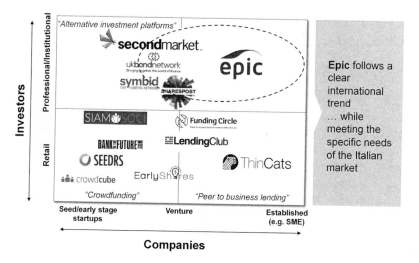

Fig. 8.2 Epic targets (Source: Epic presentation.)

relatively less crowded first quadrant: this quadrant is defined by qualified investors only and established SMEs. Epic is partially stretching its origination focus in the direction of post-seed start-up companies, thus extending its scope towards the left-hand side of Fig. 8.2.

In Italy, SMEs generate more than half of the GDP; these SMEs have historically been financed by banks. In recent years, the economic downturn has made it difficult for banks to support companies as they did in the past. The reduction in the volume of credit that companies receive from banks, however, is dangerously close to becoming a chronic issue, taking into consideration the new capital and liquidity constraints of the Basel III regulatory framework with which the latter must comply. Therefore, the need for a complementary funding channel for SMEs becomes increasingly urgent, taking into account the fact that, for most of them, accessing the capital market has very high fixed costs.

The Italian government, as with many other EU governments, has taken action regarding SME access to capital markets since 2011. Specific issues have been addressed and, in addition to a more SME-friendly regulatory and fiscal framework, systematic moral suasion has been exercised on key players such as funds, insurance companies, SMEs and pension funds. Needless to say, it will take years for the business and financial community to metabolize the required level of change fully. However, significant effects have begun surfacing since 2013, as the new regulations have been refined and have come to the attention of market participants. For example, as of 2015 some 30 specialized SME debt or equity closed-end funds have been launched; the majority of insurance companies have started investing in SME debt, either directly or through specialized funds; and over 100 SMEs have placed their mini-bonds raising over €1 billion, only counting issues of less than €50 million. Today, the Italian market is considered to be at the forefront in Europe and has taken several concrete steps. These include Development, Growth and Competitiveness Decrees, the introduction of so-called *mini-bonds* (security), and the creation of Borsa Italiana's ExtraMOT PRO (transparency of a secondary market). Additionally, the build-up of the launch of many credit funds specialized in SMEs, which act as selectors and risk managers of SME debt, and recent measures enacted by the Italian Insurance Supervisory Authority, (IVASS). The increase of the investment limit for this specific asset class from 2 % to 3 % has allowed for further investment of more insurance reserves in SMEs.

Epic performs a series of KYC and onboarding checks on all potential members that apply to the platform, whether potential issuers or investors. The status of "qualified investor" is verified by either the verification of EU-supervised intermediary status (which automatically grants the qualified investor status to many EU banks, investment companies, fund managers, insurance companies), or via a specific questionnaire, background checks and resumé analysis for HNWIs or directors of smaller non-supervised investment companies such as family concerns (see Fig. 8.3).

Epic is also standardizing the traditional private placement procedure with a more intensive use of the Internet. Multiple investors can share a common information base, will access information in compliance with issuer's confidentiality requirements and in accordance with market rules. Investors can browse a number of possible targets among new issues and secondary market opportunities across equities and mini-bonds; they do so by imposing personalized selection filters in order to focus on targets.

Membership requirements

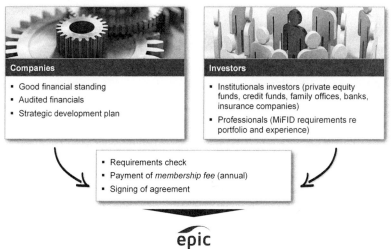

Fig. 8.3 Membership requirements (Source: Epic presentation.)

In many ways, the E-platform turns the investor in to a more active player via access to securities and to issuer's data on a shared infrastructure in totally privacy. This concept of sharing functions within the E-platform allows an investment-based crowdfunding operator such as Epic to achieve a whole series of innovations that offer wider benefits to the market as a whole:

1. Investors can research investment opportunities within a wide and deep information warehouse. As a result, they do not depend on the traditional solicitation of time-wasting securities salesmen, especially in the context of micro-investments. The SME market will tend to become a pull (by investors) market, rather than a push (to investors) market.
2. Investors will optimize their decision-making process because of the more complete and standardized set of preliminary and analytical information found on the platform. This minimizes their need to spend time on peripheral information and allows focus on a smaller number of key issues. Overall, the E-platform model saves time.
3. SMEs can access a higher number of potential investors and rely on Epic's market surveys to calibrate possible offerings and, eventually, to make more informed decisions about launching a deal. As in the case

of P2P platforms, it is likely that the liquidity build-up in Epic will provide progressively better information to issuers with regard to an investor's appetite for deals in general, as well as for key details in the offered terms and conditions, such as tenor, price, covenants.

4. By sharing costs, the model introduced by Epic brings another advantage typical of E-platforms: it minimizes fixed costs, since the platform operator typically absorbs legal, KYC, analytical, settlement and documentation costs. Epic functions like a shared procurement resource for investors. It becomes more valued since deal sizes tend to be smaller and because, in this segment, fixed costs often represent a deal-breaker, or at least discourage many investors to look into small deals.

For Epic, regardless of the product – equities, commercial papers, or minibonds – the operating mechanism is the same, and the same catalogue is shared. This process is set in four separate stages, each triggered by specific decisions made by the parties involved (see Fig. 8.4).

The Preliminary phase offers potential fundraisers a 'trial' experience that remains totally private and supports a more informed choice to move onto the next phase. The E-platform performs KYC checks, an independently managed credit analysis and an anonymous market survey on

How Epic works

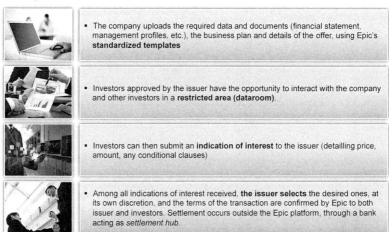

- The company uploads the required data and documents (financial statement, management profiles, etc.), the business plan and details of the offer, using Epic's **standardized templates**

- Investors approved by the issuer have the opportunity to interact with the company and other investors in a **restricted area (dataroom)**.

- Investors can then submit an **indication of interest** to the issuer (detailling price, amount, any conditional clauses)

- Among all indications of interest received, **the issuer selects** the desired ones, at its own discretion, and the terms of the transaction are confirmed by Epic to both issuer and investors. Settlement occurs outside the Epic platform, through a bank acting as *settlement hub*.

Fig. 8.4 How epic works (Source: Epic presentation)

its investor base. The feedback to the potential issuer and to the issuer's financial advisor consists of the confidential sharing of a proxy rating, as well as reflecting the investor market appetite for comparable issues.

There is then an offering phase, during which the issuer activates the process by becoming a member of the platform, thereby offering Epic an exclusive mandate to broker its offering. The issuer then uploads its financial situation, business plan and the possible terms of the proposed transaction in a dedicated area of the E-platform. Non-public information is stored in a virtual data-room and the issuer grants access to potentially interested investors that want to know more about the proposed deal.

This procedure allows an escalation of confidentiality engagements considering the nature of the information and the possibility that certain potential issuers might have previously issued publicly listed securities. During this phase, investors can interact with the issuer either via the E-platform dedicated chat-line and video-conferencing, or simply offline. Here, the E-platform function is that of facilitating and expediting the decision-making process, but does not exclude traditional methods such as a face-to-face management meetings, or a visit to the company.

Investors make the investment decision and make an offer to the issuer.

The closing phase is where the issuer chooses one or more investors and meets their terms. Transactions are then closed and settled outside the E-platform via a bank acting as a settlement hub.

As stated, Epic's aim is to connect SMEs with private capital in a direct, simple and cost-effective way, reducing intermediaries and bureaucracy; and the essential format is that of a private investment community with specific requirements necessary to join the platform.

The evolution of such private placements as Epic delivers with its "investor community" model, along with the fact that the company does not act as an issuer's advisor or creditor, determines a different brokerage model than that of traditional "one-to-one" chains where the issuer's advisor and investment bank generally contacts the potential investors individually. Investors must be "qualified" under MiFID/Consob regulation (see Fig. 8.5).

Different brokerage models

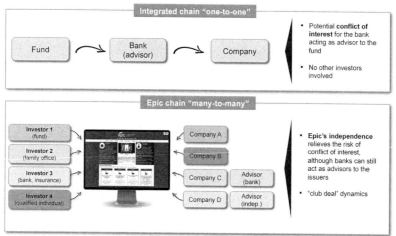

Fig. 8.5   Different brokerage models (Source: Epic presentation.)

Companies must meet the regulatory requirements for the issuance of the proposed financial instruments. Epic excludes SMEs operating in certain industries, such as real estate, financial and gambling industries.

The platform's value proposition lies in facilitating the connection, discussion and exchange of information between SMEs and investors, and participants have complete autonomy. Companies can choose which investors can access their data-room; investors can choose which companies to analyze and potentially fund; and by which amount; companies and investors may be assisted by their own advisers.

Epic's style is similar to most FinTech platforms: it is social and tries to create an ongoing channel for increased contact between SMEs and investors. The platform's technology enables the creation of a true digital network, advancing the dialogue between companies and investors, and making this process more fluid and continuous, thereby creating a community that interacts on a social footing.

This fundamental goal of simplifying the investor's workload is furthered by the adoption of a single platform where participants can find relevant information and analyze offers. The platform is thus about comparison, thereby facilitating the building of a diversified portfolio of securities.

In effect, Epic acts as a pure broker and does not handle post-trading activities. Investors are also not required to open any checking account or securities account with Epic, or with the settlement agent. Once any investment is settled, service on Epic continues. In a restricted area, investors stay in touch with companies and access post-issue updates (e.g. corporate actions, quarterly price indications, new budgets). Indications of interest can also be expressed for securities previously issued, whether originated on the platform or not.

Costs for companies are reduced due to the involvement of fewer intermediaries and to the fact that issuance costs related to bonds are deductible in the year they are incurred, regardless of the accounting policies. Issue costs include all expenses related to the issuance of the bonds – for example, the fees for the rating agency, placement fees, fees for professional services and include Epic's fees.

Epic thus offers a MiFID-regulated environment to host direct opportunities for investors or networks of qualified investors (e.g. business angels, see Fig. 8.6).

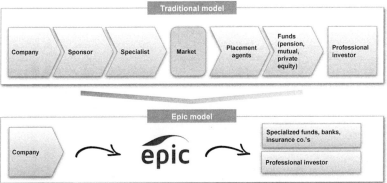

Fig. 8.6 A more direct and less expensive brokerage model (Source: Epic presentation.)

As E-platforms and FinTech market and deliver new solutions, they widen the lending business arena, allowing new investors and fundraisers to join.

Incumbents such as exchanges and banks are (slowly) reacting to the new competitive challenges. Deals such as the Nasdaq's joint-venture with Sharespost, or the partnership between Santander and Funding Circle, signal the incumbents' awareness of the structural changes.

Economic policy and regulation will encourage progressively more long-term investors such as insurance companies and pension funds to provide a structural backing to the alternative funding channel to the real economy. While retail investors' appetite for alternative finance may be subject to market cycles, the slower but steadier interest of institutional investors should grant Fintech a future. This will complement banking as a stable component of the supply chain. In the EU, this is well-defined by the Capital Markets Union's Green Paper published by the European Commission.

Emerging professional players such as specialized funds and robo-advisors will further enrich the ability of professionally managed savings to invest and continue to invest in the real economy.

The syndicate model tends to develop as a key micro-structure feature of investment-based E-platforms.

References

Acharya, Viral V., Thomas F. Cooley, Matthew Richardson, and Ingo Walter. 2011a. *Regulating Wall Street.* Hoboken: Wiley.

Acharya, Viral V., Matthew Richardson, Stijn Van Nieuwerburgh, and Lawrence J. White. 2011a. *Guranteed to Fail.* Princeton: Princeton University Press.

AFME (Association for Financial Markets in Europe), Oliver Wyman. 2013. Unlocking funding for European investment and growth.

Ayyagari M., T. Beck, and A. Demirgue-Kunt. 2007. Small and medium enterprises across the globe. *Small Business Economics* 29: 415–434.

Bamber, D. 1975. The area above teh ordinal dominance graph and the area below the receiver operating characteristic graph. *Journal of Mathematical Psychology* 12: 387–415.

Bangia, A., F.X. Diebold, A. Kronimus, C. Schagen, and T. Shuermann. 2002. Ratings migration and the business cycle, with application to credit portfolio stress testing. *Journal of Banking and Finance* 26(2–3): 445–474.

Bank of Italy. (2006). New regulations for the prudential supervision of banks, Circular n.263/2006, December.

Bardos, M., S. Foulcher and V. Oung. (2003). Exigences de capital et cycle economiques: une etude empirique sur le donnees francaises, Bulletin de la Commission Bancaire 28, April.

© The Author(s) 2017
G. Oricchio et al., *SME Funding,*
DOI 10.1057/978-1-137-58608-7

Basel Committee on Banking Supervision. 2005a. Studies on the validation of internal rating systems, Working Paper 14, Bank for International Settlements May.

Basel Committee on Banking Supervision. 2005b. Guidance on paragraph 468 of the framework document, Bank for International Settlements July.

Basel Committee on Banking Supervision. 2005c. Validation of low-default portfolios in the Basel II framework, Basel Committee Newsletter 6, Bank for International Settlements September.

Basel Committee on Banking Supervision. 2006. International convergence of capital measurement and capital standards – A revised framework, June.

Basel Committee on Banking Supervision. 2009. Strengthening the resilience of the banking sector, Issued for comment December, Bank of International Settlements.

Basel Committee on Banking Supervision. 2010a. Basel III: A global regulatory framework for more resilient banks and banking systems, December.

Basel Committee on Banking Supervision. 2010b. Basel III: International framework for liquidity risk measurement, standards and monitoring, December.

Basel Committee on Banking Supervision. 2010c. Guidance for national authorities operating the countercyclical capital buffer, December.

Beaver, W. 1967. 'Financial ratios as predictors of failures', empirical research in accounting: Selected studies – 1966. *Supplement to Journal of Accounting Research* 4: 71–111.

Beck, T., A. Demirguˇc¸-Kunt, L. Laeven and R. Levine. (2005). Finance, firm size and growth, World Bank Policy Research Working Paper No. 3485.

Bilardello, J., and B. Ganguin. 2005. *Fundamentals of corporate credit analysis.* New York: McGraw-Hill.

Black, Fischer, and J. Cox. 1976. Valuing corporate securities and liabilities: Some effects of bond indenture provisions. *Journal of Finance* 31: 351–367.

Black, Fischer, and Myron Scholes. 1973. The pricing of options and corporate liabilities. *Journal of Political Economy* 81(3): 637–654.

Blochwitz, S., S. Hohl, and C. Wehn. 2003. Reconsidering ratings, Working paper, Deutsche Bundesbank, July.

Brier, G.W. (1950). Verification forecasts expressed in terms of probability. Washington, DC: US Weather Bureau. http://juornals.ametsoc.org/

Cannata, Francesco. 2007. Il metodo dei rating interni. Basilea 2 e il rischio di credito: le regole, la loro attuazione in Italia. Bancaria Editrice.

Cantor, Richard, and Chris Mann. 2006. Analyzing the trade-off between ratings accuracy and stability, Moody's Investors Service, September.

Caouette, John B., Edward I. Altman, and Paul Narayanan. 1998. *Managing credit risk: The next great financial challenge (Frontiers in finance series)*. New York: Wiley.

Chandler, A.D. Jr. 1962. *Strategy and structure: Chapters in the history of the American Indus-trial enterprise*. Cambridge: MIT Press.

Churchill, N.C., and V.L. Lewis. 1983. The five stages of small business growth. *Harvard Business Review* May–June: 30–50.

Committee of European Banking Supervisors. 2006. Guidelines on the implementation, validation and assessment of advanced measurement (AMA) and internal rating based (IRB) approaches, GL 10, April.

Crosbie, Peter, and Jeffrey Bohn. 2003. Modeling default risk, Moody's KMV White Paper.

De Laurentis, G. 2001. Rating Interni e Credit Risk Management – L'evoluzione dei processi di affidamento bancari. Bancaria Editrice.

Durand, D. 1941. Risk elements in consumer instalments financing, Working Paper, NBER.

Dwyer, Douglas, and Irina Korablev. 2007. Power and level validation of Moody's KMV EDFTM credit measures in North America, Europe, and Asia, Moody's KMV White Paper.

Dwyer, Douglas, and Shisheng Qu. 2007. EDFTM 8.0 model enhancements, Moody's KMV White Paper.

Englemann, B., and R. Rauhmeier (eds.). 2011. *The Basel II risk parameters – Estimation, validation and stress testing*, chapter IV, The shadow rating approach – Experience from banking practice. Berlin/New York: Springer.

Engelmann, B., E. Hayden, and D. Tasche. 2003. Testing rating accuracy. *Risk* 16: 82–86.

European Commission .2006. The taking up and pursuit of the business of credit institutions, Capital Requirements Directive n.2006/48/EC, June.

Fabbris, L. 1997. *Statistica multivariata. Analisi esplorativa dei dati*. Milano: McGraw-Hill.

Gisiger, Nicolas. 2009. Risk-neutral probabilities explained, Moody's Analytics.

Gordy, Michael B. 2003. Credit risk modelling – The cutting-edge collection technical papers, published in Risk 1999–2003. Risk Books.

Gorton, Gary B. 2010a. *Slapped by the invisible hand*. Oxford/New York: Oxford University Press.

Gray, Dale, and Samuel Malone. 2008. *Macrofinancial risk analysis*. Chichester: Wiley.

Greiner, L.E. 1972. Evolution and revolution as organization growth. *Harvard Business Review* July–August: 37.

Gutierrez Girault, M.,and J. Hwang. 2010. Public credit registries as a tool for bank regulation and supervision, The World Bank, Policy Research Working Paper, December 2010.

Hosmer, D.W., and S. Lemeshow. 2000. *Applied logistic regression*, 2nd ed. New York: Johnnie & Sons.

International Monetary Fund (IMF). 2009. Global financial stability report, Washington DC, October 2009.

International Monetary Fund. 2013. Financial stability report.

Izzi, L., G. Oricchio, and A. Ratini. 2004. Il modello interno di rating del segmento retail di Capitalia. In *Rating interni e controllo del rischio di credito. Esperienze, problemi, soluzioni*, ed. G. De Laurentis, F. Saita, and A. Sironi. Roma: Bancaria Editrice.

Kealhofer, S. 2003a. Quantifying credit risk II: Debt valuation. *Financial Analysts Journal* 59: 78–93.

Kealhofer, S. 2003b. Quantifying credit risk I: Default prediction. *Financial Analysts Journal* 59: 30–44

Keenan, S., J. Sobehart, and D. T. Hamilton. 1999. Predicting default rates: A forecasting model for Moody's issuer-based default rates, Moody's Global Credit Research.

Keeney, R.L., and H. Raiffa. 1976. *Decision with multiple objectives: Preferences and value trade-offs*. New York: Wiley.

Korablev, Irina, and Shisheng Qu. 2009. Validating the public, EDFTM Model.

Lando, D., and T.M. Skødeberg. 2002. Analyzing rating transitions and rating drift with continuous observations. *Journal of Banking and Finance* 26: 423–444.

Lee, W.C. 1999. Probabilistic analysis of global performances of diagnostic tests: Interpreting the Lorenz curve-based summary measures. *Statistics in Medicine* 18: 455–471.

Li, Zan, and Jing Zhang. 2009. Investing in corporate credit using quantitative tools, Moody's KMV.

Lo, A. 2005. Reconciling efficient markets with behavioural finance. The adaptive markets hypothesis. *Journal of Investment Consulting* 7(2): 21–44.

Loeffler, Gunter, and Peter N. Posh. 2007. *Credit risk modeling using Excel and VBA*, 2nd ed. Chichester/Hoboken: Wiley Finance Series.

Lugaresi, Sergio. 2015. Review of the main European Policy initiatives, RELTIF working paper. http://reltif.cepr.org/restarting-european-long-term-investment-finance

McGuire, J.W. 1963. *Factors affecting the growth of manufacturing firms.* Seattle: Bureau of business research, University of Washington.

Merton, Robert C. 1974. On the pricing of corporate debt: The risk structure of interest rates. *Journal of Finance* 29(May): 449–470.

Merton, Robert. 1992. *Continuous time finance.* Cambridge, MA: Blackwell.

Moral Turiel, G., and R. García Baena. 2002. Estimación de la severidad de una cartera de préstamos hipotecarios'. *Banco de España, Estabilidad financiera* 3: 127–164.

Mullard, Maurice. 2012. The credit rating agencies and their contribution to the financial crisis, *The Political Quarterly* 83(1):77–95.

Oricchio, Gianluca. 2011. *Credit treasury. A credit pricing guide in liquid and non-liquid markets.* Houndmills/Basingstoke/Hampshire/New York: Palgrave Macmillan.

Pozsar Z., T. Adrian, A. Ashcraft, and H Boesky. 2010. Shadow system, Staff Report no. 458, July 2010, Federal Reserve Bank of NY.

Pozsar, Zoltan, Tobias Adrian, Adam Ashcraft, and Hayley Boesky. 2012. Shadow banking, Federal Reserve Bank of New York, Staff Paper No. 458, February 2012.

Renaul, Olivier, and Arnaud de Servigny. 2004. *The standard & poor's guide to measuring and managing credit risk.* New York: McGraw-Hill.

Resti, A., and A. Sironi. 2007. *Risk management and shareholders' value in banking. From risk measurement models to capital allocation policies.* Chichester/Hoboken: Wiley Finance.

Rostow, W.W. 1960. *The stages of economic growth.* Cambridge: Cambridge University Press.

Saaty, T.L. 1977. A scaling method for priorities in hierarchical structures. *Journal of Mathematical Psychology* 15: 234–281.

Saunders, Anthony, and Linda Allen. 2002. *Credit risk measurement – New approaches to value at risk and other paradigms,* 2nd ed. New York: Wiley

Sobehart, J.R., and S.C. Keenan. 2004. Performance evaluation for credit spread and default risk models. In *Credit risk: Models and management,* ed. D. Shimko, 2nd ed., 275–305. London: Risk Books.

Spriggs, John, Dale Sigurdson. 1985. Seller cooperation in an oligopoly-monopsony market: An analysis involving experimental economics, *Canadian Journal of Agricultural Economics* 33(3): 285–298.

Tasche, D. (2003). A traffic lights approach to PD validation, working paper, Deutsche Bundesbank, May.

References on CCRs

References on CCRs from the Bank of Italy

Banca d'Italia, Centrale dei rischi. Istruzioni per gli intermediari creditizi, Circolare 11 febbraio 1991, n. 139.

Banca d'Italia, Istruzioni di vigilanza per le banche, Circolare 21 aprile 1999, n. 229.

Banca d'Italia, Nuove disposizioni di vigilanza prudenziale delle banche, Circolare 7 dicembre 2006, n. 263.

Banca d'Italia, Relazione sull'attività dell'Arbitro Bancario Finanziario, 2011, 1° agosto 2012 • Banca d'Italia, Relazione sull'attività dell'Arbitro Bancario Finanziario, 2010, 8 giugno 2011 • Banca d'Italia, Sintesi dell'attività svolta dall'Arbitro Bancario Finanziario al 31 marzo 2010, 29 aprile 2010.

References on CCRs in English

Acharya, Viral V., Matthew Richardson, Stijn Van Nieuwerburgh, and Lawrence J. White. 2011. *Guranteed to fail*. Princeton: Princeton University Press.

Artigas, C. 2004. A review of credit registers and their use for Basel II, Financial Stability Institute, Bank for International Settlements, September 2004.

Asian Development Bank (ADB) and Organization for Economic Cooperation and Development (OECD). 2014. Study on enhancing financial accessibility for SMEs. Lessons from Recent Crises.

AFME (Association for Financial Markets in Europe), Oliver Wyman. 2013. Unlocking funding for European investment and growth.

Bassanini, Franco, and Massimo Reviglio. 2013. European Institutions and the crisis: Investing to growth and Compete, In *Le istituzioni europee alla prova della crisis*, ed. Giuliano Amato, and Roberto Gualtieri. Rome: Passigli Editore.

Bassanini, Franco, and Edoardo Reviglio. 2014. Long-term investment in Europe. The origin of the subject and future prospects, May 2014

Carmassi, Jacopo, Giorgio Di Giorgio, and Marco Spallone. 2012. SMEs and the challenge to go public, Rivista bancaria, June 2012.

Churm, Rohan, Amar Radia, Jeremy Leake, Srinivasan Sylaja, and Richard Whisker. 2012. The funding for lending scheme, Bank of England, Quarterly Bulletin, 2012 Q4.

CMS. 2013. Restructuring and insolvency in Europe, Newsletter, Winter 2013.

Denzer-Speck, David, Harald Lob. 2013. Promoting long-term investments under changing regulatory framework conditions – The case of Germany's KfW Bankengruppe, Long-term investment club.

ECB. 2013. Corporate finance and economic activity in the Euro Area, Occasional Paper Series, n. 151, August 2013.

ECB (European Central Bank). 2014. Financial integration in Europe.

European Commission (EC) 2013a. Long-term financing of the European Economy, Commission Staff Working Document accompanying the Green Paper, March 2013 (a).

EC. 2013b. Proposal for a regulation of the European Parliament and of the Council on European long-term investment funds, June 2013.

EC. 2013c. Impact assessment – Proposal for a regulation of the European Parliament and of the Council on European long-term investment funds. June 2013.

European Commission and European Investment Bank (EIB). 2013. Increasing lending to the economy: Implementing the EIB capital increase and joint Commission-EIB initiatives, Joint Report to the European Council, June 28.

European Foundation for the Improvement of Living and Working Conditions (Eurofoud). 2013. Restructuring in SMEs: Portugal, Dublin.

European Fund and Asset Management Association (EFAMA). 2013. The OCERP: A proposal for a European personal pension product, September 2013.

European Investment Bank (EIB). 2014. Unlocking lending in Europe.

European Parliament (EP) and Directorate General for Internal Policies. 2013. Access to finance of SMEs in distressed euro area Member States, July 2013.

European Security Market Authority (ESMA) and Security and Markets Stakeholder Group. 2012. Report on helping small and medium sized companies access funding, Paris, October 2012.

Fuchita, Yasuyuki, Richard J. Herring, and Robert E. Litan. (eds.). 2009. Prudent lending restored. Washington DC: Brooking Institution Press.

Garnier, Oliver. 2014. Eurozone: Promoting risk – Sharing through cross-border ownership of equity capital, Applied Economics Quarterly 60(2), Berlin, pp. 55–67.

Garrido, Jose. 2011. Out-of-court debt restructuring, World Bank, December 2011.

Giovannini, Alberto, and John Moran. 2013. Finance for growth, report of the high level expert group on SME and infrastructure financing.

Gorton, Gary B. 2010b. *Slapped by the invisible hand.* Oxford/New York: Oxford University Press.

Group of Thirty (G30). 2013. Long-term finance and economic growth.

Gutierrez, M., and J. Hwang. 2010. Public credit registries as a tool for bank regulation and supervision, Policy Research Working Paper, World Bank, December 2010.

Hernàndez-Cànovas, Ginés, and Pedro Martìnez-Solano. 2010. Relationship lending and SME financing in the Continental European Bank-Based System, Small Business Economics.

Holton, Sarah, Fergal McCann, Kathryn Prendergast, and David Purdue. 2013. Policy measures to improve access to credit for SMEs: A survey, Central Bank of Ireland, Quarterly Bulletin, no. 04, October 2013.

IIF (Institute for International Finance), B&C (Bain & Company). 2013. Restoring financing and growth to Europe's SMEs.

Industry-Led Working Group on Alternative Debt Markets (ILWGADB). 2012. Boosting finance options for business. Report of London (Breedon Report), London, March 2012.

Infelise, Federico. 2014. Supporting access to finance by SMEs: Mapping the initiatives in five EU countries, ECMI Research Report, April 2014.

INSOL. 2000. Global principles for multi-creditor workouts.

International Monetary Fund. 2009. Global financial stability report, Washington DC, October 2009.

International Monetary Fund (IMF). 2013a. Country staff report, Portugal.

International Monetary Fund. 2013b. Global financial stability report.

Kaminker, Christofer, Fiona Steward, and Simon Upton. 2012. The role of institutional investors in financing clean energy, OECD working papers of finance, insurance and private pensions, no. 23, OECD, Paris.

Kraemer-Eis, Helmut, Markus Schaber, and Alessandro Tappi. 2010. SME loan securitisation, European investment fund, Working Paper 2010.

Laryea, Thomas. 2010. Approaches to corporate debt restructuring in the wake of financial crises, IMF Staff Position Note, January 2010.

Liu, Yan, and Christoph B. Rosenberg. 2013. Dealing with private debt distress in the wake of the European Financial Crisis, IMF Working Paper, 44/2013.

Mistrulli, Paolo Emilio, and Valerio Vacca. (coordinators). 2011. I confidi e il credito alle piccole imprese durante la crisi, Bank of Italy, Occasional Papers, No. 105, October 2011.

Mullard, Maurice. 2012. The credit rating agencies and their contribution to the financial crisis. *The Political Quarterly* 83(1): 77–95.

Murphy, Pablo Lopez. 2014. Tackling the corporate debt overhang in Spain, in IMF, Spain. Selected Issues, Washington DC, July 2014.

OECD. 2011. Promoting longer-term investment by institutional investors: Selected issues and policies, Discussion Note presented at the Eurofi High Level Seminar, Paris.

OECD. 2012. SME and entrepreneurship financing: The role of credit guarantee schemes and mutual guarantee societies in supporting finance for small and medium-sized enterprises, OECD Working Party on SME and Entrepreneurship, Paris.

OECD. 2013. The role of banks, equity markets and institutional investors in long-term financing for growth and development, Report for G20 Leaders, Paris

OECD Working Party on SMEs and Entrepreneurship (WPSMEE). 2013. Credit mediation for SMEs and entrepreneurs: Final report, March 2013.

Oricchio G. 2011. *Credit treasury. A credit pricing guide in liquid and non-liquid markets*. London: Palgrave. Chapter 3.

Oricchio, G., L. Izzi, and L. Vitale. 2012. *Basel III credit rating systems. An applied guide to quantitative and qualitative models*. London: Palgrave. chapter 2.

Öztürk, Bahar, and Mico Mrkaic. 2014. SMEs' access to finance in the Euro area: What helps or hampers? IMF Working Paper, May 2014.

Pozsar, Zoltan, Tobias Adrian, Adam Ashcraft, and Hayley Boesky. 2012. Shadow banking, Federal Reserve Bank of New York, Staff Paper No. 458, February 2012.

Robano, Virginia. 2014. The role of public financial institutions for SMEs, in ADB-OECD 2014.

SMSG ESMA (Security and Markets Stakeholder Group, European Security Market Authority). 2014. Crowdfunding, position paper.

Spriggs, John, and Dale Sigurdson. 1985. Seller cooperation in an oligopoly-monopsony market: An analysis involving experimental economics, *Canadian Journal of Agricultural Economics* 33(3), pp. 285–298.

Standard & Poor's. 2014. Mid-market funding in Europe is making strides, but has far to go, April 2014.

Stiglitz, Joseph, and Andrew Weiss. 1981. Credit rationing in markets with imperfect information, The American Economic Review, June 1981.

Stringa, Marco. 2013. Thinking innovatively: A convertible loan market for SMEs, Deutsche Bank, May 2013.

Valla, Natacha, Thomas Brand, and Sébastien Doisy. 2014. A new architecture for public investment in Europe, CEPII Policy Brief, July 2014.

Van der Schans, Daniel. 2012. SME access to external finance, UK Department for Business Innovation & Skills (BIS), BIS Economics Paper, no. 16, January 2012.

Wehinger, Gert. 2012. Bank deleveraging, the move from bank to market-based financing, and SME financing, OECD Journal: Financial Market Trends, OECD, pp. 75–91.

Wehinger, Gert. 2014. SMEs and the credit crunch: Current financing difficulties, policy measures and a review of literature, OECD Journal: Financial Market Trends, OECD, pp. 153–162.

Index

© The Author(s) 2017
G. Oricchio et al., *SME Funding*,
DOI 10.1057/978-1-137-58608-7

Printed in the United States
By Bookmasters